PHILADELPHIA'S
PROGRESSIVE
ORPHANAGE

DAVID R. CONTOSTA

PHILADELPHIA'S PROGRESSIVE ORPHANAGE

The Carson Valley School

The Pennsylvania State University Press
University Park, Pennsylvania

Library of Congress Cataloging-in-Publication Data

Contosta, David R.
    Philadelphia's progressive orphanage : the Carson Valley School / David R.
Contosta.

        p.   cm.
    Includes bibliographical references and index.
    ISBN 0-271-02771-1 (alk. paper)
    1. Carson Valley School (Flourtown, Pa.)—History.   2. Orphanages—Pennsyl-
vania—Flourtown—History.   3. Child welfare—Pennsylvania—Flourtown—History.   I. Title.
HV995.F52C373   1997
362.73'2'0974812—dc21   97-6406
                                                                                 CIP

Published by The Pennsylvania State University Press,
University Park, PA 16802-1003

It is the policy of The Pennsylvania State University Press to use acid-free paper for
the first printing of all clothbound books. Publications on uncoated stock satisfy the
minimum requirements of American National Standard for Information Sciences—
Permanence of Paper for Printed Library Materials, ANSI Z39.48-1992.

CONTENTS

LIST OF ILLUSTRATIONS

ACKNOWLEDGMENTS

The author is indebted to a number of people who have made this book possible. John Taaffe, executive director of the Carson Valley School, made every effort to accommodate the project, from opening the school's records to allowing the author to spend many weeks on campus taking in the daily sights and sounds. Pat Pellicore, Carson's special assistant to administration, and Jean Tickell, director of development at Carson, helped the author in numerous ways. There was consistent support from the book committee of the Carson Valley board of trustees: Richard Collier Jr., Helen Elliott, Robert H. Haakenson, and Mildred W. Guinessy.

I am especially indebted to Yvonne Patterson, who came as a young girl to live in Flourtown with her aunt, Katherine Tucker, and Tucker's friend, Elsa Ueland, in 1918—the very year of Carson's official launching. Patterson's remembrances of "Aunt Elsa" over the course of six decades and her opening of Ueland's private papers to the author were unforeseen gifts that added a personal dimension to the book that it could not have had otherwise. Margaret Ueland, a sister-in-law of Elsa Ueland, was generous with her remembrances. Elsa's nephew Mark Ueland and her niece Clara Ueland likewise shared their memories with the author. A number of others, whose names appear in the notes, granted interviews of varying scope.

The staff of the Urban Archives of Temple University's Samuel Paley Library were both hospitable and helpful in giving access to their extensive collections of Carson materials. Dr. Helen Hayes of Chestnut Hill College's Logue Library once again shared her vast knowledge of sources and reference aids. Natline Thornton, a longtime staff member at Carson, gave repeated entry to the materials that she has collected and preserved for more than a quarter of a century. Indeed, without Thornton's decision to serve as a volunteer collector and archivist, this history of Carson would have been difficult, if not impossible, to research and write.

Peter Potter, my editor at Penn State Press, believed in this project from the beginning and guided it throughout. Marketing and sales manager, Lisa Bayer, and assistant marketing manager, Alison Reeves, prepared the way for the book with great energy and enthusiasm. Keith Monley did a thorough and thoughtful job of copyediting. Peggy Hoover did her usually fine work of steering the book through the various stages of editing and production. I also want to thank Ray Liddick Jr. for his excellent design work.

Several persons read the manuscript and made suggestions that greatly improved the final product. Among these were individuals familiar with the Carson Valley School or its immediate environs: John Taaffe, Natline Thornton, Frances E. Grant, Robert Haakenson, Mildred Guinessy, Yvonne Patterson, Marie Kitto, and Jonanna Myers. Two highly regarded academic historians read and commented on the manuscript: Robert Fishman of Rutgers University and Bruce Dierenfield of Canisius College.

My wife, Mary, as always, was unswerving in her support and encouragement. She was also a wonderful listener as I shared one story after another about the Carson Valley School and its principal players during the past eighty years.

INTRODUCTION: PAST AND PRESENT

Contrary to popular belief, the past does not repeat itself. For the personalities, movements, and events of one era will never reappear in exactly the same way. Yet it is true that the past has shaped the present. Indeed, most individuals embrace this idea as a commonsense explanation of who they are: Relatives have said that they have Aunt Sally's eyes, or that their musical ability must come from Grandfather Smith. In reality, all human beings are living testaments to the genetic impress of their ancestors, and to the times and places in which their forebears lived—going back ultimately to the dawn of humankind. Likewise, communities, institutions, and even whole nations are products of their pasts.

Because of such intimate connections between past and present, it is often difficult to tell just when a historical movement begins or ends. This is particularly true of the progressive era of reform—and of the progressive-education movement that is related to it. Although both phenomena are properly associated with the early decades of the twentieth century, it is clear that neither of them simply disappeared on a given day at the stroke of midnight.

In fact, many reforms from the progressive era remain in place as the twentieth century comes to a close: from women's vote, primary elections, the secret ballot, and juvenile courts to concern over natural resources and the environment, regulation of food and drugs, the Federal Reserve banking system, and effective antitrust legislation. Intensified concern for child welfare and for the nation's educational system are also legacies of progressivism—and of the progressive-education movement. Then there are the many physical remains of the progressive era, such as Arts and Crafts furniture and revivals of certain American and English vernacular styles in architecture. In the Philadelphia area an impressive legacy of the broader progressive movement is the Carson Valley School, formally opened in 1918 and originally known as the Carson College for Orphan Girls.

By the mid-1920s Carson College in Flourtown, Pennsylvania, was being hailed in national publications as a model progressive orphanage and school. Located just beyond the northwestern boundaries of Philadelphia, its success owed greatly to the inspiration of its first "president," Elsa Ueland (1888–1980). In addition to being an accomplished progressive educator, Ueland belonged to the larger progressive movement that inspired many young men and women, including Ueland, for the greater part of their lives. Although founded at the very end of what historians have defined as the progressive era per se, Carson College and its successor, the Carson Valley School, provide rich examples of how progressivism and progressive education have exerted an influence far beyond the period that gave them birth.

This progressive legacy is not a simple one, which befits an era marked by wide-ranging opinions and not a few contradictions among the progressive reformers themselves. One moment lauding science and technology, progressives might with the very next breath lament the passing of a simpler past, a time when communal solidarity, pride in individual craftsmanship, and an intimacy with nature had provided self-satisfaction, neighborliness, and a sense of continuity in both time and space. And while more conservative reformers advocated greater efficiency in both business and government as a cure-all for the country's ills, more liberal reformers called for extensive regulation of business and industry along with greater protection for men and women in the workplace.

There were similar contradictions and differences of opinion among progressive educators. At the same time that they embraced science as a means of problem solving and urged experiential learning with frequent field trips into the modern workplace, they also stressed such subjects as nature study, ancient handicrafts, and folk culture. While some were content to emphasize practical skills and life adjustment, others wanted students to join in social and economic criticisms of contemporary life.

The origins of Carson College (and thus of the Carson Valley School) were as paradoxical, in many ways, as the progressive movement and progressive education themselves. A large sum of money was left to establish Carson College by a Philadelphia Street railway and traction magnate named Robert Carson, who gave his name as well as his fortune to the institution. Carson made his money in a transportation enterprise that had contributed mightily to the sort of rapid urban growth and social displacement that progressive reformers so lamented. In addition, Robert Carson's huge country estate, a generous portion of which he set aside for the orphanage grounds, was itself testimony to an old Philadelphia tradition of fleeing the more objectionable aspects of urban life to a home in the country. Carson's own prescriptions for the orphanage, which he carefully set down in his will, contained forward- as well as backward-looking ideas, some of which would bedevil the institution for decades to come. Especially troublesome was the requirement that admissions be limited to white girls with both parents deceased.

Yet it was Carson's money that allowed Elsa Ueland and her staff to create a flourishing progressive institution. It was also Carson's millions that permitted the trustees to erect buildings in an elaborate (though sometimes impractical), late medieval style that formed a fitting backdrop for historical pageants even as the institution's young charges were examining the ways of modern science and industry.

Elsa Ueland's own life exemplified many of these same ambivalences. Indeed, her preparation for the job of managing Carson—and her forty-two years at its helm—are so central to understanding the institution that her life and works necessarily form a significant portion of its history. Particularly during the early decades, the story of Carson College and the life of Elsa Ueland were inseparable, presenting this author with the challenge of crafting a partial biography within an institutional history.

Of course, many forces and events beyond Ueland's (and her successors') control played crucial roles in the evolution of Carson. The depression of the 1930s, for example, exacerbated in Carson College's case by some bad investments in the late 1920s, dealt a serious blow to Ueland's progressive program. After several years of struggle Ueland had to close the highly progressive elementary school on campus and to place her girls in the local public system. But she succeeded in preserving many progressive elements within the cottages where the girls continued to live, as well as in various after-school activities and summer programs.

Meanwhile, other changes in American life compromised the existence of Carson College. Greater life expectancy, combined with aid to dependent children (provided through the Social Security Act of 1935) and a growing preference for foster care over institutional placement, led to declining enrollments for Carson College at the very time when its income was eroding. The institution managed to survive by skirting the Carson will in order to admit "half orphans," the brothers of Carson girls, then boys who were not related to Carson girls, and finally African American youngsters. Beginning in the late 1930s, it also accepted board payments from Philadelphia and the surrounding counties for children who came to Carson from public child-welfare agencies. Two decades later most of the institution's financial support derived from such public funds, rather than from the Robert Carson bequest. Although it is impossible to state the precise moment when Carson ceased to be an orphanage, it emerged after World War II primarily as an institution that cared for children whose parents, for one reason or another, were unable to fulfill their parental responsibilities themselves.

Changes in admissions policy had brought only limited relief when the whole anti-institutional atmosphere of the 1960s reinforced governmental policy, in place since the early twentieth century, of favoring foster care (or other noninstitutional alternatives) over places like the Carson Valley School (as it was known after 1946). Budget cutbacks at all levels of government in the 1980s and 1990s only strengthened the movement away from institutional child care. Meanwhile soaring divorce rates, an epidemic of drug abuse, and the breakdown of many urban families meant that numerous children continued to require outside assistance. The Carson Valley School helped to meet that need by providing institutional care for those who could benefit most from group living. It also established an innovative foster-care program in the Germantown/Mt. Airy section of

Philadelphia, which trained and assisted foster-care parents in dealing with especially difficult children. In addition, it established a program designed to help families before it became necessary to remove children from the home.

In responding to the real and changing issues of urban families, Carson continued to work within the spirit of progressive reform. Its academic school on the main campus was reopened in the mid-1980s because the local public schools could not address the emotional problems and learning deficiencies of many of the children they were now receiving. In its program, Carson's school emphasized life-coping skills that were also close in spirit to the old goals of progressive education. Of course, there was not a full return to the sort of progressive program that had flourished at Carson before the Great Depression. Times had changed, and there was no going back to the days of the traditional orphanage, despite calls to that effect by some conservative politicians like the newly elected Speaker of the U.S. House of Representatives, Newt Gingrich, in early 1995.

The past would not repeat itself. Knowing this and being willing to adapt to new realities have allowed Carson to flourish long after the day of the orphanage has passed, while many other institutions with similar origins (but that had refused to move with the times) were forced to close their doors. Unfortunately, the dearth of competent histories of individual orphanages and child-care institutions has made it impossible to draw many fruitful comparisons between Carson and its counterparts in the region and beyond.

Clearly, not every event in the seventy-five-year history of the Carson College for Orphan Girls and the Carson Valley School can be neatly examined within the context of progressivism and its legacies. Many other forces have left their marks on the institution, from the qualities of its leaders and the late romantic architecture of its buildings to national and world events and the development of the child-welfare system itself. Yet the theme of progressivism does provide a real and compelling focus for studying the evolution of Carson and, through it, a microcosm of the child-welfare system in the United States during this century.

Although this progressive institution is located just beyond the official boundaries of Philadelphia, more Carson children have come from the City of Brotherly Love than from any other locale. Benefactor Robert Carson made the bulk of his money in Philadelphia, and numerous members of the Carson board have lived in the city. For all these reasons, the school has been essentially a Philadelphia institution since the beginning, a fact that receives due emphasis in the title for this book: *Philadelphia's Progressive Orphanage: The Carson Valley School.*

Like many of the author's earlier works, this study is written with several audiences in mind: alumni, staff, and friends of Carson, general readers in the greater Philadelphia area, students of the child-welfare system, and historians of the progressive movement, as well as educational, urban, and architectural historians.

CHAPTER ONE

DIFFICULT BIRTH

As with most historical questions, those which seek to establish the precise beginnings of an institution can be difficult to answer. There is invariably a seminal idea, or cluster of ideas. From this point, years or even decades can elapse before the first shovel of earth is turned and buildings begin to arise. A welter of legal documents, provisions for governing boards, the hiring of staff, and some plan of operation necessarily precede opening day. In Carson's case, the birth date is even more difficult to ascertain because of protracted court battles over the Carson will, followed by war, inflation, shortages of building materials, transportation difficulties, and labor strikes. Thus an array of formative events command the historian's attention: Robert Carson's first apparent musings about founding an orphanage for girls (1890s); the writing of the Carson will (1903);

Carson's death (1907); the death of Carson's widow (1912); receipt of the institution's charter of incorporation and appointment of its first board of trustees (1914); the acceptance of the first few orphans into care (1916); the beginning of construction (1917); the official opening (1918); or completion of the initial set of buildings (1920).

Thus the beginnings of Carson College were characterized by many difficulties and uncertainties. Nor were there any clear indications during this period of gestation that an exciting experiment in progressive child care and education would emerge during Carson College's first years of operation. On the contrary, many of the stipulations set down by its benefactor were anything but progressive, while numerous elements of the architecture that was adopted for the buildings exuded a dreamy romanticism, including decorative themes that depicted women solely as wives and mothers. At the same time, the interiors of these first buildings were not arranged in every aspect with an eye to the practical, everyday needs of an enlightened orphanage. Progressive forces would prevail at Carson despite these travails. Indeed, the lack of any clear vision of schooling and residential life during what one might call Carson College's prehistory would frequently present difficulties for its later progressive program.

In any case, early accounts of the institution must begin with its benefactor, Robert Niedermark Carson (1846-1907). Surprisingly little information about this man has survived, despite the fact that he was a wealthy and important entrepreneur in his day. He was born in Philadelphia and apparently grew up in rather modest circumstances.[1] Nothing is known about his education, but by the 1870s he was associated with the successful Philadelphia banking and brokerage firm of William H. Shelmerdine and Company. In 1876 Carson and the Shelmerdine firm began to invest in what were then called street railways (a term that is confusing for later generations, since these street railways were actually cars pulled by horses along iron rails).[2] From these early investments in horsecar lines, Carson went on to become president of the People's Passenger Railway Company, which was a consolidation of various horsecar operations. Most of these routes were electrified in the 1890s and were thereby transformed into electrical trolley-car lines.[3]

Carson resigned his presidency of People's Passenger in 1893, though he continued to own considerable stock in the company. He then turned his attention to creating electrically powered interurban rail lines that ran out to the Philadelphia suburbs, as well as to various towns and cities beyond. As part of this venture he established the Interstate Trolley Com-

Fig. 1.   Robert N. Carson. CVS.

pany, which operated interurban routes from Philadelphia to Chester, Norristown, Reading, and Wilkes-Barre (all in Pennsylvania) and to Wilmington, Delaware—among other destinations. An amusement park outside Reading that was owned by the company (a device commonly used by traction companies in those days to lure weekend riders during the summer season) bore the name Carsonia Park in his honor.[4]

Worth an estimated $5 million at the time of his death in 1907, Carson lived his later adult life like many other rich men of his day. He and his wife, Isabel Frances "Fannie" (Flickinger) Carson, spent their summers among other wealthy families at Newport, Rhode Island. And like many of Philadelphia's more prosperous families, the Carsons owned both a country estate and a home in the city. Their downtown residence was at the Hamilton Apartments, a handsome and well-appointed building that Carson himself owned at 1234 Walnut Street.[5]

Carson's country seat was the 225-acre Erdenheim Stock Farm, which he purchased in 1896 for an estimated $100,000. The property lay just northwest of the Philadelphia city limits, near the village of Flourtown and adjacent to the Philadelphia neighborhood of Chestnut Hill. The stock farm had been established in the early 1860s by Aristides Welsh, whose finely bred racehorses were internationally renowned for their first-place showings at Ascot (in England), the Kentucky Derby, and many other famous race courses. This winning tradition had been continued under the farm's next owner, Louis Kittson, who obtained the property about 1890 and then sold it to Carson some six years later.[6]

The breeding and racing of horses, like owning a fine country estate, was one of the ways in which wealthy Americans at the turn of the century tried to imitate the British upper classes. Fox hunting was yet another genteel, Anglophile pursuit for the American rich, a pastime in which Robert Carson indulged as a member of the local Whitemarsh Valley Hunt Club. Their colorful autumn hunts frequently ranged across his own fields and adjoining properties.[7] Set amidst picturesque rolling hills, the fox hunts and fine horse flesh of the Erdenheim Stock Farm exuded an upper-class English aura that would later extend to Carson College itself.

Although newly rich according to the standards of the time, Carson seemed well on his way to making it into the Philadelphia upper class. Besides owning an impressive country estate and belonging to the local hunt club, he was a member of Philadelphia's Union League and the Corinthian Yacht Club, both marks of the proper Philadelphian. He was not a member of the city's most exclusive gentlemen's club, the Philadelphia Club; nor did he and his wife appear in the *Social Register.*[8] Yet Carson had risen far into the city's polite society in the space of several decades.

It was after purchasing his country estate that the childless Robert Carson came up with the idea of establishing an orphanage for girls. According to Frances Carson, her husband wanted to establish an orphanage, to be located on a portion of his property, "as a monument to himself."[9] His explicit model was Philadelphia's Girard College, which had been founded through the beneficence of the wealthy merchant and banker Stephen Girard (1750-1831).[10] In his will Girard left $2 million to establish a school for white orphaned boys. Girard College opened in 1848 in magnificent Greek Revival buildings designed by one of the renowned practitioners of that style, Thomas U. Walter. Although the institution kept its orphans only through what later generations would call the high school years, Girard had used the word "college" in the French sense, which denoted an elementary or secondary school, a somewhat unfortunate choice that would cause much confusion in the decades ahead.[11]

According to several newspaper accounts, Carson's admiration for Girard College had come through his close friendship with Joseph L. Craven, a Philadelphia banker and a member of the Board of City Trusts, which oversaw Girard College. It was reportedly while on a visit to Girard sometime during the 1890s (in the company of Craven) that Carson struck upon the idea of creating a similar institution for orphaned girls. In the years that followed, Robert Carson often visited Girard College and met with Craven to discuss plans for what would become Carson College.[12]

In his will, the main portions of which were completed in 1903 (the same year that he was diagnosed with serious heart disease), Carson left the bulk of his estate to establish an orphanage. Its name, according to his specific instructions, was to be "The Carson College for Orphan Girls." The word "college" came directly from Girard's will, a designation that would create as much confusion for Carson College as it had for Girard, and that would ultimately lead to the decision, a half century later, to change the name to "The Carson Valley School."

The will set down a number of other specific provisions and restrictions. Although many of Carson's ideas were enlightened for the time, several would prove regressive as well as troublesome—and in some cases nearly fatal for the institution. The college was to be located on "not less than fifty nor more than one hundred acres" of Carson's Erdenheim Stock Farm; this acreage was to be on the easternmost portion of the estate, which was closest to the village of Flourtown. The college was to be directed by a board of trustees, comprising seven men appointed by the trustees of the Carson estate and approved by the courts. If possible, Carson desired that three members of the board "be of my own blood, and members of my own family."[13]

One million dollars was set aside for the erection of buildings. The remainder of his estate (less a number of small bequests and a generous income to his wife during her lifetime) was to be held in trust by what was then called the Real Estate Title Insurance and Trust Company of

Philadelphia, with the net income paid to support and maintain Carson College. Specifically mentioned by the will were cottages for the girls—each including dormitory, study, and recreation rooms—and "ample grounds and lawns, with flower beds." There was to be a separate residence for the superintendent and his family. In addition, Carson proposed a school building and "a chapel, assembly or lecture room, for religious services."[14] The latter could be housed in a separate structure or be included as part of a school building. Construction costs not covered by the $1 million would have to be taken from income so as not to make further inroads against the principle. Any surplus not used for Carson College would go to "erecting and furnishing dormitories for sick children in the various Children's Hospitals."[15]

The object of Carson College, according to the will, was "the care, education, maintenance and support of *poor, white, healthy girls, both of whose parents shall be deceased*" (emphasis is added). Preference in admissions was to be given to girls born in Philadelphia and Montgomery County (Carson College's home county), then to natives of other Pennsylvania counties, and last to those from elsewhere in the United States. No orphans could be received from any other institution, and none could be admitted *"under the age of six years or over the age of ten"*[16] (emphasis is added).

As to their education, the girls were "to be given the benefit of a good moral training and taught all the common English branches, including the elements of algebra and geometry, with so much of applied physics, chemistry and natural history as they may be able to comprehend."[17] The elements of instrumental and vocal music would also be made available. In addition to these, the girls were to be taught, "thoroughly and practically, all the domestic arts, including laundering and dressmaking, and also, as far as possible, the domestic sciences, in order that [they] may be prepared to take up successfully housekeeping and nursing." A course in woodworking should also be offered so that the girls could become "familiar with the handling of tools, or any light work."[18] Finally, the girls should learn something about flower and vegetable gardening and the care of chickens, cows, and other farm animals.

As to religion, Carson girls were to receive training in "the fundamental doctrines of Christianity," but the college was never to fall under the control of any religious denomination, nor could there be on the grounds religious services associated with any particular church. Unlike the Girard will, which forbade clergy even to enter the grounds, clergy could visit Carson so long as they did not attempt to indoctrinate or convert.

The will specified that the girls should live in cottages of not more than twenty-five children, headed by a housemother, with much of the work in cottages to be done by the girls themselves as part of their domestic training. There was to be no "uniformity of dress . . . in order to avoid the appearance of charity."[19]

Mandating cottages for Carson College was particularly enlightened, since nineteenth-century orphans commonly had resided in huge buildings, where they slept in dormitories, took their meals in large halls (often in silence), and had to wear identical uniforms.[20] Despite its being a model for Carson in many instances, Philadelphia's Girard College was a good example of such an "unenlightened" institution. Although there was no uniformity of dress, the Girard boys took their meals in large dining halls and slept in dormitories rather than in smaller bedrooms. Several of the buildings at Girard housed as many as one hundred boys each.[21] According to Neva R. Deardorff, in an article for the April 1924 issue of the *Survey* (a leading progressive magazine of the day), some 1,200 of the older Girard boys were "fed in a great barnlike building with long tables and small round stools." Continuing with her description of accommodations at Girard during the mid-1920s, Deardorff wrote, "They are housed in dormitories, each with thirty to thirty-five cots; sometimes the cot has a chair beside it. The boys keep their few personal possessions in lockers in the dormitories and study rooms in the building. The three-hundred younger boys all live and have their lessons in one large building. . . . They, too, have one large dining-room, and dormitories."[22] The massive Greek Revival temples that sheltered the boys only reinforced the lack of anything resembling a homelike atmosphere at Girard.

Carson College would not be the first orphanage to break from a "congregate" model like Girard's and replace it with a cottage arrangement. Rather, the cottage system had been introduced on an impressive scale at the New York orphanage at Hastings-on-Hudson just after the turn of the century, but Carson College would be one of the first to follow this example.[23] Whether Robert Carson took his inspiration from Hastings-on-Hudson is unknown.

Whatever his source for the idea of cottages, the first event in actually implementing the proposed Carson College unfolded dramatically on the evening of October 15, 1907, when Robert Carson slumped over dead in his seat at Philadelphia's Chestnut Street Opera House while watching a performance of *The Merry Widow*. Accounts of his death, along with the contents of his will, were reported in detail by the Philadelphia metropolitan press. The initial public reaction to his philanthropy was very positive, with women's clubs in the city being especially pleased about the projected Carson College for Orphan Girls.[24]

Yet by early December of 1907 strong objections to Carson's plans began to appear in the Philadelphia newspapers. The most significant criticisms were over the requirement that admission be limited to young, healthy girls with deceased parents. According to child-welfare organizations in the city, these were the very sorts of orphans who were the most easily placed into good homes. In the words of Miss Mary E. Richmond of Philadelphia's Society of Organizing Charity (and one of the foremost pioneering social workers in the United States), "There are a great many professional people who have no children and who, if they can be assured that a child has no serious physical defect, and that there will be no interference from parents, will readily take the child into their homes. There is no difficulty placing such healthy girls when both parents are dead." Furthermore, Richmond believed that such attempts to set down restrictions in perpetuity were bound to spell trouble for Carson College: "The whole history of charitable bequests is an interesting illustration of the futility of trying to restrict the boundaries of beneficence for, say, more than thirty years after the testator's death. If Mr. Carson had looked around him he would have found that the whole orphan [one who had neither parent] is in a rather peculiar position."[25]

In addition to Richmond's concerns were those of child-welfare professionals generally, who, at that time in the United States, were already beginning to turn against the very concept of orphanages and to advocate foster care as a far more desirable alternative. Indeed, just two years after Robert Carson's death, the 1909 White House Conference on the Care of Dependent Children, hosted by President Theodore Roosevelt, declared that "children from unfit homes and children who have no homes . . . should, so far as practicable, be cared for in families."[26] Thus it appeared that Carson College would be opening at the exact moment when the child-welfare community was turning against the idea of institutional care.

Such concerns were quickly seized by certain of Carson's nieces and nephews in an attempt to break the will and to claim a substantial portion of the estate for themselves (a course that had been unsuccessfully pursued eighty years earlier by relatives of the childless Stephen Girard).[27] In fact, Carson had provided modest sums for them: Those nieces and nephews whose parents had died during Carson's lifetime were each to receive the annual interest or dividend income on $20,000; grandnieces and grandnephews whose parents were still alive at Carson's death were each to receive the annual income on $10,000.[28]

On August 5, 1910, nine of these heirs filed suit before Judge William F. Solly in the Montgomery County Orphans Court at Norristown, asking that the registrar of wills be enjoined from probating the will. Besides citing the impracticality of launching an orphanage as stipulated in Carson's will, they contended that those who had witnessed the signing of the will had exercised "undue influence," in that they were either officers or stockholders of the Real Estate Title Insurance and Trust Company, which had been designated to administer the Carson estate and subsequent trust, and who stood to earn large commissions from both.[29] At least some of the heirs also believed that Mrs. Carson had disliked her husband's family and had pressured him to exclude them from the bulk of his estate.[30]

Although ill herself at the time of the dispute over the will, Carson's widow, Isabel Frances Carson, testified against the nieces and nephews. She related to the court that her husband had made her promise never to try to break his will, adding that he had wanted to create an orphanage for girls "as a monument to himself." She added that her husband "always felt sure he was right in everything he did."[31] Mrs. Carson, who had appeared in court against the advice of her physician, had to curtail her deposition from the witness stand because of faintness, details of which were reported widely in the Philadelphia newspapers, including the fact that her nurse had to administer some medication as she helped her out of the courtroom.

When the Montgomery County Court upheld the will, the nieces and nephews appealed the decision to the Pennsylvania Supreme Court. Those attending the session on February 2, 1912, as well as those reading about the proceedings in the newspapers, received an additional bit of drama when Pennsylvania attorney general John C. Bell "was overcome" while arguing on behalf of the Carson will and was forced to retire for a short rest.[32] The court went on to rule that the appeal was premature, since Mrs. Carson was still living, and that therefore the provisions for creating an orphanage for girls—the most important aspect of the contested will— had not yet gone into effect. The death of Isabel Frances Carson on July 4,

1912, seemed to remove this obstacle, but the high court ruled again in May 1913 that an appeal was unwarranted, this time until a second accounting of the estate, occasioned by Mrs. Carson's death, had been completed and presented to the Montgomery County courts.[33]

This accounting came in September 1913, allowing the dissenting heirs to renew their legal battle at the Montgomery County Court House, while newspaper reporters telegraphed the continuing saga of the Carson bequest to their editors in Philadelphia in order to make the late afternoon editions. On November 29 Judge Solly again upheld the will. By February 1914 the nieces and nephews were back before the Pennsylvania Supreme Court with yet another appeal. After hearing the various arguments, the high court ruled in favor of the will on March 9.[34]

Nearly seven years after the death of Robert Carson, the way now seemed clear to realize his dream of an orphanage for girls. Yet litigation was not quite at an end. Substantial income had accumulated since the death of Mrs. Carson in 1912 (but before Carson College could go into operation), and the trustees wanted to apply this income to the principal of the trust. They too appealed their case all the way to the Pennsylvania Supreme Court, which ruled in May 1916. In this instance the court held that the accumulated income (by then some $300,000) must go to children's hospitals in Philadelphia and elsewhere in Pennsylvania, since the Carson will had directed that any funds not used by Carson College must be turned over to such institutions.[35]

Meanwhile a board of trustees had been appointed, a charter of incorporation had been secured from the state of Pennsylvania, and bylaws had been adopted by the board—all three steps accomplished in 1914.[36] The charter, as directed by the Carson will, provided for a board of trustees "composed of seven reputable and experienced white male citizens of the county [Montgomery] in which said college is located, and of the City of Philadelphia."[37] Their successors would be nominated by the trustees of the Carson estate (as distinguished from the board of trustees of Carson College) and approved by the Court of Common Pleas of Montgomery County. The bylaws directed that there be monthly meetings of Carson's board of trustees, held on the third Friday of each month, and an annual meeting on the third Friday of January. Officers of the board were a chairman, vice-chairman, secretary, and treasurer, all elected by the board. There were standing committees for buildings, finance, and management.

The charter members of Carson College's board of trustees were James P. Carson, Walter W. Perkins, Thomas M. Thompson, Theron I.

Crane, Otto T. Mallery, John Gribbel, and George Vaux Jr. The majority of these men were well placed among the socioeconomic elite of Philadelphia—and even of the nation at large. Indeed, they seemed to leap from the pages of *The Protestant Establishment,* a book by the Philadelphia historian and sociologist E. Digby Baltzell.[38] Four of the seven board members (Crane, Mallery, Gribbel, and Vaux), for example, appeared in the Philadelphia *Social Register,* and four of them (Mallery, Gribbel, Vaux, and Perkins) made *Who's Who in America* at some point during their lives.[39] So far as can be determined, all seven men were Protestants. The only two board members who did not appear in either the *Social Register* or *Who's Who* were members of Robert N. Carson's "family": his brother-in-law Thomas M. Thompson and his nephew James P. Carson (neither of whom were among the Carson heirs who had brought suit against the will).[40] James P. Carson was a partner in the M. H. Carson and Son Real Estate and Insurance Company.[41] Thompson, it appears, was a former Philadelphia city councilman, city controller, and director of public works.[42]

Perkins's occupation is unknown, but his large and fashionable residence in the Germantown section of Philadelphia suggested that he was a man of some wealth. As to the occupations of the other four board members, Crane was an industrialist; Gribbel was a successful banker and manufacturer of gas meters; and Vaux appeared to be independently wealthy, as did Mallery. Crane had founded Pilling and Crane Iron and Steel Company and sat on a number of industrial boards. At the time of his death in November 1929 he left an estate valued at just over $4 million.[43] Gribbel, like Crane, was on the boards of several industries and financial institutions other than his own, in addition to being president of the socially exclusive Union League club of Philadelphia.[44]

Vaux was active in various Quaker charities, served as chairman of the U.S. Board of Indian Commissioners, and was a member of the board of the Eastern State Penitentiary. In addition, he was a "gentleman naturalist" associated with the Academy of Natural Sciences of Philadelphia and was best known for his research on the glaciers of Colorado.[45] Mallery reportedly inherited about $2 million around the time that he joined the Carson board. He spent his life serving on public commissions and civic boards, along with holding several subordinate cabinet positions with the state and national governments. In Philadelphia he was associated most with the promotion of public playgrounds and recreation centers, causes closely connected with the progressive movement in urban areas. Mallery would be one of the mainstays of the Carson board, serving continuously from his appointment in 1914 to his death in 1956, a forty-two-year record that has not been equaled since.[46]

In the context of the times, it made sense to appoint men of high social and economic status to the Carson board. It was such men who managed the commercial and financial affairs of the city and who were thought to have the skills, experience, and personal contacts that would allow them to govern a well-endowed institution like Carson College. The impressive size of the Carson bequest, and the prospects of creating a philanthropic enterprise on a vast scale, doubtless appealed to these men of means and could only add to their reputations as substantial members of the wider Philadelphia community. In any case, Robert Carson himself, a wealthy man of affairs, would surely have affirmed such a selection.

Although these board members were men of wealth and high social standing, several of them appear to have been somewhat forward-thinking individuals of the progressive type. This seems particularly evident in the cases of Mallery and Vaux. In fact, Vaux was reportedly dubious about the whole idea of establishing a new orphanage, and was quoted a number of years later as having said more than once that "there is no place today for the Orphan Asylum."[47] According to a document from the middle 1930s, it would also seem that most of the other board members had shared Vaux's belief that "the day of building orphanages was over."[48] As genuine progressive reformers, Vaux and Mallery probably agreed with the White House Conference's recommendations in favor of foster care. Learning of such sentiments, the practical businessmen on the board may not have been too confident about investing money in what looked to be a declining or discredited method of dependent-child care. Indeed, if they were like many other captains of industry in the region, they probably shared the practical, no-nonsense worldview of leading Quakers, even if they themselves did not belong to the Society of Friends.[49]

Yet stating such doubts in public or challenging the provisions of the bequest would only have given ammunition to those Carson heirs who had filed suit against the will. Thus, with no real alternative but to work within the confines of the bequest as presented to them, the board decided to use Robert Carson's money to create a wholly enlightened program. Besides caring for needy children, Carson College would provide "an opportunity for experimental teaching," which "might be a contribution . . . to current social work thinking."[50] At the same time, the college might "contribute to the life of all the young people in the [Flourtown] community, and [to] better neighborhood planning."[51]

Whatever the case, the Carson board assembled for its first organizational meeting on October 21, 1914, at the offices of the Real Estate Title Insurance and Trust Company in downtown Philadelphia. Meetings continued to be held there until the board rented its own offices in the fall of 1916 in room 718 of the Witherspoon Building, likewise in downtown Philadelphia.[52] (In 1924 the offices would move to room 1803 of the Packard Building.)[53] The board elected John Gribbel as its first chairman, James P. Carson as secretary, and Walter W. Perkins as treasurer.

The board had much to do before Carson College could open its doors. In preparation for its many tasks, the board agreed to hold a joint conference with the board of another projected orphanage for girls to be known as the Charles E. Ellis Memorial School, which was eventually located in Delaware County, Pennsylvania, near the community of Newtown Square. At its disposal was approximately $4.5 million, which had been provided in the will of Charles E. Ellis, who had died in 1909, just two years after Robert Carson.[54] Although Ellis, like Carson, had made his money in the traction business, the two men had apparently not known anything of each other's plans, thus raising the specter of a redundant and possibly wasteful expenditure of resources. In order to explore common difficulties, as well as the possibilities for cooperation, both the Carson and Ellis boards called upon Dr. Hastings H. Hart, director of the Child Helping Department of New York's Russell Sage Foundation. Hart organized a joint conference, attended by some one hundred educators and experts in child care, at Philadelphia's newly built and lavish Bellevue-Stratford Hotel for October 13-14, 1915.[55]

On the eve of the Carson-Ellis conference Dr. Hart lamented to the *North American,* then an outspokenly progressive newspaper in Philadelphia, that the two bequests had added some $9.5 million to the $10 million that already existed in the Philadelphia area for the care and training of orphaned or otherwise handicapped girls. These sums made a grand total of nearly $20 million, estimated to be the largest amount available for such purposes in any city in the world.[56] In other words, there appeared to be little real need for either the Carson or Ellis bequests. Unfortunately there are no figures on the numbers of children needing care in the Philadelphia area at the time, and on the number of beds in the city's various orphanages.

Under the circumstances there was talk of having the courts—or even the Pennsylvania State legislature—intervene to consolidate some or all of these institutions, along with their funds. On the eve of the Carson-Ellis conference, even Pennsylvania governor Martin G. Brumbaugh promised to throw his influence behind one or more merger schemes, though nothing came of the idea.[57]

In its final report on the Carson-Ellis conference, the Committee on Conclusions repeated Hart's admonitions, made a brief comparison of the Carson and Ellis bequests, and ended with several recommendations to the two boards. Among the observations was the fact that neither of the wills had designated women to sit on the institutions' boards of trustees, even though both were intended exclusively for girls. However, the Ellis will had mandated a "Board of Education," one or more of whose members might be women. It also authorized a separate "Advisory Board of Women." Although the Carson will did not envision such additional boards upon which women might serve, the conference report indicated that there was nothing to prevent the Carson authorities from creating an advisory group of women.

As to troublesome restrictions in the two wills, the conference report noted that both institutions were open exclusively to the white race. Another difficulty in both was that admissions were limited to certain age groups: girls had to be between six and ten to enter Carson College, while Ellis forbade admission to girls over the age of thirteen. Carson could admit girls from a wide geographic area, with first priority going to Philadelphia and Montgomery County, then to Pennsylvania, and then to the United States as a whole; Ellis was limited to Philadelphia and environs. But Carson was more restrictive in its limitation to whole orphans, while Ellis required only that the girls be "fatherless."

The conferees believed that such encumbrances would prevent both Carson College and the Ellis School from acquiring sufficient numbers of children to use their resources fully and efficiently, with Dr. Hart suggesting that the institutions would need to serve about five hundred girls each for optimal operation. The conference thus advised the two boards to consider legal proceedings to remove restrictions in the wills, thereby allowing them to take girls of widely varying ages and to accept nonorphans whose parents, for a number of reasons, could not care for them at home.[58]

The report also offered advice in other areas. Doubtless with Girard College in mind, it warned against "large monumental buildings." In addition, only those structures that were necessary for immediate needs should be erected, and these should be placed in a villagelike setting. The girls should be housed in cottages, each one of which would be "a complete unit of family life." All schooling ought to be carried out in accordance with the most modern practices, thereby preparing the girls to become self-supporting. Finally, the two institutions were urged to cooperate with each other whenever possible. Although the terms of the two wills would not allow them to merge completely, there was no reason why they could not work to avoid wasteful duplications.[59] (Perhaps because they would both compete for a limited pool of potential applicants, neither institution would seek close cooperation in the future.)

Several of the conference suggestions had already been envisioned in the Carson will, namely, proposals for cottage living and a practical education. When it came to restrictions in the will, however, the Carson board would not move to break or even skirt its benefactor's instructions for many years, despite the numerous early warnings that would later be borne out by events. Most of all, they may have feared that any challenges to the will on their part would only strengthen the claim of those Carson heirs who were insisting that the whole idea of Carson College was impractical.

By the time the Carson-Ellis conference took place, the Carson board had already begun to take steps for building and staffing the Carson College for Orphan Girls, though they continued to confer with Dr. Hart of the Russell Sage Foundation about details. Any particular advice to them has not survived. In all probability Hart reiterated his proposal, given at the Carson-Ellis conference as well as in his earlier writings, that the girls be housed in small, homelike cottages.[60] In December 1915, the board hired Leonard W. Coleman as superintendent, or business manager, at a salary of $2,500 per year.[61] This was the only senior staff position that had been mentioned in the Carson will, and at first he was responsible for overseeing the entire operation.

The first crucial decision in getting the institution up and running was the choice of an architect for the buildings. In the summer of 1915 the board approved and sent out a "Program of Competition."[62] This program envisioned an impressive array of structures: an administration building, a school, a boiler and power house, a superintendent's cottage, eight cottages for girls, a chapel, a greenhouse, an infirmary, and two farmers' (or tenants') houses. The administration building was to include a "Carson memorial Room" that would serve as a museum and meeting place for the board of trustees. In the school building there were to be ten classrooms and an auditorium for three hundred people, along with a gymnasium, shops, playrooms, and teachers' offices. The superintendent's residence was to be "aloof from the general cottage life," with seven family bedrooms and two rooms for servants. Each of the eight cottages would accommodate twenty-five girls and come equipped with two classrooms (assumedly for teaching domestic subjects), a playroom in the basement, a dining room large enough to seat thirty, and a living room "capable of being divided into two parts." Each cottage must come with two acres of land, three-quarters of an a acre for a play area (with "sand piles" and trees), one-quarter of an acre for a vegetable garden, and the rest in grass, flowers, shrubs, and trees. A central power plant would heat these and the other structures by means of ducts that ran through underground passageways, which should be large enough to be used as sheltered walkways in bad weather (a feature that had been specifically mentioned in the Carson will).[63] Such features were a far cry from the bleak institutions, with their dormitories and large dining halls, that had been integral parts of American orphanages during the past century.

Given the fact that the board envisioned spending $300,000 on such buildings (an impressive sum in 1915), the competition was very keen. On October 8 the board selected Albert Kelsey (1870–1950), who was already a well-known Philadelphia architect.[64] Born in St. Louis, Missouri, he had graduated from the University of Pennsylvania in 1895. He did architectural apprenticeships with Theophilus P. Chandler and with the firm of Cope and Stewardson, both successful Philadelphia establishments. Kelsey then joined with two other architects to form the firm of Kennedy, Hays, and Kelsey. Around 1905, Kelsey became associated with Paul Cret, collaborating with him, as a junior partner, on the design of the so-called Pan American Building in Washington, D.C. He continued to work with Cret in planning the Benjamin Franklin Parkway, a grand boulevard lined with neoclassical buildings that was Philadelphia's most important contribution to what is known as the City Beautiful movement. Kelsey also designed a number of private residences, including a large country house for Jay Cooke III not far from the Carson campus.[65]

Despite his designs for neoclassical structures like the Pan American Building, Kelsey might be viewed from the perspective of the 1990s as a late-romantic architect whose designs were as firmly rooted in associationist concepts of art and architecture as were those of most nineteenth-century practitioners. Broadly defined, associationism was an approach to the arts that held that paintings, sculpture, buildings, and decorative objects could affect the well-being of individuals, as well as entire

Fig. 2.   Albert Kelsey, original architect of Carson College, standing in front of Stork Hill (Primrose) Cottage, with primrose tiles around doorway. CVS.

societies, by causing people to *associate* themselves with certain thoughts, feelings, and values. By extension, unattractive and badly built structures reflected a basic dishonesty and ugliness of spirit within the society that had given rise to them. At the same time, this dishonesty and ugliness were perpetuated in the hearts and minds of all who beheld such misbegotten works. (An associationist approach to architecture and decoration continues to be employed in theme parks like Disney World or in restaurants where diners are made to feel that they have entered a faraway time or distant land.)

Although there were many apostles of associationist theories in the English-speaking world, such ideas were most closely linked with the voluminous writings of the English social reformer and art critic John Ruskin (1819–1900).[66] Ruskin was widely read by educated Americans well into the twentieth century, and his views about art and architecture were doubtless familiar to someone like Albert Kelsey. Thus Kelsey intended his neoclassical edifices along the Benjamin Franklin Parkway to exude a sense of order, power, and beauty at a time when many parts of the city were plagued by dirt, overcrowding, crime, and disease. In similar fashion, he and other late-nineteenth- and early-twentieth-century architects could turn to medieval English themes or American colonial styles in order to convey their own as well as their clients' distaste for the less savory aspects of the modern city with its increasing number of immigrants who were not from the British Isles, or even from northern and western Europe.

It was within this tradition that Albert Kelsey set out to create a "fantasy" village at Carson College. For his buildings he chose an English Tudor Gothic motif then in vogue among wealthy Americans, including many in nearby Chestnut Hill and in the more distant suburbs of the Philadelphia Main Line, as a statement of their British roots, Anglophile tastes, and upper-class standing.[67] As a late medieval style it also seemed to decry the ugliness of sooty factories and urban slums, which many members of the middle and upper classes were seeking to escape by moving to the suburbs. A growing list of colleges and universities had also turned to English Gothic designs in order to associate themselves with ancient seats of learning in the British Isles such as Oxford and Cambridge. In Philadelphia the University of Pennsylvania had adopted Gothic in the late nineteenth century, and Villanova College, on the Main Line, had taken up the idiom around 1900.[68] Beyond the region, both Princeton and Yale were donning Gothic garb. There is thus good reason to believe that the Collegiate

Gothic style was one of the sources of Kelsey's building designs for Carson College.[69]

Kelsey also embraced various decorative schemes from the so-called Arts and Crafts movement, which echoed a late-romantic distaste for many aspects of industrialization, and especially for machine-made goods. According to arts-and-crafts advocates, such as Ruskin himself and fellow Englishman William Morris, mass-produced furnishings and decorative objects were stultifying, uniform, and frequently unattractive. The decline of handcrafted goods, it was claimed, had also deprived skilled artisans of their independence and creativity, thereby forcing most workers into a dreary industrial regimen where they were robbed of their manhood and self-esteem.[70]

Of course, this hearkening back to the past for architectural and decorative ideas had its limitations. For example, late-romantic architects, including Kelsey, had no qualms about using the latest building materials, such as reinforced concrete, about applying false half-timbering on gable ends, or about installing all the latest utilities (which his clients would have demanded in any case). Nor did Kelsey or anyone else seem to realize the incongruity of constructing a seemingly preindustrial village with the money that Robert Carson had made through investing in the latest technology of his day, namely, electrified street railroads and interurban lines. In this sense Kelsey and the Carson board were not unlike wealthy suburbanites in nearby Chestnut Hill or the Main Line, who used money earned in modern industrial pursuits to build romantic houses in semi-rural retreats. During the early decades of its existence, certain aspects of Carson College's program would reflect these same ambivalences and contradictions, as would many progressive educators and progressive reformers (see Chapters 2 and 3).

Although Kelsey submitted plans for all the structures outlined in the Program of Competition, the board chose to proceed cautiously. The Carson will had asked that buildings be erected only as they were needed, and it was impossible for the board to know just how many orphans the institution would enroll during its early years. Thus they authorized only three cottages and a superintendent's residence in late 1915.[71]

Kelsey put great thought into arranging these first buildings, along with the other structures envisioned for the future. At the time he began his work, the Carson grounds amounted to some eighty-seven acres, in the middle of which was a shallow bowel-like valley. Kelsey ran his main road along the eastern rim of this valley, in some cases banking up earth along the edges in order to increase the steepness of the decline. When completed, one entered the grounds from Wissahickon Avenue, on the south, through a three-acre woodland of hemlocks, which screened the property from the road at the same time that it served as a gateway into Kelsey's children's village. Opposite this entrance one could originally view two church spires off in the distance in Chestnut Hill, those belonging to Our Mother of Consolation Roman Catholic Church and to the old First Presbyterian Church (both of which had been dismantled at the time of this writing). In order to improve the area immediately opposite the entrance, the Carson board purchased a two-acre strip of land just across Wissahickon Avenue in the summer of 1917 and planted it in white pines.[72]

Upon emerging from the evergreen plantings at this south entrance, a series of curves in the road treated the beholder to changing vistas as the buildings appeared and then disappeared behind low hills. Where the road exited on the north—the Mill Road side of the property—there was another screen of trees, made up largely of white pines. Various broadleaved trees lined the roadway at points along its winding path or embraced the various cottages in seemingly random clumps. (Some of these roadway plantings, it would appear, were not made until 1925, in accordance with a plan drawn up by Arthur Folsom Paul, a local "landscape engineer.")[73]

Other landscape features were the "Moon Well" and "Star Well," connected by a "wonder walk" of soft pine needles. The wells are in fact round slabs of stone, with raised carvings of a star on one and the moon on the other. These rested on a small rise at the north side of campus, in a thicket of white pines. According to the *Architectural Record*, which published a long illustrated article on Kelsey's work at Carson in July 1921, "Here in the young forest are the Moon Well and the Star Well, . . . which, when the trees are grown, will lie sunken at the bottom of a dark forest circle. . . . They will be quite druidical sort[s] of places. For the imaginative life of children, there is a promising subtlety and oddity in the idea."[74] The extension of a small grassy meadow into one area of the pines near the two wells made for an outdoor theater that would soon be known as Sherwood Forest (doubtless because of the many Robin Hood plays put on there by the girls).

Toward the southwest corner of the property, where the land started to rise out of the valley (near the present Lower Beech Cottage), Kelsey designed a sunken garden that featured a walkway lined with parallel rows

Fig. 3.   Aerial view of Carson College, October 22, 1938, showing landscape features: the Wissahickon Avenue entrance through a hemlock grove is near the lower-left corner; Sherwood Forest is near the upper-right corner; the four cottages designed by Albert Kelsey and built 1917–20 are just above center (l. to r., Thistle, Stork Hill, Red Gables/Mother Goose); the two later cottages designed by Pope Barney and completed in 1931 are just below center (l. to r., Lower Beech and Upper Beech). Photo by Victor Dobbins, Hagley Museum and Library.

of linden trees. These were to be part of the grounds of the superintendent's residence, which had originally been planned for this site but which was not erected there (because Carson's first president, Elsa Ueland, objected to such an extravagance).

Reflecting on an interview with Kelsey in January 1917, a writer for one of the Philadelphia newspapers waxed eloquent on the architect's village for orphaned girls: "Every little girl who comes to Carson . . . and who has lain awake at nights wondering just what the man in the moon

Fig. 4.   Front elevation, by Albert Kelsey, of a projected administration building and school for Carson College that were never executed. *AR,* July 1921, 6.

was saying if only he could be heard, and . . . just what tune that tiny star way off in the corner twinkled to, will only have to take a stroll in the wonder-walk to know these things. I shouldn't be at all surprised if Peter Pan and Wendy and the Blue Bird children didn't all vacate their present quarters and come to the wonder-walk to live."[75]

Kelsey arranged his buildings, like the winding roadway through the property, along the rim of the shallow, central valley. All the structures were rendered in Chestnut Hill stone—also known as Wissahickon schist—a locally quarried material that had been used in and around Chestnut Hill since the earliest days of settlement, and that tied its various types of architecture together in both texture and color. It is a warmly colored stone, with gray, brown, and sometimes bluish layers, containing a great deal of mica, which glistens in the sunlight. In using this stone, as well as in employing late medieval English motifs that were then all the rage among Chestnut Hill's prosperous residents, Kelsey connected the Carson campus stylistically to this neighboring community.[76]

But unlike Chestnut Hill's stately Tudor Gothic residences, Kelsey's buildings were conceived more on a children's scale. Thus, in addition to the standard low Gothic arches and steep gable ends, Kelsey covered his roofs with multicolored, rounded pentiles, with reds prevailing toward the top and then gradually shifting to greens and blues at the lower ends. The triangular areas between the gables were decorated in low reliefs, showing Mother Goose on one building and storks with babies in their beaks on another.

Since the school would be inhabited by girls, Kelsey employed a number of decorative themes that any cultured Victorian would have easily associated with the so-called feminine character. Indeed, Kelsey's basic idea could have come straight out of Ruskin's essay "Of Queens' Gardens," which had been well known and widely read on both sides of the Atlantic for two generations. Here, and in several other works, Ruskin had asserted the familiar romantic belief that women were innately closer to nature than were men, and had frequently compared them to flowers. Thus he wrote that a girl "grows as a flower does."[77]

Although one can only surmise that Kelsey was familiar with Ruskin's ideas, the architect's beliefs about women and their place in the world were clearly romantic and Victorian. For instance, each of his four structures carried the name of a flower. These were Cornflower, Narcissus, Primrose, and Thistle. Only the latter designation would survive in common

Fig. 5.   A portion of Red Gables Cottage (Narcissus) in foreground, with portions of Mother Goose Cottage (Cornflower) on far left. Photo by Graydon Wood, April 8, 1986. CVS.

usage, as both faculty and students would soon give the other buildings nicknames that corresponded to their most noticeable features. Thus Cornflower became Mother Goose, Narcissus became Red Gables, and Primrose became Stork Hill. The floral motifs remained, however, with the appropriate bloom appearing in specially designed glazed tiles set around the main doors of each building (with the exception of Thistle, which had only one small thistle image on the upper left side of its doorway). The flower designs were also repeated in wooden carvings as part of the colorful gables on each cottage.

The tile work came from the Enfield Pottery and Tile Works, located nearby in the Springfield Township community of Enfield (now more commonly known as Oreland). Its founder and principal owner was J. H. Dulles "Joe" Allen (1879–1940), who had explored several types of clay and sand on his farm at Church and Paper Mill Roads in 1906 and soon thereafter set up a pottery studio on the site. Allen and his artisans specialized in handmade products for a given project or commission, both characteristics of the Arts and Crafts movement and of the emphasis placed by some progressives upon restoring honest craftsmanship. (The Great Depression of the 1930s—and the virtual halt in lavish building projects—would lead to Enfield's demise in the mid-1930s.)[78]

One of Allen's closest friends since childhood had been Otto Mallery, among the most influential members of the Carson board of trustees. In 1913 Mallery invested in Enfield Tile and became vice-president of the company. At about that same time Enfield was working with Albert Kelsey and Paul Cret on the decoration of the Pan American Building in Washington. Allen collaborated with Cret on a number of other projects over the years. Among Enfield's most important commissions were decorative tiles for the Detroit Museum of Art, the Philadelphia Museum of Art, the Barnes Foundation (in Merion, Pennsylvania), and the Bok Tower, a two-hundred-foot carillon near Lake Wales, Florida.[79]

One is left to surmise that Enfield Tile and architect Kelsey, both of them well known to Carson board member Otto Mallery, came together as an artistic package and that Kelsey was something of an "inside" candidate for the Carson commission from the very beginning.[80] Kelsey's use of Enfield tiles to execute his floral themes at the various Carson cottages is thus not surprising. Lending further support to the close connections between Kelsey and Allen is the fact that Allen was also a consultant on furniture and interior decoration for Carson College.[81]

Fig. 6. A gable end of Mother Goose Cottage (Cornflower), with Mother Goose pargeting, decorated vergeboard, and carved cornflower inset. Photo by Graydon Wood, April 8, 1986. CVS.

Fig. 7. Children at the entrance to Mother Goose Cottage (Cornflower), with floral tiles visible to the right of the doorway. Photo 1930s. CVS.

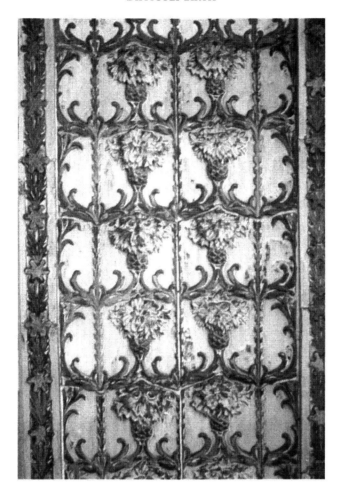

Fig. 8.   Floral tiles, detail, Mother Goose Cottage. Photo by the author, 1994.

In addition to the floral designs executed in tiles (as well as in wood), Kelsey had carved under the side gables of two cottages sayings that likewise reflected his romantic views of women. At Narcissus (Red Gables) are the words "Quiet Strength," and next door at Cornflower (Mother Goose) the phrase "Une Femme Doit Plaire; C'est Son Bonheur" (A woman ought to please; that is her happiness").

Kelsey also planned several allegories to be portrayed in exterior relief panels as well as on an elaborate tower. In yet another gesture to his romantic views of womanhood, these would depict a woman's life from

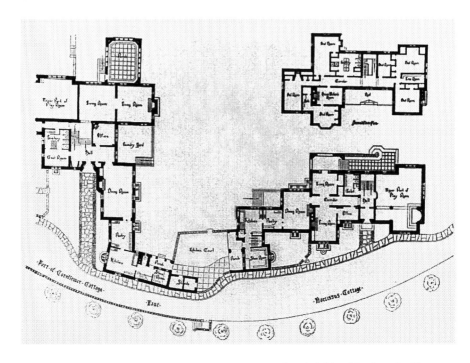

Fig. 9.   Floor plan of Mother Goose (Cornflower) and Red Gables (Narcissus). *AR*,
July 1923, 7.

the time she was born until she herself gave birth to a child. Only one of
these, the so-called Sun Baby, by Swiss-born sculptor Otto Schweizer
(1863–1955), was actually executed. Schweizer was a highly respected
sculptor of the day whose other works include the Pennsylvania State
Memorial at Gettysburg, relief work in the Lincoln Memorial Room of
Philadelphia's Union League, and numerous commemorative medals.[82]

Schweizer's Sun Baby at Carson is located on the wall of what Kelsey
called a Gothic ambulatory at Cornflower (Mother Goose) Cottage. It was
vividly described by Kelsey himself in a newspaper interview given in
May 1917:"It is in brightly colored, delicately modeled terra cotta.... Suggesting heat and light, a golden sun casts its rays upward and to the right
and left. Out of the blazing eye of this rising sun the girl baby is born.
Between the rays of the sun, alternate flutters of butterflies and chains
and fetters—symbolizing the pleasures and troubles of life."[83]

The other four allegories, as projected by Kelsey, were to be called
Childhood and Play, Girlhood and Study, Maidenhood and the Melody

Fig. 10.   Front gable of Stork Hill Cottage (Primrose), showing one of two stork panels in pargeting and ornamented vergeboard. Photo by Graydon Wood, April 8, 1986. CVS.

Fig. 11.   Gothic ambulatory at Mother Goose (Cornflower), with Sun Baby seen through arches. Photo by Graydon Wood, April 8, 1986. CVS.

of Life, and *The Glory of Motherhood and the Mystery of Time and Space.* This last work would appear as a statue atop a high memorial tower to Robert Carson, the tower itself to be part of a combined school, administration building, and chapel. Never executed, the structure was slated to occupy the highest point on the institution's grounds, which was just about in the center of the campus on the eastern edge of the campus's shallow valley. Exuding great excitement over the tower and its figures, Kelsey related to the newspapers, "I want to suggest the perpetuation of all things through woman, and it will be a sort of review of that endless chain which is life. The top of the memorial tower is to be light and airy Gothic architecture, crowned by a proud young mother holding her baby triumphant over her head. Four supporting female figures on a lower level, garlanded together with swags of flowers, will represent '[t]he Dawn Maiden,' 'the Zenith Maiden,' 'the Eventide Maiden,' and 'the Maiden of the Night.'"[84]

The writer of an article on Carson for the *Architectural Record* believed that the tower figures, the floral motifs, and the romantic landscaping were not so much for the children's benefit—at least directly—as they were a means of inspiring the Carson staff: "The ideal of the architecture and the plan of the grounds should have a tendency . . . to keep alive [a] resistance to the 'institutionalizing' of childhood. When the spirit of the place has been built into its architecture, cut into its stone and molded into its panels—these things do not change."[85]

In any case, it was all very romantic, all very Ruskinian, and all awash with Victorian neomedievalism, with its partly pagan and partly Christian idealization of woman as fertility goddess and Virgin Mother. Both these allegorical themes and the Tudor Gothic architecture of the buildings themselves were clearly intended as a counterpoise to an urban industrialized world. Thus, in Albert Kelsey's mind, Carson College would become a beautiful, soothing, rural retreat from the stresses and strains of the modern world that had buffeted Carson's little orphans. At Carson College they would be healed and restored through constant association with what was most beautiful and inspiring about the preindustrial past.

As it turned out, Kelsey's fantasy was never fully completed. Ironically, its failure to materialize stemmed from one of the ugliest realities of human existence, a murderous war in Europe that the United States had just joined in April 1917. Spiraling inflation, a lack of building materials, and a shortage of transportation would initially undermine Kelsey's program.[86] (Subsequent economic difficulties and the outspoken opposition of Carson's first president, Elsa Ueland, who believed that Kelsey's buildings were much too impractical for the day-to-day workings of an orphanage, would keep the project from being renewed a decade later.)

The more mundane task of construction on the Carson grounds began in the spring of 1916, when the board received bids from some nine contractors. In July the board selected Jacob Meyers and Sons, an accomplished and well-known Philadelphia firm. Meyers proposed to do the job for approximately $350,000. Fees for the architect and engineer, in addition to other expenses, raised the total cost of the buildings to about $450,000. Construction was to begin as soon as possible in 1917, with completion slated for the following summer.[87] Although construction did begin with the coming of good weather in 1917, there is no record of an official groundbreaking ceremony, perhaps because the American declaration of war in April 1917 would have made such festivities unseemly.

Even before the declaration of hostilities, the Carson board was forced by rising prices and labor shortages to scale back its immediate construction project to two cottages (Mother Goose and Red Gables), a superintendent's residence (Stork Hill), and a maintenance garage with mechanic's cottage attached (Thistle).[88] The situation grew predictably worse once the United States entered the war. In November 1917, for example, the board learned that the Akron Roofing Tile Company, in Akron, Ohio, which had contracted to supply roof tiles for the Carson buildings, was going to have trouble meeting its delivery schedule. In March 1918, the company still did not have the tiles ready, explaining that they had been forced to shut down their factory altogether because they could not obtain clay for making tiles or coal to fire the kilns.[89] As if this were not enough, the Carson board failed in its request to the War Industries Board to obtain priority for shipping the tiles by rail.[90] Thus, when Carson officially opened on July 1, 1918, only one building was ready for occupancy. This was Primrose (Stork Hill) Cottage, which (after the abandonment of the earlier site) had been slated as the superintendent's residence but which was now pressed into use as a cottage for girls. Soon thereafter the so-called mechanic's cottage, known as Thistle, was taken over as a cottage for girls, yet another change in plans for building use.[91]

Up to this point the principal shapers of Carson College had been Robert Carson himself and architect Albert Kelsey. But this would change with the selection of Elsa Ueland as president in the spring of 1916. She would preside over Carson for the next half century, leaving her mark on virtually every aspect of the institution. More than anyone else, she would make Carson College into a widely admired progressive school and orphanage.

CHAPTER TWO

THE
EDUCATION
OF A
PROGRESSIVE

For fifty-one years Elsa Ueland (1888–1980) was at the center of Carson College (and the Carson Valley School), first as president (1916–58) and then as a member of the board of trustees (1958–67). In the years following her resignation from the board and until her death in 1980, she remained vitally interested in the institution, continuing to live just a few blocks from its gates. It was her intelligence, her enthusiasm, and her vision that made Carson a leading progressive institution and that attracted nationwide attention to its work. In order to understand Carson and its mission one must get to know Ueland during her formative years.

In many ways Elsa Ueland's childhood, youth, and education paralleled the backgrounds of many other progressives. According to the historian Robert M. Crunden, progressive reformers were likely to be Protestants from professional, upper-middle-class families in the northern states. The majority of progressives, according to Crunden, also grew up in Republican households, though in Elsa's case her father was a prominent Democrat.[1] In addition, Elsa's mother was an outspoken social and political reformer who held advanced ideas about teaching that anticipated many aspects of progressive education.

Elsa herself was born on March 10, 1888, in Minneapolis, Minnesota, the second of seven children (three girls and four boys) of Andreas Ueland and Clara Hampson Ueland. Andreas Ueland was a native of Norway who had immigrated to Minnesota in 1871 at age 18. The Uelands had known some prominence in the old country: Although they were only farmers of modest means, Andreas's father (Ole Gabriel Ueland) had been the leader of the Norwegian parliament for several decades.

Once in the United States, Andreas read law in Minneapolis and went on to practice with several prestigious firms in the city. At one time he was the partner of John Lind, the much celebrated progressive governor of Minnesota.[2] A two-year stint as a probate judge in the early 1880s gave Andreas the moniker Judge Ueland, which he carried with him for the rest of his life, although he never again served on the bench. Andreas also became involved in banking, serving as both a director and legal counsel for several large Minneapolis banks. By 1928 he was general counsel to the Federal Reserve Bank of Minnesota. As a young man in Minneapolis he had converted from his native Lutheranism to the Unitarian Church and had become something of a freethinker who delighted in attacking what he considered to be the ridiculous and often frightening beliefs of more traditional churches.[3]

Although Andreas Ueland provided well for his large family, it was Elsa's mother, Clara Hampson Ueland, who was the most important influence in her young life. Born in Akron, Ohio, in 1860, Clara was descended on both sides from colonial American ancestors, including a pre-Revolutionary governor of New York. Yet Clara had grown up in pinched circumstances because of her father's death in 1864 (when she was only four) from an illness contracted while in the Union army during the Civil War. About 1869 Clara moved with her mother and sister to Minnesota to join an aunt and uncle who were living there. They eventually settled in Minneapolis, where Clara met Andreas Ueland at the Young People's Society of the local Unitarian church. They were married in 1885.[4]

In 1890, when daughter Elsa was two, the Uelands built a new house (demolished in 1953) on a three-acre tract of land on the south shore of Lake Calhoun, located about four miles from downtown Minneapolis.[5] Perched on a high ridge overlooking the lake, the house was a spacious three-story wooden structure, with sixteen rooms, designed in an early Colonial Revival style. Many years later Elsa's younger sister Brenda remembered the "tennis court[,] and . . . the enormous elm trees . . . by the pellucid summer lake, shining like yellow glass at sunset," and "having tea and sponge cake under the apple trees on the western lawn."[6] The house was "painted bright yellow with a white balustrade porch that looked over the lake." Inside was a large library and dining room, where they sat down to "lordly dinners around [a] Georgian mahogany table that came from England."[7]

Most memorable was the hall, with its "elaborately carved oak mantel piece" that reached to the ceiling: "Here the handsomely carved staircase mounted to the second floor[,] turning halfway up at 'the landing.'. . . [I]t was just here that there was a series of three huge windows more than

Fig. 12.   Childhood home of Elsa Ueland on Lake Calhoun, Minneapolis, Minnesota. Copy of photo postcard, early twentieth century. EUP.

twelve feet high, with shafts and golden wires of sunlight flooding the upstairs hall and slanting down into the stately lower hall. Here one looked out to the south over the pasture.... [With] the light pouring in ... [it] was gloriously cheerful, especially on a winter day."[8]

The floods of sunlight had probably been Clara Ueland's inspiration, for she wanted her children to grow up in sunny, happy surroundings. Elsa's later insistence on sunshine and fresh air at Carson College may have begun with this bright upstairs hall in the house overlooking Lake Calhoun. It was in this hallway, too, with a long blackboard running along one wall, that Elsa and the other children had their first schooling, in a kindergarten taught by their mother.[9]

Clara Ueland was already an experienced teacher, having taught elementary school in Minneapolis before she married. She was intensely interested in various philosophies and methods of education and read widely on the subject. She studied Jean-Jacques Rousseau, Johann Heinrich Pestalozzi, and Friedrich Froebel, all of them advanced educational reformers in their day, in addition to numerous other authors who were not directly associated with pedagogical theories. Like many other Victorian Americans, she was much taken by John Ruskin's social and aesthetic theories.[10] Clara recorded her gleanings from such writers in a series of notebooks, which also included many of her own thoughts on education and child rearing. An entry from the early 1890s is particularly revealing because of the way in which it seems to anticipate Elsa's later devotion to progressive education: "Grown people are very sensitive to fault-finding, to criticism and to allusion to their imperfections. Why, then, should we expect and demand of children that they receive constant reproof and criticism amiably, and with forbearance which older people do not practice? Are not many children's dispositions seriously injured by these constant reprimands and reproofs?"[11]

Even more redolent of a progressive approach to schooling was the paper that Clara read before a group of Minneapolis mothers in the fall of 1890, at a time when a number of teachers' and parents' groups in the city anticipated many of the practices and concepts that would become an integral part of progressive education.[12] In her presentation to one such group, Clara proposed that "a child is not a piece of clay to be moulded and forced into any desired shape. He is rather like a plant which should have as nearly as possible the right conditions, and then be allowed to grow freely and naturally into his own symmetry." "To develop self-reliance and strength," she continued, "a child should have as much liberty as possible, as much as is consistent with the rights of others." [13]

According to Brenda, their mother had practiced what she preached. On rainy days she allowed the children to play hockey in the large, oak-paneled hall and to go wherever they wanted after school without reporting home first, asking only that they be back in time for dinner at 6:30.[14]

Clara also had some definite ideas about the proper relation between childhood and work, likewise progressive in spirit. Speaking before her audience of mothers she advised, "As early as possible children should have tasks assigned to them [so] that they may be led to feel that mankind must work and that even small children may help a little. There is nothing in child training that requires more tact and insight on the part of the mother than to ask of him what is just suited to his strength and development. If she asks too much, he is disheartened and loses faith in her judgment; and yet he should have to try to develop his growing powers in order to have confidence in himself." [15]

In making such remarks, Clara may have been thinking of daughter Elsa, who was very clever with her hands. One winter she used the *American Boy's Handbook* to build an iceboat for skimming across Lake Calhoun. It was not "just a junk little thing made of broomsticks and three-girls skates," Brenda later wrote, "but a big one with true runners and a tiller." [16]

Not surprisingly, Clara believed that boys and girls were equal in almost every way, and that it was ridiculous to place restrictions on their physical activities, especially when freed from constricting Victorian dress.[17] Thus Brenda remembered that both she and Elsa were regular tomboys: "Elsa was a kind of boy and I was more so. Mother let us wear knee-pants and we played baseball." [18] Once, when a wagon driver passed the two of them playing ball, he was heard to mutter that Elsa was either a boy with braids or a girl in pants.[19] Brenda herself thought that Elsa looked like a "boy angel," with her tall athletic frame, bright blue eyes, and golden curls.[20]

Reminiscing further about their mother's views of daughters and sons, Brenda wrote:

> Girls . . . were just as precious as boys. We never felt that girls had to do housework and boys outdoor work. [Mother] made no distinction between them in actions, freedom, education, or possibilities. Elsa and I could be presidents and admirals, just as much as

[brother] Sigurd, if we happened to feel like it. . . . The girls could hitch up the horse and climb trees and show their underpants as much as they wanted to. She never told us to be careful, cautious, [or] prudent. . . . We were never warned about "awful men," and told not to go places alone, or in the dark.[21]

The Ueland children also escaped the religious fears often visited upon many of their young friends, for there was never any talk in the Ueland household about sin, human degradation, or hellfire and damnation. Nor did they have to endure endless gloomy Sabbaths, but were free to romp and make as much noise as they wanted on Sundays. They did, in fact, attend the Unitarian church in downtown Minneapolis with some frequency, making the eight-mile round trip in the family's horse-drawn carriage. Their minister, a Dr. Henry Simmons, was "a wonderfully sweet-natured man and a remarkable scholar," recalled Brenda, "whose sermons were about Evolution, history, Matthew Arnold, Emerson and such things."[22] None of the Ueland children was baptized, and they never said prayers at home—either as a family or as individuals at bedtime—as was the custom in many homes of that era.[23]

Yet there was one area where Clara Ueland drew the line. Both she and Andreas shunned alcoholic beverages. Indeed, Clara opposed "stimulants," as she called them, including coffee and tea, forbidding all such drinks to her children with the exception of very weak hot chocolate at bedtime. Her idea of a good snack was a piece of raw fruit—and especially apples—which she dispensed to the children from a barrel all winter long.[24]

As an advocate of freedom and equality for both girls and boys, it seemed only natural that Clara Ueland would champion women's suffrage. She first became interested in the movement after meeting Carrie Chapman Catt, Anna Howard Shaw, and other leading suffragists who came to Minneapolis in 1901 for the National Women's Suffrage Convention. But it was daughter Elsa's great enthusiasm for the suffrage cause in 1907, a result of her attendance at meetings of a suffrage club at the Unitarian church in Minneapolis, that spurred Clara to take the movement seriously and to join it in earnest several years later.[25] Indeed, it was Elsa's persuasion, more than any other factor, that convinced her mother to take up the cause of women's vote.[26] Clara eventually became president of Minnesota's Equal Suffrage Association and then of the state's League of Women Voters. She marched in parades, testified before legislative commissions, and traveled throughout the state (and other parts of the nation) on behalf of women's vote, as well as other reforms to benefit women. Following her death in 1927 the local newspapers said that she had been the best-known woman in Minnesota for a generation.[27]

According to Brenda, Andreas Ueland was not always pleased about the time and effort that Clara gave to "politics," and became less sympathetic about her causes as he grew older. He was often critical of the amounts of money that she spent on such activities, as well as on the children and various household expenses, and was especially given to outbursts of temper, around the first of every month, when the bills came due.[28]

Although Andreas may have been unhappy about the extent of his wife's feminist activities, he agreed that his daughters deserved good educations. Elsa, like the other Ueland children, attended a public elementary school in the neighborhood and then went on to Minneapolis's Central High School, which was also part of the public system.[29] Although she left no account of her school days, a letter that she wrote to one of the local newspapers during her first year of high school reveals an early preference for realistic literature. "My favorite author," she declared,

> is one who paints real life in its true colors. I think that Charles Dickens entirely fulfills this requirement. . . . Dickens has written two books which I like almost equally well, "A Tale of Two Cities" and "David Copperfield". . . . [I]n "David Copperfield" Dickens has painted his characters in more vivid tones than in any other book I have read. This book is a story of his life with very little variation; it is probably for this reason that his characters are so plainly original; they were real people. Here we have the life of the lower class of people, neither modified [n]or exaggerated.[30]

Such sentiments foreshadowed Elsa's later preference for reading biography, history, and nonfiction in general. Dickens's use of "realistic fiction" to expose urban poverty and social exploitation may have helped to point Elsa toward a career in progressive education and various social reforms, as it did with many other young men and women on both sides of the Atlantic in the late nineteenth and early twentieth centuries.

This thirst for realism may have also played a part in Elsa's refusal to attend a women's college in the East, as was the custom for college-bound girls of genteel or wealthy families. According to Brenda, Elsa found such institutions "too ladylike, too seminary-like. She wanted to be where there were law and engineering schools and poor people and coeducation."[31] Thus Elsa enrolled at the state-sponsored University of Minnesota in the fall of 1905.

At college Elsa took full opportunity of both academic and extracurricular activities. She specialized in sociology and psychology, in addition to pursuing a year of legal courses. Studious habits and high native intelligence earned her election to Phi Beta Kappa, but she also found time to edit the student newspaper, to serve as captain of the basketball team, and to join the dramatic club and the Alpha Phi sorority. In 1907 she became president of the university's College Equal Suffrage Club, and in 1909 she organized the state's Congressional Union for Women's Suffrage, a lobbying group set up to pressure national legislators to pass a women's suffrage amendment. At the same time, she joined her mother in numerous suffrage events.[32]

It may have been at the university that Elsa first encountered the writings of economist and social critic Thorstein Veblen (1857–1929). According to Elsa's future sister-in-law, Margaret (Mrs. Rolf) Ueland, she counted Veblen as one of the most important influences on her intellectual life.[33] Although the precise impact of Veblen on her is unclear, Elsa's later writings would suggest that she sympathized with Veblen's attacks on "conspicuous consumption" and on classical, laissez-faire economics in general.

In any case, Elsa must have struck her college classmates as an especially bright young woman with healthy good looks. She was tall—five feet eight or nine—and rosy-cheeked, with luminous blue eyes and hair that was now a golden brown. Trim but largely built—and slightly more handsome than pretty—one can imagine her striding through campus filled with energy and cheerful determination, looking very much like one of the young beauties made famous by the illustrator Charles Dana Gibson.

Such impressions of Elsa were reflected in a letter of recommendation written on her behalf by the dean of women at the University of Minnesota:

> Miss Ueland is a young woman of splendid strength and physique. Her mental qualities may be judged from her record in scholarship. Both mentally and physically she was a leader in her class in college. But to say that is to describe her imperfectly; her character is perhaps the most notable thing about her. She is so gen-

erous and enthusiastic, so sensible, so honest and straightforward, that she wins immediate love and respect. I have known very few young women whose powers were so evenly developed and whose promise was so great.[34]

Even allowing for the exaggeration that often creeps into such recommendations, one can conclude that Elsa Ueland had made an extraordinarily good impression at the University of Minnesota.

Soon after graduation in June 1909, Elsa went to visit some friends in Weymouth, Massachusetts, a trip that would forever change the course of her life. While there, she was invited to visit the Richmond Hill Settlement House in New York City. She was impressed by the place, excited about the city, and genuinely ready to leave home. Although her mother

Fig. 13. Elsa Ueland in her twenties. EUP.

had brought her up to be a capable and independent young woman, both parents were unnerved about her plan to become a settlement-house worker. According to sister Brenda, "Their darling Elsa was now to enter a path that troubled them.... [It] was not *their* picture for her. The course she was to move through now seemed too grubby, too democratic. It did not go with her golden-red complexion and her straight nose and her free, long-striding gait." [35]

But Elsa would not bend. Insisting upon her independence, she wrote them from New York that summer: "I am sorry that you and Father feel as you do about the New York Settlement.... I suppose I have the wild 'get away' feeling. If you knew the wild longings and dreams [I have] of the Philippines and Turkey and Alaska, you would realize how mild is the Richmond Hill House.... I am writing this letter outdoors and as the mail man is now due, I will leave some exciting things such as a ghost—a real one—that has been discovered on our third floor, to another letter." [36]

Beyond mentioning her wild feelings to get away, Elsa gave no complete explanation for her wish to move so far from home. Her parents had certainly given her every advantage, and there was no doubt that the Uelands were now one of the leading families of Minneapolis. All this must have been a source of pride and encouragement. Yet if Elsa remained at home, there was a real danger that she would forever be seen as a Ueland daughter rather than as a person in her own right, with unique talents and accomplishments. The move to New York would allow her to become her own person, at the same time that it would afford her what psychologist Erik Erikson has called a late adolescent moratorium, a period of several years when she could be free to postpone any final decisions about her future and to explore various alternatives on her own. [37]

Though hers was an individual decision that sprang from her own needs and experiences, spending several years in an urban settlement house had become something of an adventurous yet acceptable option among the daughters of upper-middle- and upper-class Americans. Like Elsa, most settlement-house workers were single women in their early to mid-twenties, well educated, and from prosperous families in the Northeast or Midwest. They also tended to come from cities or from suburbs near major metropolitan areas. Like Elsa's mother, many of their parents were involved in charitable activities or reform movements. [38] (Two generations later many of the same kinds of young people would join the Peace Corps or civil rights movement.)

When Elsa took up residence at the Richmond Hill House in the fall of 1909, settlement houses were at their peak in numbers and influence, with some four hundred of them scattered in cities across the country. This idea of having well-educated young adults living in poor areas and assisting the local residents in a variety of ways had actually originated with Toynbee Hall in London, founded in 1884 and staffed by young graduates of Oxford and Cambridge Universities. In many respects these young people (men in this case) had been inspired by the social and aesthetic ideas of John Ruskin (the same John Ruskin who had so enthralled Elsa Ueland's mother and whose ideas had influenced the architecture and landscape of Carson College). The settlement-house concept quickly made its way across the Atlantic, and in 1889 the first such facility, the College Settlement in New York City, opened its doors.[39]

At the time that Elsa moved to New York to take up settlement-house work, the United States was in the midst of a multifaceted reform movement commonly known as progressivism. According to the historian Allen F. Davis, in his insightful study of the settlement houses and their connection with urban reform, the settlement houses played a major role in both launching and sustaining the progressive impulse.

Although progressivism was an extraordinarily complex phenomenon, virtually all progressive reformers could agree that the United States, in the early decades of the twentieth century, faced serious problems that had been brought about through the rapid industrialization and urbanization of the country during the past several decades. Political corruption, business monopolies, the erosion of democracy in general, the exploitation of workers (many of them women and children)—and the poverty, ignorance, crime, and disease that afflicted large segments of the urban population—were all grist for the progressive mill. Yet there was much disagreement and even contradiction within the movement. For example, some progressives believed that the public exposure of problems through investigative reporting would be sufficient to promote private solutions that required little or no governmental intervention. As time went on, an increasing number of progressives—though by no means all—looked to the states and then to the federal government for solutions to the nation's most pressing needs. Among those who preferred private initiatives were members of the business and professional communities who called for greater efficiency in all aspects of American life, including government. Many progressives also exhibited contradictory tendencies, such as longing for a simpler past at the same time that they called for modern scientific solutions to social and economic afflictions. Consequently, a growing number of historians have despaired of crafting any simple definition of the progressive movement, and some have advocated that the term be abandoned altogether.[40]

There was no better place to observe and assist the progress to be made against a host of contemporary evils, many idealistic young people believed, than in the urban settlement houses. Sharing many of the contradictions of the wider progressive movement, settlement-house workers often admired a preindustrial past at the same time that they had faith in the ameliorating possibilities of science and technology. Thus, while they made empirical studies of working conditions and helped their clients to organize labor unions and other pressure groups, they sought to restore ancient craftsmanship through teaching such things as pottery, wood carving, spinning, and hand weaving. In like manner, they believed that city children could be strengthened and ennobled through exposure to the rural countryside—in their minds a survival from a simpler time. As a consequence, many settlement houses ran summer camps in the country, or even operated farms that employed urban youth. In this sense, the future Carson College, with its gardens, working farm, handicrafts, and summer camps, would share many impulses of the settlement-house movement—as conveyed to it by Elsa Ueland in particular.[41]

More than once Ueland expressed her own sense of the nation's having lost a better past. One example of such thinking appeared in a letter that she wrote to her mother from Akron, Ohio, where she had gone to speak before a women's club. Remembering that her mother had spent her earliest years in Akron, Elsa searched out the modest childhood home, only to find that its once semirural surroundings were now a smoky urban slum. For Elsa this degraded neighborhood symbolized what urban life was doing to the American people, and especially to their children. Thus she lamented to her mother, "I couldn't help but feel that that house was symbolic in a way of what our cities are doing to our children. Forty-five years ago that back garden, set in the lovely Akron Valley, must have been an ideal place for children. [But] today railroads, coal yards, heavy traffic, and soot have crowded up to the very doorsteps of the house. . . . Children are *still living there*, . . . but they have to go *over a half a mile* to find an open space to play"[42] (emphasis is in the original).

Although somewhat different, living conditions were just as trying for the neighbors around the Richmond Hill Settlement House, where Elsa

finally went to live in the fall of 1909. Located in Manhattan at 28 Mac-
dougal Street, just south of Washington Square, the facility was under the
direction of "head worker" Elizabeth Roemer (c. 1870-1961), a Danish
immigrant who would become one of Ueland's closest friends in the
years to come.[43]

Most of the neighbors with whom they worked at Richmond Hill were
poor Italian immigrants.[44] Elsa conjured up a colorful scene for her
parents:

> Here I am installed at Richmond Hill Settlement House, a typical
> New York tenement with all its rattle and smells and confusion
> and tom-cats. . . . New York is a place where you live *fast.* You
> think that you have had a long day and ought to be tired when
> some one suggests "tea" at Fleishman's and off you go. . . . And
> when you get back and are ready to drop[,] you begin to talk
> Socialism, or Miss Roemer talks about Europe and America in her
> beautiful and ideal way; and then everybody gets a second wind
> so to speak, and you *can't stop.*
>
> New York is so refreshingly frank in its likes and preferences to
> one who has any hesitation about doing what he wants to do[,]
> whether it is going to a saloon, or speaking to a lady. But the same
> delightful independence is *yours* too. So absolute solitude or ab-
> solute sociability are always at your command.[45] (Emphasis is in the
> original.)

Elsa did not go home for Christmas in 1909 and was so busy exploring
her new surroundings that she did not appear to miss the family at all. In
a letter that somewhat shocked her parents, she painted a vivid picture of
Christmas with her Italian neighbors:

> Christmas here has been wholly delightful. The Italians do know
> how to have "a party" even if it is six people sitting in a perfectly
> bare room with nothing to eat. But the fiddle begins, little girls . . .
> do a "tarantella" in costume and then—"Everybody up for the
> tarantella!" someone sings out. A little weazened woman begins
> to dance with a stocky little man, a heavy man pairs off with a
> twelve-year-old girl, a fat woman joins in for a few breathless
> moments and some boys, too bashful to ask for partners, are danc-
> ing in the hall.

After that everything *goes*. Solos are volunteered[;] the dancing gets faster and faster and everyone wants to help pass the ice-cream. And when it is time to go, your hand is nearly shaken off with wishes for a Merry Christmas and a Happy New Year. The party I went to last night was actually one of the best parties I ever went to, for mellowness and joy.[46] (Emphasis is in the original.)

That Elsa herself, a tall Scandinavian beauty, must have added to the incongruities of the scene apparently did not occur to the enthusiastic letter writer.

During her years in New York (1909–14), Elsa continued to revel in her freedom and in the excitement of the city itself. In fact, this was a heady time for a talented young person to be in New York. Greenwich Village, where the Richmond Hill Settlement stood, was moving toward its peak as a mecca for artists, social critics, and intellectuals, who were attracted by its cheap rents and freedom from Victorian, middle-class restraints.

That Elsa participated in this culture is evident from what sister Brenda wrote about her at Richmond Hill. When visiting, she and Elsa went for dinner at "an Italian restaurant and had red wine and . . . smoked cigarettes" (both activities forbidden by Clara Ueland). In the winter of 1913 Brenda joined Elsa at Richmond Hill and was soon having a great time prowling around Washington Square and Greenwich Village. Although she does not say directly that Elsa joined her and others on these forays, there is no reason to think that Elsa hung back. In Brenda's words, "We went to suffrage and socialist meetings. We picketed with factory girls. We went to night court and were indignant and sorrowful over the prostitutes. 'My Lord! why don't they arrest the *men* as well as the poor girls?'"[47] (emphasis is in the original). At a restaurant one night in the Village they met and talked to John Reed, who would later go to Russia as an idealistic revolutionary. (John Reed would be "revived" for later generations in the movie *Reds,* with Reed played by Warren Beatty.) On other evenings in the Village they would run into Max Eastman, Big Bill Haywood, or Emma Goldman, all radical intellectuals of the day.[48]

Elsa herself kept a diary during her early months in New York. After taking up residence in the city on Sunday, October 24, 1909, she lost no time throwing herself into reform causes. The very next day she served as an usher for a suffrage meeting at Carnegie Hall featuring the famous British suffragette Emeline Pankhurst. On Tuesday of that same week she volunteered as a "watcher" at the Triangle Shirtwaist strike, a protracted labor action by female garment workers then in progress. That Friday, only five days after her arrival in New York, she was a delegate to a city suffrage convention.[49]

Accounts of suffrage meetings and labor strikes continued to find their way into her diary in the ensuing weeks. On January 11, 1910, she joined several other women in picketing a garment shop despite a court injunction forbidding such actions. Elsa expected to be arrested and seemed disappointed when they were not.[50] Sometimes her reform activities took her out of town, as in April 1910, when she went to Washington, D.C., for a large suffrage meeting where she heard speeches from the young and militant crusader Alice Paul, among others. On April 18 she joined a procession to Capitol Hill to present suffrage petitions and attend a hearing before the House Judiciary Committee on women's vote. In her diary Elsa wrote, "Real thrills [as] we present our loads of petitions[,] passing up the avenue in bannered automobiles."[51]

Fig. 14.   Suffrage parade in New York City, 1915. The photo, which may include an unidentified Elsa Ueland, was found among Ueland's private papers. EUP.

Meanwhile she continued her work back at the Richmond Hill Settlement House, where her main assignment appears to have been supervising separate youth clubs for boys and girls, and directing plays put on by both groups. During the summers she ran a girls' camp on Staten Island, which presumably enrolled children from her own and other settlement houses.

Yet along with the suffrage meetings, strikes, and work at Richmond Hill, Elsa and her friends found plenty of time to take in New York's high culture, including the opera *Aida,* with the starring role sung by the great Caruso. They also went to some of the best stage plays of the era, often returning home for a nightcap of cheese, beer, and animated discussion. In 1913 Elsa viewed the famous International Art Exhibit, more commonly known as the Armory Show, which touched off wild controversy and introduced the American public to cubism and other products of contemporary art. Just what Elsa thought of Marcel Duchamp's *Nude Descending a Staircase,* or other sensational works at the show, was not recorded.[52] In any case, this contradiction in working and living among the poor while taking advantage of the best that New York had to offer apparently did not strike Elsa as odd. Just how she afforded this lifestyle is unknown, though it is probable that she received some form of allowance from her family back in Minnesota. A letter that Elsa wrote to her father in February 1911, asking for $100 with which to make several purchases, would seem to show that such was the case.[53]

In addition to all these activities, Elsa found time to continue her education. As soon as she arrived in New York, she enrolled in the city's School of Philanthropy, a pioneering institution to train social workers that had been founded in 1898 by the New York Charity Organization. (In 1919 it became the New York School of Social Work and in 1940 the Columbia University School of Social Work.) The school's director was Samuel Lindsay, a professor of political science and economics at Columbia University. In 1910 Lindsay resigned as director and returned full-time to Columbia. It was perhaps through Lindsay that Ueland presented her research for a master's degree in economics from Columbia, which she received in 1911.[54]

Whatever the arrangement, Ueland took as a research project the shirtwaist trade (that is, dressmaking industry), a topic that was doubtless suggested by the dramatic shirtwaist strike during the winter of 1909–10. A condensed version of her findings was published in the *Journal of Politi-*

Fig. 15. Elsa Ueland (bottom row, third from right) as a student at the New York School of Philanthropy, c. 1910. EUP.

cal Economy for December 1910, written in collaboration with another student named Pearl Goodman.[55]

Both the journal article and the thesis itself bulged with charts and statistics, a typical device of many investigators during the progressive era, who placed much faith in the mere publication of facts as a way of producing reform. Most of these figures concerned wages and working hours in order to show that shirtwaist workers were both underpaid and overworked. Although the recent strike had allowed workers to make some headway, Elsa concluded that only powerful unions could protect the welfare of laborers in this exploitative industry.

The decision by Ueland to pursue formal training at the New York School of Philanthropy and Columbia University was increasingly typical of settlement-house workers, making her part of a transition in the early twentieth century between amateur volunteers and professional social workers.[56] As such, Ueland was in the forefront of the social work profession, a group with which she would identify throughout her adult life.

Like many young social workers, Ueland had come to believe that much of the misery in the world came from selfish capitalists, who were intent on making money at all costs. The sinking of the *Titanic* on April 14–15, 1912, with the loss of over 1,500 lives, was only one of the more hideous examples of such greed. Elsa felt outraged at the inadequate number of lifeboats and at the other proofs of disregard for passenger safety by the immensely wealthy Cunard Line, which owned the ship. In a letter to her mother, she tried to explain how shaken she was by this monumental catastrophe: "Do you know this Titanic disaster has in a way *unnerved* us all[?] It is still the constant subject of conversation. Life seems to be hanging just by a thread! Personally I find myself in an emotional state. Aren't you astounded by the lack of equipment, of search-lights, spy glasses for the look-out, sufficient life boats?"[57] (emphasis is in the original).

No one could know that death would become organized on a grand scale a little more than two years later, when the great powers of Europe plunged themselves into the maelstrom of war in August 1914. Like most other young progressives, Elsa was horrified by the war, but unlike many of her contemporaries, who believed that they might use the crusading spirit unleashed by the war to further their reform agenda, she did not change her mind about the conflict once the United States entered it in April 1917. In a letter addressed to her entire family, she set forth her opposition in no uncertain terms.

She began by blaming the U.S. government for abandoning strict neutrality more than two years before in siding with Great Britain on trade restrictions and loans. Nor had the United States really tried to understand Germany's feelings of encirclement by the Triple Entente of Great Britain, France, and Russia. As to the charges against German imperialism, Elsa reminded the folks back home that Britain was the most imperialistic country in modern times, and that the United States itself had recently pursued an outspoken imperialist policy under President Theodore Roosevelt. Under the circumstances, she believed that her country's declaration of war was "an example of the pot calling the kettle black," adding, "I see no more reason to fight Germany, because of her past sins, than to fight England."[58]

As to President Wilson's proclamations about crusading for democracy, Elsa cited the fact that Britain and France had been fighting on the side of autocratic Russia, which had gone through a revolution just in the "nick of time" to save the United States from allying itself with the czarist regime. She would believe Wilson when he and the government demanded genuine democracy at home: "Let's bring about more equitable taxation," she insisted, "wider opportunities for women, better education for our children." And if the war were really a noble crusade, she insisted, then no one would make money out of the conflict, and added, "If there is a repetition of the graft and profiteering of our previous wars, while you boys [that is, her four brothers] are butchered to preserve our trade, then I am ready to go into violent revolution here at home." [59] She never did become reconciled to her country's participation in the slaughter, as letters home continued to make clear. [60]

Elsa's reform activities also embraced education, for education was a natural step for a progressive like Elsa, who placed a high value on the dissemination of information as a powerful tool for bringing about reform. And if some members of the older generation were deaf to calls for change, the progressives could hope to shape the future by working with children and youngsters in the schools. Many progressives also saw the schools, like the settlement houses themselves, as institutions that might help children as well as their parents to meet the challenges of an urban, industrial world. Indeed, the settlement houses, including Elsa's Richmond Hill, organized a network of "visitors" who attempted to serve as liaisons between the public schools and parents in the neighborhoods. [61]

In the process of this involvement with the schools, settlement-house workers realized that there was a pressing need to help guide young people toward a suitable vocation, especially at a time when many of the schools offered a curriculum that was largely irrelevant to the needs of the day. In order to respond to this problem, a settlement-house worker in Boston named Frank Parsons, in 1910, published a book called *Choosing a Vocation.* This book was instrumental in launching a Vocational Guidance Association, with branches in several large cities. [62]

In 1911 Ueland herself began work as an "investigator" for a survey undertaken by the Vocational Guidance Association in New York, while continuing to live at the Richmond Hill Settlement. [63] Funds for the survey came from the Public Education Association of New York City, a private organization that worked closely with the city's board of education. The survey's director was Alice P. Barrows (1877–1954). Barrows had studied under John Dewey at Columbia University and would become one of the hardest working and most outspoken supporters of progressive education in the United States. She would also become a lifelong friend of Elsa Ueland.[64]

Ueland's part in the guidance survey resulted in a lengthy report called "A Study of Eighty-Seven Working Paper Boys Who Left One School in District 9, Manhattan, in the Year 1911–1912."[65] Like her study on the shirt-waist trade, it was filled with figures, this time on family incomes, the pay of boys who quit school before graduating, and the reasons why they left to go to work. Eight decades later these numbers are not so important as Ueland's growing understanding of adolescence and her belief that the schools could and should play a significant part in guiding youth through this difficult stage. Although not a startling idea as the twentieth century comes to an end, it was something of a novel concept when she completed her report. In Elsa's words:

> The age of adolescence is the most plastic period of life. It is a time when new forces are born; when almost a new personality emerges. . . . But adolescence is also a period of great vulnerability, when outside influences leave their mark most irretrievably. . . . In truth the whole future of the child's life depends upon how these new powers of adolescence are husbanded and directed. . . . If conditions are pointed out which are destructive of youth and the new forces of adolescence, they are outlined here because we believe that the *school* will be the organization to remedy these defects.[66] (Emphasis is in the original.)

Elsa's idea of using the schools to remedy problems in the larger society was, of course, not original to her. Many progressives espoused similar ideas, as did an emerging body of thought and practice known as progressive education. As its name suggests, progressive education had many things in common with the wider progressive movement, though it would be a mistake to see it as a mere subtheme of progressivism without a history and life of its own.

According to John Dewey (1859–1952), the philosopher and educator who has been most closely associated with the progressive movement in education, the school needed to adjust to the realities of the urban, industrial age. Because the world had changed so rapidly, and would doubtless continue to do so at an ever accelerating pace, it no longer made sense to have students merely memorize a body of knowledge that educators had believed was eternally true and permanently useful. For Dewey, who was much influenced by Charles Darwin and other evolutionists, "truth" itself had evolved in response to changing realities. In order to prepare students for the future, education should equip them with the mental tools (or instruments) that they would need to understand the world of tomorrow and thereby to find solutions to problems that no one had yet imagined. (This did not mean that Dewey opposed all memorization, or that he did not believe students had to learn certain skills in order to succeed, as critics of progressive education would later charge.)

It followed that schools should not exist in a vacuum, isolated from the rest of life, but should be a part of the living, working community around them. Otherwise, students would see education as something apart from reality, with no connection to making a living or solving problems in the future. Besides, Dewey believed that children were naturally curious about their world, a curiosity that was often stifled by too much rote learning that had little or nothing to do with their lives. Finally, by tapping into youngsters' natural curiosity, progressive educators could show respect for their students' individual interests and needs, and in the process strengthen the child's self-worth and self-esteem. Above all, perhaps, children did not have to feel like helpless pawns in an utterly mysterious world.[67] (This emphasis upon self-esteem would come under fire a century later from some psychologists and educators who believed that children also needed to experience a degree of failure and disappointment as part of their preparation for life, or who feared that too much emphasis upon self-esteem could foster selfishness and even antisocial behavior.)[68]

That Ueland would become involved in the progressive-education movement is understandable, given her work at the Richmond Hill Settlement and with the Vocational Guidance Association, not to mention her own mother's advanced ideas on education and child rearing. In the fall of 1914 Ueland made a major step toward gaining practical experience in a progressive school when she signed on as an English teacher in the public schools of Gary, Indiana.

Ueland left no written explanation for why she took the position, but it seems certain that she had heard about the exciting educational experiments there under the direction of Superintendent William Wirt (1874–1938) from the tremendous and generally favorable publicity that the so-called Gary Plan was receiving from coast to coast. Alice Barrows, under whom Elsa had worked as an investigator for the Vocational

Guidance survey, was a major advocate of the Gary Plan and, in fact, directed the Gary School League, a group of educational reformers in New York City who wanted the New York public schools to adopt the Gary system.[69] There is also every reason to believe that Elsa heard Wirt give the keynote address at a vocational-guidance convention in New York in 1912, while she herself was working on the guidance survey.[70] In addition, Elizabeth Roemer, the head worker of the Richmond Hill Settlement and by now a close friend of Elsa, was an enthusiastic supporter of the Gary Plan and joined Ueland in the fall of 1914 as a teacher at Gary.[71] Since there was considerable interest at the time in having New York City adopt the Gary idea, it may be that both Ueland and Roemer went to Indiana with the idea of gaining firsthand experience under Wirt and then returning to help implement the plan back in New York. (As it turned out, intense opposition from teachers and other groups in New York, including riots, forced school authorities to abandon the idea. Many teachers opposed such sweeping reforms imposed from above, while parents feared undue interference with their children and with family life.)[72] Whatever her motives, Elsa stayed at Gary from 1914 to 1916, becoming Superintendent Wirt's secretary, or main assistant, toward the end of her stay there.[73]

John Dewey himself believed that the Gary schools, as operated under Wirt (who himself had been one of Dewey's prized students at the University of Chicago), were a model of progressive education.[74] Thus, in his book *Schools of Tomorrow,* written in collaboration with his daughter Evelyn Dewey and published in 1915, Dewey devoted a chapter to the Gary experiment.[75] A year later Randolph Bourne, who was a close friend of Alice Barrows, published an entire book on the Gary schools, which was also very positive in its appraisal. The book emerged from a series of articles that Bourne had written about the Gary Plan the previous year for the *New Republic,* then an avant-garde, reform magazine in the progressive tradition.[76]

Of course, not everyone who observed the Gary Plan was impressed. Among the most important detractors was Abraham Flexner, the then famous critic of American education best known for his scorching indictment of medical schools in the United States. Flexner charged that the Gary Schools did not always deliver what they promised, especially when it came to coordinating practical experiences with classroom work. He also charged that the shops and laboratories were not always well supervised, that dropout rates were about the same as in other public schools, and that many of the teachers continued to use old-fashioned methods of instruction.[77]

Despite such criticisms, many reform-minded educators continued to see the Gary Plan as a model of progressive education. Because Elsa Ueland would adapt many of its features for Carson College, it is worthwhile to review the major features of the Gary system—in theory if not always in practice.

The opportunity to create this progressive program in Gary owed in large part to the fact that the place was virtually a new city. It had been created almost overnight when U.S. Steel built a huge new plant on the site, a slice of Indiana shoreline along Lake Michigan, only twenty-five miles or so from downtown Chicago. The company named the new town Gary, after its first chairman of the board, Elbert H. Gary. Since the community and the steel plant were both brand-new, there were no educational traditions to overcome, and thus Gary's school board was willing to hire an educational innovator like Wirt and to give him virtually a free hand. U.S. Steel, which was the largest taxpayer in the city, was also happy that Wirt's scheme would make maximum use of facilities and thus keep taxes at modest levels.[78]

In Wirt's plan the school experience had four major parts: play, exercise, intellectual study, and special work, all of them woven together in as many ways as possible. In order to accomplish this ambitious program, children attended school eight hours each day. The schools also opened in the evenings for adult-education classes, in addition to a wide array of community activities. Thus the school plant was used as fully as possible.

In order to break down the sense of an artificial distinction between school and the outside world, there were many attempts to bring the community into the school and the school into the community. Thus the Gary schools were situated on or near parkland, where students could play during the school day as well as after hours, on weekends, or during vacations. This arrangement also avoided the wasteful duplication of two sets of playgrounds, one for the schools and another for the community as a whole. In like manner, Gary's public libraries were inside the school buildings, where both children and adults could come together to share the facilities.

Teachers also conducted frequent field trips to local museums and work sites in order to make use of such resources outside the school and, once more, to help break down the distinction between the often arbitrary worlds of the classroom and workplace. As yet another extension of this idea, teachers in the various school shops were skilled artisans hired from the outside. In addition to instructing students, such teachers maintained buildings and grounds and might actually use students to assist in their various jobs. In this way students learned gardening, with actual garden plots in the spacious school grounds or in parklands adjoining the educational facility. The school system even boasted a working farm, where students interested in agriculture could learn firsthand. There was also a constant effort to have older students help the younger ones—yet another method of saving money while helping to combat the sort of snobbery and age discrimination that was typically visited upon younger children by older ones. (Critics, however, saw this arrangement as merely a cost-cutting scheme that deprived students of proper supervision.) Indeed, each of the Gary school buildings contained all twelve grades under one roof.

In addition, there was supposed to be constant effort to integrate the different student experiences. Thus a history lesson and a writing assignment might be coordinated with an art project, drama presentation, or field trip into the community. Frequent assemblies—or auditorium time, as they were called—were a central part of this concept, in that the students themselves presented plays and projects to their classmates. In order to accommodate these various parts of the daily schedule, Wirt developed a "platoon system" whereby a grade level made up two or more platoons. Thus, while some students went to the auditorium or shops, others were in academic classrooms, an arrangement that again had the effect of using school facilities to their fullest.

As in the wider progressive movement, there were contradictory aspects to Wirt's educational theories. By stressing vocational education and by supplying Gary's school shops with the latest equipment, he shared the faith of many progressives in technology. Yet Wirt, like so many other progressive reformers and educators, felt ambivalent about the urban industrial world and wanted to use the schools to restore a sense of pride in workmanship. He also believed that keeping children busy much of the day would help to remove them from the immoralities and empty pleasures of modern urban life. In this respect a deeply conservative current wound through Wirt's educational ideas, a conservatism that would grow with the years. In the words of Ronald D. Cohen and Raymond A. Mohl, who have studied Wirt and the Gary Plan in much detail, "The school would be sort of an oasis, the... building protected from its hostile surroundings by a public park in front, athletic fields and playground in back, and gardens on the sides."[79]

Ueland herself was wildly enthusiastic about teaching at Gary, even though she frequently worked from six in the morning until eight at night.[80] In addition to teaching English, she had charge of the auditorium programs beginning in the fall of 1915. For this she earned all of $120 a month. Yet it was enough for her to rent a six-room apartment with another teacher (probably Elizabeth Roemer) and to hire a housekeeper and cook.[81] It was also clear that she much admired Superintendent Wirt, and especially after she became his assistant in January 1916. To her mother she wrote in August of that year, "I had a talk with Mr. Wirt yesterday—which always leaves me in [a] seventh heaven of enthusiasm."[82]

Elsa described her new position as that of Wirt's "literary assistant." None other than Elbert H. Gary, still chairman of the board of U.S. Steel, had just given Wirt $10,000 to disseminate the Gary Plan nationwide, and he wanted Elsa to help him compose as well as to edit promotional materials, including the captions for six "reels of moving pictures which present the whole Gary philosophy."[83] Wirt also wanted her to write her own articles in support of the Gary Plan and to place them in leading metropolitan newspapers. As if this were not enough, he asked her to meet with various groups of teachers, to draw conclusions about what had been the most important elements of their most recent experiments, and then to write a report on them for publication.[84] Although this would entail a great deal of work, Elsa explained to her father why she thought the experience would be beneficial: "The intimate association with *general* problems of school administration, and problems in teaching other subjects besides my own; the advantageous position for writing on my own account; and the chance to make good in this general field of publicity; all determine me to accept the position and give up teaching"[85] (emphasis is in the original).

During her brief stint as Wirt's assistant, as well as before, Elsa did in fact write several articles about the Gary Plan. These included an article on the Gary kindergarten for a periodical called the *Kindergarten and First Grade* and another entitled "Physics Taught to Fifth Grade Children" for the *Municipal Review.*[86] She also contributed a short piece as part of Randolph Bourne's series on the Gary schools for the *New Republic.* In the latter she discussed the benefits of the Gary Plan for teachers. Most important in this regard was the independence that it gave to teachers, who presented just one subject to several sections of students, rather than many subjects (and therefore several preparations) to one classroom of students, as was typical of public elementary schools at the time. The teacher was also free to adapt lessons to the interests of the students, either as a group or as individuals.[87]

In an article for the *New York Evening Post,* Elsa concentrated primarily on the advantages of the Gary Plan for students. In place of strict, old-fashioned discipline, which was not adapted to the natural energies and curiosity of young children, the Gary schools allowed their students to move about and explore, to learn naturally, and to respect the abilities of others, be they boys or girls. As Elsa explained, "Life in the Gary schools gives more than discipline. It has given our boy an interesting respect for girls, for one thing, because girls handle tools in the shop and play baseball as cleverly as the boys. And it has added to his fine nine-year-old eagerness about everything he sees and does. No walk in the woods is complete without bringing back cricket, cocoon or cactus to the nature study teacher. Sewing is just as interesting as sawing. And books, unspoiled by over-emphasis, are as entrancing as the creatures in the woods."[88]

Elsa, who was twenty-seven years old when she wrote these words, remained a lively and attractive woman. Thus it is not surprising that she had had several serious suitors over the years. A classmate at the University of Minnesota named Harold Taylor remained interested in her after her move to New York. He wrote frequently and sent Elsa violets at the settlement house.[89] But in early 1911 she turned down his proposal of marriage. She also had a suitor at Columbia University, whom she likewise rejected. In a letter to her mother in February 1911 she referred somewhat dramatically to both men: "Do I want to marry him [Harold] or don't I? I am afraid sometimes that I am blindly and stupidly throwing away a very big thing. Perhaps I am morbidly depressed about the whole thing. That Foley incident—you remember my Columbia suitor who was so insistent?—turned out so disagreeably that in a more primitive society I would have killed him."[90]

In another letter to her mother soon thereafter she explained that she would not marry until she was certain of caring enough for a man so that "the step is fair to him."[91] Just why her Columbia University suitor turned out so disagreeably is unknown. As to her beau from Minnesota, Elsa probably did not want to give up her independence at a time when married women, at least of the middle and upper classes, were still expected to devote most of their energies to child rearing and managing the household.[92] Years later she told her sister Brenda that their father's monthly fits of anger over their mother's expenditures probably played a part in her aversion to losing financial independence through marriage. Reiterating what she took to be Elsa's own thoughts on the matter, Brenda wrote, "[Elsa] be dependent on a man for money, for support? I guess not! Not on your life!"[93]

Although Elsa would never marry, she had a great capacity for friendship, and she made several lasting friends during her twenties—particularly in New York—some of whom would play an important role at Carson College. Besides cultivating this network of friends, Elsa had become a woman of impressive accomplishments by her late twenties. She had obtained firsthand experience as a social worker in New York and had become part of one of the most exciting (if also controversial) educational experiments of the day—the Gary Plan. Furthermore, she was a respected scholar and published author and displayed an intelligence, energy, and optimism to all who met her. As both a progressive reformer and educator, she would soon apply her already rich fund of knowledge and experience to the development of the Carson College for Orphan Girls in Flourtown, Pennsylvania.

CHAPTER THREE

LAUNCHING
THE
PROGRESSIVE
ORPHANAGE

Looking back over her long life, Elsa Ueland must have seen the dozen or so years after Carson's official opening in 1918 as something of a golden age for the institution as well as the high point in her own professional life. It was during this time that Carson was best known as a model progressive orphanage and school, attracting attention far and wide from educators and the social work community. It was also a period of great prosperity for the country at large, when a growing income from the Carson bequest allowed Ueland and her staff to provide a rich and innovative program. It was these funds that allowed Carson College to overcome many of the doubts about founding a new orphanage, as expressed, even before the facility opened, by relatives of Robert Carson, by the board of trustees itself, and by many in the child-welfare community.

Although the Carson will had stipulated that there should be a superintendent of the institution, the board decided in the spring of 1916 to engage a separate person (specifically a woman), to be known as the president of Carson College, who would direct the educational and living arrangements of the girls. Because there would now be two high-ranking positions, the board drew up separate job descriptions for superintendent and president. The superintendent was to act as a general business manager, to keep accounts, to oversee the physical plant of the college, to prepare an annual budget under the direction of the president, and to attend board meetings when invited. The president was designated as the "chief executive officer." As such she was to submit all general policies, including the budget, for approval by the board. She was to "nominate" all employees, with final assent reserved to the board, and was in charge of discipline for all employees and children. She also had the right to suspend any employee. Unless otherwise directed, she was to attend all board meetings.[1]

Just exactly how a young progressive educator like Elsa Ueland came to the attention of the directors of Carson College as a prospective president is open to some conjecture. It may have been through William Wirt, to whom Carson sent some promotional materials in October 1915. Ueland's friend Alice Barrows also received a copy of this promotional literature.[2] Or it may be that another of Ueland's friends, Katherine Tucker, whom she had met in New York and who was now working in Philadelphia, alerted Elsa to the position.[3] Yet according to an account that appeared in the Philadelphia press and seems to be confirmed by Carson records, a delegation from the board simply decided to visit the Gary schools, as part of a larger tour of orphanages and schools, in order to see if any of the Gary programs would be applicable to Carson College.[4] Since one of their principal tasks was to educate orphaned girls from mainly working-class backgrounds (as spelled out in the Carson will), Gary's large working-class population may have made its program of compelling interest to members of the Carson board. It was Elsa Ueland, according to press accounts, who took the Carson delegation on a tour of the facilities and so impressed them that they asked her to consider becoming president of their fledgling institution.[5] In the end, it may have been a combination of several factors that resulted in Ueland's applying for the job.

Whatever the exact scenario, Ueland received an invitation to visit the Philadelphia area in May 1916 to meet with other members of the board and to learn more about Carson College firsthand.[6] During this visit she seems to have stayed at the home of George Vaux, who then chaired the management committee of the board. She was charmed and somewhat amused by the Vauxs' Quaker simplicity, which she described for her mother with her usual flair for detail: "The Vaux's [*sic*] have been Quakers since William Penn. They live in this grey-stone, flower-filled house near Bryn Mawr, surrounded by acres of woodland. Dressing plainly, eating plainly, saying 'thee' to all members of the household, silent grace before eating and scripture reading after dinner—besides wonderful old silver, old portraits, old furniture and a rarely beautiful house."[7]

Elsa went on to explain in the same letter that the board had expressed some misgivings about her Unitarianism, a religion that many more-traditional Christians then equated with freethinking. In addition, the board seemed to fear that Elsa's liberal religious beliefs would keep her from observing a quiet and respectful Sabbath at Carson. Under the circumstances, she was somewhat worried about her own personal liberty as head of Carson College. She also thought that several provisions of the Carson will were bizarre or unworkable—for example, that admissions were restricted to girls between six and ten, both of whose parents were dead, along with the mimicry of certain outdated parts of the Stephen Girard will.[8]

Yet the salary of $4,000 per year—worth perhaps $80,000 in the 1990s—was attractive to Ueland, as she confessed to her parents.[9] It was evident, too, that she wanted to use the position as a platform from which to disseminate the highly progressive Gary Plan throughout the local schools—and perhaps beyond, into Philadelphia itself. As she wrote to her mother on April 17, 1916, "Mr. Wirt wants me to take the [Carson College] position. He believes I can do more to organize public education [in accordance with the Gary Plan] in such a position than as principal of a school in Minneapolis, for instance, where I could appear to have some personal axe to grind and all the time might be blocked by my superiors."

Indeed, Ueland was so intent on spreading the Gary system in and around the Quaker City that she initially supposed her decision about whether to remain at Carson for any considerable period would turn on her success or failure in introducing the Gary system locally. Thus she would take the Carson position, she wrote to her mother, "with the understanding that if I could do nothing for the *public* schools in two years, I would then quit"[10] (emphasis is in the original). In any event, Ueland was pleased to inform her parents in late May of 1916 that the Carson board had unanimously elected her to lead the new institution. Her official title would be "President of The Carson College for Orphan Girls." [11]

The Uelands were very proud of their daughter's latest success, but her father, at least, worried about the effects of such a job on her prospects for marriage. "The only draw back," he wrote to her in June 1916, "is that it may stand in the way of your marrying. If you could do that too and have a family and children, my hopes for your future would indeed be completely realized." [12] She was, according to the conventional wisdom of the day, quickly passing the age of eligibility, a fact that had not escaped her father's notice. Given her qualms about losing her independence, it is probable that Elsa had given up altogether on the idea of marriage. It is also quite unlikely that Carson College would have hired a married woman as president, given the prevailing attitudes about the proper role of a married woman as a mother and homemaker. (These assumptions about Ueland are borne out by the fact that she turned down yet another suitor only two years after taking the job at Carson. He was none other than Carson board member Otto Mallery, who befriended Ueland when she arrived in Philadelphia and asked her to marry him sometime in 1918.) [13]

Although Ueland had written on educational topics, had made herself an expert on progressive education, had taught in the Gary schools, and had done a brief stint in school administration (as Wirt's assistant), she concluded that some further preparation was in order for the Carson position and spent several months trying to gain additional knowledge. She thus went to New York in July, where she participated in what was described as a "Round Table discussion or Seminar," on whose precise nature she did not elaborate. [14] While there she visited with several old friends from settlement-house days, and attended a dinner that included Randolph Bourne and the young Walter Lippmann, who would go on to become one of the most respected writers on public affairs in twentieth-century America. [15]

After spending August back in Gary winding up her life there (and the first two weeks in September with the family in Minnesota), Ueland apparently arrived in Philadelphia during mid-September, since her employment began officially on the fifteenth of that month. She found temporary accommodations downtown in the Hotel Adelphia, at 13th and Chestnut Streets, and later a room in the College Club, at 1300 Spruce Street, both within easy walking distance of Carson College's downtown office. [16] She then spent several weeks visiting various orphanages, including the Andrews Institute, near Cleveland, Ohio, and the New York Orphan's

Asylum at Hastings-on-Hudson, but apparently left no record of her impressions.[17]

The Philadelphia newspapers gave extensive coverage to Ueland's arrival in the city, in part because of all the earlier publicity about the Carson bequest and the protracted legal disputes over the will. Several reporters were struck by Elsa's youth, with the writer from the *Bulletin* referring to her as a "girl of twenty-eight."[18] The *Bulletin* reporter also marveled that she looked nothing like the proverbial orphanage super-intendent—from her bright and sunny smile to the lively blue dress, designed by herself, that she had worn for the interview. A writer from the *Public Ledger* added that she radiated all the good health and energy of an athlete who loved the out-of-doors: "She walks with almost a stride; the walk of a basket ball player who is never ill."[19]

Ueland spent part of this introductory press conference sharing her ideas about education and child care. She wanted to inspire freedom, imagination, and independence in her girls, she told the reporters, and intended to use some of the insights that she had gleaned from studying the "Montessori method," which she had seen in action at several schools.[20] She added that more-open classrooms, where children were free to move about, would solve most discipline problems.

Ueland also spoke about her hopes for cooperation between Carson College and the surrounding neighborhood in Flourtown—and especially its schools. Such cooperation was not only practical and economical, she explained, but it would save her girls from the isolation that typically came with "orphan asylums." Greatly impressed, one of the reporters pre-dicted that it would only be a short time "before educators [turn] their eyes to Carson College."[21]

Finally, Ueland was outspoken about her belief in coeducation, despite Robert Carson's insistence that the institution accept only girls. She her-self had attended the coeducational University of Minnesota, where men and women learned to work "shoulder to shoulder." At Carson she would compensate for the all-girl atmosphere by inviting boys from the local neighborhood to participate in various activities. "I shall have parties and games and dances," she explained. "I want the college at Flourtown to be a definite factor in the community life. I want my girls to know their neighbors."[22]

Missing from Flourtown was anything like an urban atmosphere, despite the fact that it was only a dozen miles or so from downtown Philadel-phia. For all intents and purposes, Flourtown was what might be called a strip village, hugging both sides of Bethlehem Pike as the road made its way north out of the Chestnut Hill section of Philadelphia. Maps from the early twentieth century show several old taverns that had once catered to stagecoach travelers, along with a few local stores and modest dwellings, many of them former farmhouses.[23] There were only a few cross streets, such as Wissahickon Avenue and Mill Road, which contained modest-sized houses for half a block or so on either side of the pike. Completely absent were urban town houses, suburban villas, tall office buildings, or sophisticated commercial establishments.

The manuscript of the federal census for 1920 further supports such a view of Flourtown.[24] According to this census, 427 people were living in the village.[25] Nine of them (2 percent) were listed as black, and forty-seven (11 percent) as foreign born. Of the foreign-born population, thirty-eight gave Ireland as their place of birth. Six were from Germany, two were from England, and one was from Scotland. Significantly, none was from southern or eastern Europe, from Latin America, or from the Orient. The vast majority of the native-born population listed Pennsylvania as their place of birth. Although there was no record of religious affiliation in the census, one might conclude from their places of origin that the vast majority of Flourtowners were Protestants, with only a few Roman Catholics, who were largely of Irish birth or descent. Indeed, the only place of worship in the village itself was a small Presbyterian church on the northeast corner of East Mill Road and Bethlehem Pike.

Using occupation as an indication of economic standing, one would have to conclude that Flourtown was not a particularly wealthy community. One hundred sixty-seven of the adult residents listed employment. Of these, fifty-two persons (31 percent) were unskilled workers (that is, laborers, factory workers, teamsters, and the like). This figure included the five black employees in Flourtown, who worked as either farm laborers or housemaids. Forty-one individuals (25 percent) were in skilled or semi-skilled occupations (ranging from trolley drivers and printers to plumbers and masons). Thus over half (55.5 percent) of the employed residents in the village were members of what one might call the working class. Five others (3 percent) put themselves down as farmers, though it is impossible to tell from the census how much land they owned.

Fifty-nine individuals (35.5 percent) worked in what might be considered lower-middle- and middle-middle-class occupations (from stenographers and telephone operators to shopkeepers and the local florist). Only nine persons (5.5 percent) reported managerial or professional positions: the public school superintendent, the village doctor, two lawyers, an architect, and the Presbyterian minister, who together constituted Flourtown's upper middle class. So far as can be surmised from the occupational listings in the census, there was no wealthy upper class in the village, at least not in comparison to the Philadelphia metropolitan area as a whole.

Elsa Ueland would later claim that Flourtown was in fact the kind of community where Carson College's orphaned girls could gain a realistic idea of what to expect in later life. In many ways she was right, for the occupational stratification of Flourtown was similar to that of the United States as a whole, except for the absence of any kind of real upper class, a somewhat larger number of unskilled workers than the national norm, and a smaller upper middle class than usual. According to the social historian Edward Pessen, a normal social-class distribution in the United States in general would have been 21 percent unskilled workers, 34 percent skilled workers, 32 percent lower middle and middle middle class, 9-10 percent upper middle class, and 3 percent upper class.[26] Since Carson College's orphans were without the sorts of accumulated advantages that arise from family connections, and even from small amounts of property and savings, Ueland may have reasoned that her girls would have few prospects of rising into the wealthier classes. In this sense she was probably correct in declaring that the families of Flourtown were convenient models of what her girls might expect when they grew up.

Just beyond Flourtown itself was Philadelphia, whose vast municipal limits had been expanded in 1854 to fill all of Philadelphia County. In 1920 Philadelphia thus reached to within two miles of Flourtown and coincided with the boundaries of neighboring Chestnut Hill. Although Chestnut Hill was officially within the city of Philadelphia, it remained essentially a wealthy suburban enclave, with large tracts of open land and impressive country estates, along with suburban villas and some smaller houses for its shopkeepers and artisans—in contrast to Flourtown's more modest socioeconomic profile.[27]

In 1920 Philadelphia was still the third largest city in the United States, behind Chicago and New York, with a total population of about 1.8 million. Although the city had received large numbers of immigrants over the past half century, they represented only 25 percent of its residents in 1920, as opposed to nearly 33 percent in Boston and approximately 40 percent in New York. The city also enjoyed a generally high level of prosperity, and remained one of the leading industrial centers of the nation, specializing in a variety of finished goods rather than heavy industry. With its Baldwin Locomotive Works, Cramp shipyards, scores of textile mills, and hundreds of small manufacturing firms, the Quaker City could still boast that it was a "workshop to the world." Although there was certainly grinding poverty in some sections of the city, Philadelphia's slums were smaller than what one might imagine for a city of its size, in part because the vast expanse of land extending out from the center of the city in every direction contributed greatly to modest housing costs. Indeed, with home ownership higher than in any other major city on the east coast, Philadelphia proudly called itself "the city of homes."[28]

Such an impressive degree of home ownership, a large native-born population, overall prosperity, and a variety of industries and business interests had all given rise to a tradition of moderate politics in Philadelphia. The city had its share of political corruption, and although progressive reformers had mounted several seemingly successful crusades against the bosses, their victories were neither profound nor long lasting. Thus, in the 1920s an entrenched Republican machine ran the City of Brotherly Love, as it had for the most part since the end of the Civil War, and most Philadelphians were content to let it rule in peace.[29]

If Philadelphia was not a bastion of reform in the 1920s, residents of Flourtown were even less likely to demand change. Governed as part of Springfield Township, residents were content with township trustees and other elected officials who confined themselves to a minimal and predictable round of responsibilities, such as providing a basic public school system and maintaining local roads. Thus neither Flourtown nor Philadelphia seemed to offer fertile ground for the sorts of school reforms that Elsa Ueland had in mind—or for any advanced progressive ideas that she might espouse. Whether Ueland appreciated such limitations when she took the job is unknown. In any case, such knowledge would probably not have kept her from pushing ahead to create a progressive orphanage while making whatever impact she could in the surrounding community.

Ueland appears to have moved into semirural Flourtown in the spring of 1917, when Carson College rented a house for her, with a barn and a vacant side lot, along Wissahickon Avenue.[30] Located on a piece of property directly abutting the Carson grounds, the dwelling (now number 35) served as an on-site office for the still uncompleted institution and a storage area for farm equipment, in addition to a residence for Ueland. For a short time it appears also to have housed other members of the staff. The structure itself was a two-story farmhouse with stuccoed walls (painted gray in the mid-1990s) and a wooden porch across the front. Elsa called it the Maples, in honor of the two large maple trees in the yard.[31]

Ueland shared the Maples with her friend Katherine Tucker (1884–1957). Ueland and Tucker had met each other in New York, where Tucker, a graduate of Vassar College and a trained nurse, was director of the Social Service Department of the New York State Charities Association. In 1915 or 1916 Tucker had moved from New York to Philadelphia as head of the city's Visiting Nurse Association, a progressive institution with nationwide branches that had emerged, like so many other social programs of the period, out of the settlement-house movement. In 1929 she would become executive director of the National Organization for Public Nursing, a post that she held until 1935, at which time she became director of the Nursing Education Department of the University of Pennsylvania, holding that position until stepping down in 1949.[32]

Elsa and "Kate" would remain lifelong friends and would share a household most of the time until Tucker's death some four decades later. Both of them loved their little "farmhouse," as Elsa sometimes called the Maples in her letters to the folks back in Minnesota. Just east of the house they had a huge garden in the vacant lot, which was far more Kate's preserve than Elsa's.[33] As Elsa described it, "There is almost nothing in the vegetable kingdom which we are not raising, from the staple potato and bean to sage and thyme and esoteric salads."[34] They were living, she wrote, a "real 'back to the hearth,' and 'back to the soil' existence."[35] Although she could revel in their old-world pursuits, Elsa thrilled at obtaining one of the more modern pieces of technology, a new Ford automobile, which she purchased in the spring of 1924.[36]

As it turned out, Ueland and Tucker were the pioneers in a group of unmarried professional women who settled in Flourtown over the next few years and formed a close-knit set that was remarkable for its talent and mutual support. In the spring of 1921, Elsa and Kate were joined in Flourtown by two other women they had probably met in New York, Jessie Taft and Virginia Robinson, both of whom were trailblazers in the social work profession. Taft and Robinson bought a modest house on the north side of East Mill Road, just beyond Bethlehem Pike.[37]

Taft (1882–1960) held a doctorate in psychology from the University of Chicago, and had been the assistant superintendent of the reformatory for women at Bedford Hills, New York, during the time that Ueland was in New York City. In 1918 Taft became the director of the new Child Study Department and Mental Hygiene Clinic of the Children's Bureau

Fig. 16.   Elsa Ueland, on left, with Kate Tucker beside her and
Bobby Ueland with back to camera. Jessie Taft is the woman
on right, with Martha Taft in her arms, beside unidentified man.
Photo c. 1920. EUP.

of Philadelphia and Children's Aid Society of Pennsylvania. Later she
became a professor at the Pennsylvania School of Social Work, which was
eventually absorbed by the University of Pennsylvania. Taft would be
widely hailed as a pathfinder in child psychology, whose many articles
and books were well received among her contemporaries.[38]

Robinson (1883–1977) was a graduate of Bryn Mawr College and held a
doctorate in sociology from the University of Pennsylvania. Like Taft she
was in the forefront of professional social work and social work education,

teaching at the University of Pennsylvania's School of Social Work and also serving for some time as its associate director. She would later become Taft's principal biographer, besides authoring numerous articles and books on social work and particularly its connections with psychology.[39]

In fact, both Taft and Robinson appear to have spent some time in Flourtown before moving there permanently, since both of them were employed part-time by Carson College in 1917 and supplied with room and board (probably at the Maples) when they were working on site. Taft did psychological tests and consulted on difficult cases. Robinson worked as supervisor of admissions and discharge and was, for all intents and purposes, Carson's first social worker.[40]

Several other professional women of considerable ability would settle in Flourtown and become friends or acquaintances of Robinson, Taft, Tucker, and Ueland, but the four of them would remain the closest-knit of the local group. Besides the companionship that the women offered one another, the relatively cheap real estate in the sleepy village of Flourtown and the beautiful, rolling countryside that surrounded it helped attract all of them.

In addition to the Flourtown circle, Ueland frequently invited old friends from her New York days down to Flourtown, and especially for Christmas and other special holidays. These included Elizabeth Roemer and Alice Barrows. Roemer, who was a Danish immigrant, always cooked a Christmas goose, Danish style, "with apples and plum pudding." On Christmas Eve, Elsa provided a Norwegian supper, using recipes sent from the family in Minnesota.[41]

Although they were all single, several of these women reared orphaned children in their own homes. Elizabeth Roemer adopted a boy named Merle. Jessie Taft and Virginia Robinson took two children into their home, Everett and Martha Taft, whom Jessie legally adopted. (Martha would also attend the elementary school that Carson established on the grounds.)[42] Elsa and Kate likewise became "parents" in this way. Soon after moving to the Maples, Elsa took in a small boy named Carl, whose death from influenza in October 1918 was a crushing blow.[43] In February 1919, she accepted another little boy named Robert, whom Jessie Taft had referred to her. In 1924 Elsa enrolled him in school under the name of Robert Ueland, though she did not formally adopt Robert at that time or, apparently, at any later date.[44] In the fall of 1918, Kate's eight-year-old niece by marriage, Yvonne Patterson, also came to live with them. Yvonne took the name of Tucker at school, but was never officially adopted by her "Aunt

Kate," and went back to the name of Patterson in young adulthood. (This taking of responsibility for children by single women, whether through formal adoption or not, did not seem to be controversial at a time when many widowed or abandoned women reared children alone—or at a time when women were seen as the principal caretakers of children in any case.) The Maples thus rang with the sounds of childhood, as did the dinners and festive gatherings of Elsa, Kate, and their friends.

Living as single, independent-minded professional women in Flourtown must have been difficult at times. One of Ueland's own early experiences at Carson College surely emphasized this fact. In February 1919 complaints came before the board that Ueland and eight housemothers at the college had been smoking and drinking on New Year's Eve, and had held what were described as wild bohemian parties on the grounds.[45] (Ueland herself admitted in a letter to her mother that she and her friends had shared some sherry and cigarettes on New Year's Eve, but that all the children were away from campus on holiday visits.)[46] At the time, however, conservative members of the older generation still considered smoking by women to be unseemly—and even daring. Such persons likewise

Fig. 17.   On the front porch at the Maples. Yvonne Patterson is on the left (next to dog). The girl in center is Martha Taft, and the boy is Bobby Ueland. Photo early 1920s. EUP.

would have disapproved of drinking by women in this year just before the nationwide prohibition of alcohol was slated to take effect.

The two members of the Carson family then serving on the board, James P. Carson and Thomas M. Thompson, who were probably disgruntled over the terms of the Carson will, pounced on these complaints as an opening to charge that the entire school was being mismanaged and to demand the dismissal of Ueland and the other offenders. According to Ueland, a third member of this cabal was Carson College's superintendent, Leonard Coleman, who was doubtless angry at having been superseded in authority by Ueland herself, as well as at having been denied use of the superintendent's residence when it was co-opted as a children's cottage, now known as Stork Hill.[47] In a telling letter to her mother in September 1918, Elsa referred to "some old quarrels" with James Carson, who had now allied himself with the disaffected Coleman.[48] In January 1919, some two weeks after the New Year's Eve party, she wrote to her mother that Coleman and Carson were trying to have her removed, and added that Carson "has preferred charges against me for having called him 'a crook and a grafter.'"[49] In a subsequent letter to her mother, she wrote that James Carson was "like a wild animal that has tasted blood." Besides carrying his complaints to the newspapers, he had tried to get at her through Coleman, and was now attempting "to stir disloyalty [among] members of the staff."[50]

The board stood by her, however, and instead of firing Ueland, they asked James Carson to step down as a trustee.[51] He did in fact tender his resignation, as did Thomas Thompson. Soon thereafter, Superintendent Coleman also left, much to the relief of Ueland and the remaining board members, who could now proceed to govern the orphanage without meddling from the Carson family or the embittered Coleman.[52]

Just how this incident may have affected Ueland is unknown. Although single, she still had an image to uphold as the head of a girls' orphanage and would have to be extremely careful about her personal conduct on campus—or anywhere else in the Philadelphia area. If the twenty-nine-year-old Ueland needed any reminders that she was no longer a young settlement-house worker living in Greenwich Village, this incident would certainly have sufficed. As she admitted to her mother, "It was a crazy thing to do, . . . for in Flourtown and in an institution[,] one can have no personal life whatever."[53]

During the two years before this incident occurred, Ueland had been working hard to get Carson College up and running. According to her, the board placed most of the responsibility for executing the details squarely in her lap, prompting her to write back home in January 1917, "I dream of plumbing fixtures."[54] In addition to the plumbing and other utilities, there was a staff to assemble, landscaping to complete, furniture and equipment to be secured.[55]

In selecting furniture, Carson followed the Tudor Gothic themes employed by architect Kelsey on the exteriors of the buildings—in consultation with J. H. Dulles Allen of Enfield Tiles, who had been engaged to oversee the decoration. Thus Carson purchased such items as settles, trestle tables, rush-bottomed ladder-back chairs, and gateleg tables with spooled carvings. Some of the tables were especially designed for Carson by the Chapman Decorative Company, with the monogram "C C" (for Carson College) carved into them at various places.[56]

Since construction had proceeded so slowly on the campus buildings, Carson had to rent some six houses in Flourtown that were near or just outside the grounds. In addition to Ueland's residence at the Maples were three properties in the 1400 block of Bethlehem Pike and two just off the pike on intersecting West Mill Road. The rentals on Bethlehem Pike included a modest stone residence (now number 1415) that Carson College named Darwin Hall, no doubt in honor of the famous scientist Charles Darwin, a choice probably made by Ueland herself, who had admired Darwin since childhood.[57] Moving north along the pike, the next rental property was called Tanglewood, probably in reference to the tangle of trees and vines around the site. Now demolished, Tanglewood stood at the southwest corner of Bethlehem Pike and College Avenue, on the present location of Friendly's restaurant. Directly across the street from Tanglewood was the third rental on the pike. This was Marigold Cottage, so named, according to one source, for the orange-yellow color of its stuccoed walls. Marigold has likewise been torn down, in this case replaced by Flourtown's state liquor store. The fifth and sixth rentals were dwellings on Mill Road, one of them called Mill Road and the other Ninth House (because it became the ninth cottage acquired by Carson).[58]

As early as 1916, Carson College was caring for five orphans in Flourtown, probably in the old Goss farmhouse on Bethlehem Pike, which the institution would soon purchase and name Orchard Cottage.[59] And although the official opening day would not come until July 1, 1918, the college continued to care for a handful of girls during 1917 and the first half of 1918.[60] Indeed, more than six months before Ueland came to Philadelphia, in February 1916, Superintendent Coleman had invited vari-

Fig. 18.   Fireplace, ladder-back chair, wall sconce, and other
details, dining room of Mother Goose Cottage (Cornflower).
AR, July 1921, 18.

ous court officers and charity organizations in southeastern Pennsylvania
and southern New Jersey to consider referring orphaned children to Carson College.[61] Even as Coleman was sending out these letters, he was
happy to report to the board that they now had enough applications to
open a first cottage.[62]

Given the growing preference for foster care as opposed to institution-
alized orphanages—and especially since the 1909 White House Conference on the Care of Dependent Children—it seems surprising that Carson
received so many applications even before its formal opening. Still more
impressive was the rate of admissions after the official launching on July 1,

1918. On opening day there were 10 children enrolled, with 23 more by the end of the month, for a total of 33 on August 1. The board decided to admit 10 to 12 new girls each year thereafter, with a maximum goal of around 100.[63] In January of 1919 the number stood at 42, and rose to 54 in January 1920, to 66 in January 1921, to 78 in January 1922, to 82 in January 1923, to 95 in January 1924, and to 102 in January 1925. By renting Ninth House, on West Mill Road, Carson was able to go beyond the 100 mark, and by early 1928, 112 children were under care.[64] As planned, the enrollment remained slightly over 100 during the rest of the 1920s, but doubtless could have risen higher if Carson College had been able to provide additional space.[65] Those children who lived at Carson during this period came from various Pennsylvania counties, but the great majority of them were from Philadelphia and its immediate environs.

The reasons for this success were several, despite many initial doubts about Carson's viability, and despite the growing opposition to institutional orphan care among the social work community. Of great assistance, no doubt, were the close connections that Ueland had with child-welfare authorities, doubtless enhanced by her friendships with Jessie Taft and Virginia Robinson. It is also evident that from the beginning Carson College enrolled girls who were not entirely proved to be full orphans. For example, a number of Carson girls had lost their mothers, but their fathers had deserted their families some time before and could not be found. Though it was possible that such fathers had died, there was no legal evidence of death, and thus the distinct possibility remained that these absent fathers were very much alive at the time their daughters went to Carson. Then there were those children who were illegitimate and whose fathers were unrecorded. When their mothers died, these children were considered to be full orphans, even though their biological fathers might have been alive and well at the time.[66]

In addition to such factors, the numbers of dependent children in institutions throughout the United States (both full and half orphans) continued to rise during the 1920s, despite the mounting preference for foster care. This occurred because the number of children needing care increased faster than the supply of foster-care homes. The continued growth of urban areas, and the socioeconomic dislocations that accompanied this growth, resulted in more orphans as well as neglected and abused children. At the same time, a relative decline in the country's rural population meant that there were fewer farm families, who traditionally had taken foster children free of charge in exchange for the labor on the farm. Only later, when substantial amounts of public money became available to compensate foster parents, would the supply begin to catch up with the demand.[67]

Not only were there plenty of girls in need of Carson College during its first years, but many of them required close attention. As Ueland wrote to the management committee of the Carson board in September 1918, "Many of these children came to us with only their clothes on their backs, in poor physical condition, and with very little education."[68]

Typical of those admitted during the early years was a ten-year-old girl who had lost both her parents during the influenza epidemic in 1918. Her maternal uncle had taken her into his home, but he himself died several years later, and the aunt, who had four children of her own, could no longer support the niece.[69] Another child, seven and a half, was orphaned when her mother committed suicide and her father died of a stroke the following year.[70] Yet another, aged eight, entered Carson after her father had died of tuberculosis and her mother expired following a gall bladder operation.[71] Then there was the case of a nine-year-old girl, both of whose parents had burned to death in a house fire.[72]

Once a new girl's basic physical needs were met, Ueland deemed a good education and a warm yet well structured cottage life to be of utmost importance. Given her recent experience with the Gary Plan and her own desire to implant some of its features in the local public schools, it is no surprise that she immediately went to work trying to generate some kind of cooperative arrangement with the public school in Flourtown. Indeed, because Carson's approximately forty girls threatened to overwhelm the village school, Ueland believed that a joint program with the public system was a genuine necessity.

There was in fact only one public school in Flourtown at the time, a small elementary building, originally constructed in 1879, that had received an addition in 1907. (Another wing would be erected in 1921.) It stood on the north side of Wissahickon Avenue and directly adjoined the Carson grounds. It was so close to Carson College that, except for its architecture, one might have assumed that it was part of the Carson complex. Such close physical proximity must have seemed ideal to Ueland, in that her girls could walk across the fields to the village school for some of their classes, while the village children could just as easily walk over to Carson for part of their instruction. Both facilities would receive maximum use, thereby avoiding wasteful duplication and extra expense to Carson and to the local school district. Such a cooperative arrangement would also help to integrate Carson girls into the local community, one of Ueland's goals from the beginning.

There seemed to be some prospect for such an arrangement when the Springfield Township School Board (which had jurisdiction over the Flourtown School) agreed in May 1918 that Carson could use its schoolhouse for a summer program during July and August. Carson would pay all utilities, along with the custodian's salary, and admit children from the community free of charge.[73]

The summer school was an apparent success, with several children from the village attending alongside Carson girls. This first summer program was the beginning of an annual series of cooperative summer schools at Carson. Yet when it came to a full-scale cooperation during the regular academic year, the local board refused to go along. The first hint of trouble came in late July of 1918, when the Springfield Township School Board announced to Ueland that they were under no legal obligation to finance the education of Carson girls out of local funds. If, however, Carson would agree to pay tuition for its children, either the school board would erect a new building on its property for both the Carson students and the local children, or it would rent a suitable building in Flourtown to handle the overflow.[74]

For Ueland, who had witnessed the efforts in Gary to make maximum and efficient use of all educational resources in the community, such a proposal from the school board made little sense. Thus, in late August she responded in a letter that proposed an experimental plan for one year in order to see if they could work together for the benefit of both groups of children, at the same time avoiding unnecessary expenses. Although she had been advised by Carson College's own lawyers that Springfield Township could be made to educate Carson girls without tuition payments, Ueland tactfully proposed that Carson would render such payments in the event that they were required. But much of her letter concentrated on explaining how they might join forces in such a way as to benefit all concerned: "Either you employ a[n extra] teacher, rent a room, find desks, and send us the bill, which we will pay. . . . Or we can plan our program in such a cooperative way that by using our teachers for 'out-of-school' activities, for all the Flourtown children, you need employ no new teachers, rent no new room, find no new desks, spend not one extra cent for the school in Flourtown, and yet be sure that every grade has the same number of minutes for work, in the prescribed studies, as it had last year."[75]

Fig. 19.   Carson girls, and boys from Flourtown village, at the cooperative summer school, 1922. CVS.

Although the precise reasons have not survived, the school board turned down Ueland's offer. She tried again in 1920–21 to forge some kind of cooperative schooling, but failed once more.[76] It may be that the school board found Ueland's ideas about education too advanced, or it may be that there had been some community opposition all along to the idea of an orphanage in Flourtown and that some parents objected to having their children go to Carson for part of their educational program. Whatever the case, this disagreement between Carson and the local school would prove only the first salvo in a series of difficulties over the next few decades. That the school board's position greatly exasperated Ueland is clear from a letter to her mother in the summer of 1918 in which she wondered "if the President of the United States has any more difficult job [with] the Russian situation than I now have . . . with the Flourtown School Board."[77]

With Carson's subsequent unwillingness to place children into the public school as it then existed, there was no alternative but to create its own elementary program. (Since Carson was forbidden by the Carson will to admit any children over age ten, it would be several years before they had to worry about high school instruction.) Though frustrated at the lack of cooperation from local school officials, Ueland confessed to being "fascinated by the new [educational] problems."[78] In having to create its own school program, Carson College would also have far more freedom to implement the latest ideas in progressive education and even to experiment with various plans.

Although Ueland was the main author of the elementary program at Carson, she received permission from the Carson board in September 1918 to hire Mrs. Phoebe Crosby Allnutt (1884–1974) as "teaching principal." By 1923 Allnutt's title had been upgraded to that of school director.[79]

Allnutt and Ueland also used the expertise of Lucy Sprague Mitchell (1878–1967), yet another of Elsa's friends from the New York days. A disciple of John Dewey, Mitchell launched the Bureau of Educational Experiments in New York in 1916, which she later renamed the Bank Street College and still later the Bank Street College of Education (located in an old spaghetti factory on Bank Street in Greenwich Village). In addition to experimenting with teaching methods and generating new curriculum materials, the Bank Street School became one of the most important progressive teachers colleges in the United States. Carson College obtained a variety of teaching materials from Bank Street and also took student teachers from that institution throughout the 1920s and 1930s. In addition, Ueland and Lucy Mitchell visited frequently with each other, in both Flourtown and New York, and sometimes took lengthy trips together. Between 1918 and 1920 Ueland herself served as a member of Bank Street's advisory council.[80]

In deciding, of necessity, to create their own elementary school at Carson College, Ueland and her staff freed themselves to embark upon their own progressive experiment, which would join the classrooms, residential life, and community activities in as many ways as possible. Within several years, it would be widely hailed as one of the most successful and enlightened programs in the country.

CHAPTER FOUR

THE
PROGRESSIVE
YEARS

Although the progressive-education movement
evolved over the years and contained many
strands, there were several characteristics of
the movement, according to the educational
historian Laurence Cremin, that were widely
shared by progressive educators. These were
(1) a desire to broaden the scope of the school
to include direct concern for such things as
health, recreation, family life, and the quality
of the local community; (2) an application of
new pedagogical techniques based in psychology and the social sciences; (3) a recognition
of the need to tailor instruction to individual
students, as well as to different social and economic backgrounds; (4) a belief that American
culture should be made more democratic in
that all students would be introduced to the
best that modern civilization had to offer in
both the arts and sciences.[1]

In carrying out these ideas, Elsa Ueland and Carson College worked hard to meet the individual needs of each girl, while offering a well-integrated program that linked school to other aspects of the child's life. Thus classroom instruction, field trips, cottage activities, recreation, religious training, and contacts with neighbors in the Flourtown area were coordinated as much as possible so that each aspect of life would enrich the others and provide a sense of security, competence, and self-esteem for the Carson girl. At the same time, Carson College tried to provide realistic vocational training and job experiences so that its graduates could find gainful employment once they left the campus, a need that was doubtless reinforced by Ueland's earlier work in vocational guidance.

All the full-time teachers at Carson were single women. Some had never been married, while others were widowed or divorced. Throughout the nation at the time, most educators and parents believed that elementary school children, who were already used to being cared for primarily by mothers, would more naturally be attracted to women teachers—in effect, substitute mothers during the day. At the same time, many school districts frowned on married teachers, whose principal duties were thought to be in their own homes. Furthermore, teaching was one of the few professions open to women at the time. Finally, since Carson could only pay its teachers modestly, virtually all of them had to live on the grounds or share in some kind of rental housing in Flourtown, yet another factor that would militate against the hiring of married women as teachers.

In the early 1920s, Carson teachers received about $100 per month plus "living" (that is, room and board), some of them residing with the children as a part of a "cottage family." (These salaries were purposely higher than in other orphanages and were more or less equivalent to what elementary school teachers received in Philadelphia at the time.) Those who did not opt for the living on campus earned approximately $130 a month, but had to find their own accommodations in Flourtown. In the fall of 1924, for example, four Carson teachers shared a house that they called the Crow's Nest, located next door to Jessie Taft and Virginia Robinson's residence on East Mill Road. (In later years the Crow's Nest was the residence of Phoebe Allnutt, who shared it with Frances Jones, the orphanage's social worker.) In 1927 another house in Flourtown known as the Beacon (the location of which is now forgotten) was being rented by three teachers.[2]

From all accounts, Ueland treated her staff almost as if they were part of an extended family. Directives were often given informally and in person, and there was much socializing among the staff, most of whom lived on or very near campus during the early decades. According to Dorothy Moore (Fenstermacher), who began working in the business office at Carson in 1930 and later succeeded Ueland as head of the institution, Ueland ran a "low-key operation."[3]

What stands out in retrospect about Carson's progressive-education program is its many resemblances to the Gary Plan.[4] As at Gary, there was a long school day. During the academic year 1921–22, Carson girls went to school from 8:45 in the morning until 4:45 in the afternoon, with an hour and a half for lunch (12:15–1:45). The reason for this extended day, as at Gary, was to allow for the teaching of traditional as well as nontraditional subjects. (The long lunch break was necessary so that the girls could help with noontime chores back at the cottages.) Also as at Gary, the various grade levels divided into two groups, or "platoons." While one platoon engaged in academic work, the other took part in nontraditional courses such as physical training, sewing, laundry, music, weaving, or pottery.[5]

Increasingly, the academic subjects were paired with allied activities. For example, during the fall of 1922 the ninth-graders (who then formed the senior class of Carson's on-campus school) learned history, geography, English, and printing all during one period of two hours and forty-five minutes. The idea here was that students needed to read and write (that is, study English) in order to pursue history and geography, two related subjects that often overlapped in content. Printing on their own press allowed the students to publish compositions about history and geography and, in the process of setting type and reading proof, to become more proficient with their language skills.[6] In 1928 the eighth grade carried out a similar project when they researched, wrote, and printed their own study of Flourtown.[7]

Carson arrived at such an integration of studies, as Ueland explained in her annual report for 1923, somewhat through trial and error: "We have always realized the importance of hand-work, of learning primarily through vivid concrete experience, and only secondarily through books. And to secure this, we have hitherto departmentalized our work so that the children have gone from [the] classroom . . . to work-shop or studio or laboratory with [a] special teacher and special equipment; and then back again to [the] classroom. . . . But its danger, in over emphasis, is that it may also bring a scattering, a lack of relation and cohesion to the day's experiences."

Fig. 20. Carson girls operate their own printing press, mid-1920s. CVS.

In order to obviate this danger, the ninth-grade class, taught by Florence E. Whitney, had combined history, geography, English, and printing. Besides integrating these activities closely, the combined class had engendered tremendous pride, enthusiasm, and self-initiative among the students. Again, according to Ueland, "They feel that they are 'writing for publication' and, therefore, take pride in a correct and finished piece of work. They are learning to work independently. . . . They are asking relevant questions, not questions which are beside the mark. . . . And, with it all, they are getting a foundation of knowledge of printing itself."[8] In other words, the girls had come to see their studies as something real rather than as an empty exercise forced upon them by the teacher and devoid of any connection to the outside world.

Music classes also combined more-standard academic fare with exciting practical exercises, such as having the girls make their own musical instruments during the summer of 1921. This project was undertaken by, in Ueland's words (from a letter to her family in Minnesota), "a genius of a manual training teacher," whom she unfortunately did not name. "The

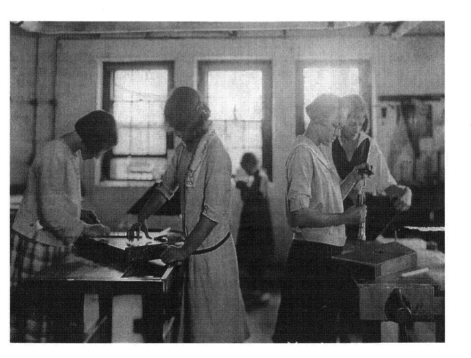

Fig. 21.   Carson girls making musical instruments, 1921. CVS.

children," as she described the class, "are making musical instruments—
wind, percussion and string—and begin to play [them]. Of course it is
crude, but most fascinating. They get the principles of all musical instruments and are understanding the early attempts at music made by the
human race." [9]

Even the youngest children combined practical exercises with learning. In 1926–27, for instance, the primary class built their own little town
as part of a unit on communities and how they functioned. According to
the children themselves, who contributed an article to the school newspaper (doubtless edited by one of the teachers), "We built a town to see
how towns are built, and because we wanted to play with a little town of
our own. And because we wanted to be good workmen. And because we
wanted to bring our dolls to school and make them walk up and down
the streets and go to church." [10]

Their little town had streets made of small stones, which the girls had
seen crushed at a nearby quarry. They named their thoroughfares Pebble
Street, Shady Lane, Carson College Avenue, and Church Street, and lined
them with houses and other buildings. There was a butcher shop, grocery
store, drugstore, post office, clothing shop, firehouse, and church. The

Fig. 22.   "Clopsville," the miniature town built by the primary class, 1926–27. CVS.

girls drew plans for each structure, measured and sawed wood, drilled holes, pounded nails, painted and stuccoed walls, and even planted little gardens. In the course of putting up the town, they visited a lumber mill to see how logs became boards, and also went to inspect the house (later called South Fields) then under construction by Carson College as a residence for "Miss Ueland" (see Chapter 5). The girls decided to call their town Clopsville, after their pet goat, Cloppity, who enjoyed running down the pebble streets and climbing on the roofs of the little houses.[11]

As this project demonstrated, Carson College, like the Gary schools, used resources in the surrounding community whenever possible. Carson's school director Phoebe Allnutt explained the practice in an article that she published in June 1923: "Concrete experience," she wrote, "is needed to train and discipline the imagination.... Trips to the banks of a neighboring creek, ... to dairies, factories and museums, help to acquaint [students] with the world they live in."[12] During the 1920s and early 1930s there were field trips to the nearby Corson lime quarries, to the Breyer's ice cream factory in Philadelphia, to the Philadelphia City Hall, to the Delaware River docks, to a facility in Norristown where they trained "Seeing Eye dogs," to the Container Corporation of America in the Manayunk section of Philadelphia, to a retail grocery establishment in the city, and to the Widener farm next door to Carson College itself.[13]

One set of trips in particular, those revolving around a unit on water, made a vivid impression on several teachers, who recalled them fondly many years later in reminiscences solicited by Ueland. They and the students had begun with their own Wissahickon Creek, sought out its source, and traced it to the Schuylkill River. Then they went to the top of the Philadelphia City Hall, where they could see the Schuylkill flowing into the Delaware River several miles to the southeast. Pursuing the Delaware further along its course to the sea, they took a boat trip down the river to Wilmington, Delaware. Other trips took them to a spring, where they made lemonade from the water, and to the local waterworks, where they could see how water was purified and sent on its way to hundreds of homes. The girls also staged a musical play, "How the Singing Water Got into the Tub."[14]

Students shared these experiences (in addition to the projects that they carried out in the classroom or in the cottages) with one another during morning assemblies—the so-called auditorium periods at Gary. In 1921-22 the assemblies took place on Monday, Wednesday, and Friday mornings from 8:45 to 9:15. The location was, in all probability, the large playroom in the basement of Mother Goose Cottage, known more popularly then and now as "the gym." In addition to the spacious Cinderella fireplace (created by Enfield Tile) on the west wall, the room contained a series of three Gothic arches at the north end of the gym, with a small stage behind. It was probably in this portion of the large room that the various presentations took place.

A brief account of these assemblies appeared in a document called "Notes on School Program, 1921-1922":"Assembly will be [coordinated by] a committee of seniors [that is, ninth-graders]. . . . There will be an opening hymn, prayer and psalm, roll call, announcements and a short program given by the different classes in turn." [15]

A sampling of topics presented by the children at assembly time survives from a list drawn up for the fall of 1924. On November 4, the first and second grades talked about how they had made and cared for their aquarium, and what they learned from the experience. The third and fourth grades had their chance two days later, when they recounted, for the other children, their recent trip to the zoo. Sometimes the presentations came from the girls as members of a particular cottage, as when Red Gables gave a program on December 11 about how to care for a baby, seemingly complete with a real infant named Charles. From time to time outside speakers gave talks. On what was then called Armistice Day (November 11), the assembly heard Miss Edith Leach from the very liberal Women's International League for Peace and Freedom (to which Ueland belonged) address them on the topic of "War and Peace." [16]

In addition to brief accounts of their projects at assembly time, the students often recorded their results in scrapbooks, notebooks, photographs, and publications from their own press, in addition to numerous plays, pageants, and tableaux. Among such items that have survived is "The Record of Our Mice," as set down by the first and second grades in June 1926. In it they described the mice in great detail, including their sleeping and washing habits, and the way in which they nurtured their young. As successive generations of mice were born, the children named them and created a family tree for them. [17]

Other project accounts included photographs. During the 1926-27 school year, for example, the fifth grade did a project on wool and documented each stage with snapshots. The pictures showed them shearing the sheep, washing and carding the wool, spinning and dying it, and then weaving it into cloth. A separate series of photographs depicted a group of girls dressed up like Indians in front of teepees while making dyes from local plants. Still another set of photographs showed a play called

Fig. 23. "The Agricultural Age," a scene from the play *Yesterday and Today*, enacted by Carson girls during the 1920s and 1930s. CVS.

Yesterday and Today, put on by the eighth grade throughout the 1920s and 1930s. The five acts took their audiences through the "Fear Age," the "Pastoral Age," the "Agricultural Age," the "Industrial Revolution," and the "Present Day." [18]

Such dramas allowed the students to "reenact history" at a time when historical reenactments and pageants were very popular in the United States. During the progressive era in particular, pageants tried to show a sense of continuity and community between past and present, and to show a kind of inevitable progress from the past into present and future times. [19]

Such pageants and historical reenactments could also convey a nostalgic theme and sometimes stressed the idea that the past was in certain ways better than the present. [20] This sentiment was not altogether at odds with the progressive ideas of Elsa Ueland, who like many reformers and educators of the day often held ambivalent views of the industrial revolution and of the rapid urbanization that accompanied it. Indeed, Carson College itself, with its semirural location and Gothic Revival architecture, made about as powerful an antiurban and anti-industrial statement as one could imagine.

Bespeaking this more nostalgic spirit were the medieval pageants and plays that became annual events in the life of Carson College. The most colorful of these was the May Festival, which received extensive coverage in the Philadelphia newspapers during the early 1920s. The account that appeared in the *Public Ledger* on May 22, 1920, was particularly full and descriptive:

> On the hills of Carson College . . . children . . . frolicked yesterday in a May festival. More than 500 persons watched the efforts of six weeks preparation. . . .
>
> The procession of the May revelers formed at Mother Goose cottage . . . and proceeded to Sherwood Forest, where the "Gooseherd and the Goblin" was presented. . . . From Sherwood Forest the town crier led the visitors to fair Nottingham Town [the lawn behind Mother Goose and Red Gables], where the second part was presented. There Robin Hood outwitted the sheriff in the shooting match.
>
> Lettie Laughlin, a child of eleven years, was then crowned Queen of the May. All the formality of the court was expressed in these solemn exercises. She was attended by a corps of ladies-in-waiting, who were all gorgeously costumed. While seated on her jeweled throne, ten nimble misses danced the banquet dance before her. The exercises closed with a maypole dance.[21]

In future years the play most often presented at the May Festival was Robin Hood, invariably performed in Carson's own Sherwood Forest.[22]

Another seasonal presentation was the annual Christmas tableau in the Mother Goose playroom/gym, attended by the whole school as well as the board of trustees and other invited guests.[23] They used live animals (cows, sheep, and horses from the Carson farm) for the manger scene, while Ueland read the Christmas story from the Bible, her voice filled with emotion.[24]

Such celebrations, like so much else at Carson, were integrated into the school's curriculum as vehicles for studying history and culture, as ideas

Fig. 24. May Festival in Sherwood Forest, 1921. CVS.

for writing assignments, or as topics for presentation at assemblies. During the period 1927–31, one of the English classes wove the theme of festivals into its work. Students researched the history of festivals from ancient civilizations (that is, the Egyptians, Chinese, Greeks, and Romans) through the Middle Ages and up into modern times. They also associated certain modern festivals with those of the past, thereby helping them to identify with former ages, as well as to see how the past played an important part in fashioning the present. For example, they connected the American Thanksgiving not only with the Pilgrims and other early settlers, but also with harvest celebrations going well back to antiquity. They also associated certain aspects of Christmas with pagan rites revolving around the winter solstice, an exercise that doubtless would have dismayed a good many orthodox Christians at the time—as well as later.[25]

What is not evident from the curriculum materials that have survived is whether the teachers at Carson College endeavored to inculcate what might be called progressive political ideas as a part of their instruction. Since Ueland had been and would remain a liberal and a reformer, one

Fig. 25.   May Queens in Gothic ambulatory of Mother Goose Cottage (Cornflower),
with Sun Baby behind them, 1921. CVS.

might suppose that she hired teachers who shared her views in general
and that these views would find their way into the classroom, though
there is no solid evidence that this is what happened.

Besides what transpired in school, there were many activities for Carson girls that involved the everyday operations of the institution, and
especially in the cottages where they lived. Because the girls lived as well
as learned on campus, there was an opportunity to connect learning in
the classroom with "home life" far more intimately than in progressive
schools where children returned at night to their own families.

Superintending these home activities were the housemothers. They were not professional child-care workers or persons with formal training in social work, but were women who drew upon their own experiences as mothers. From what can be gathered, they were widowed (or possibly divorced) and were attracted to positions at Carson because they included room and board at the cottages, as well as a modest salary (averaging about $80 per month in the early 1920s). Many of the housemothers—six of the nine in 1927—brought their own children to live with them in the various cottages.[26]

Ueland believed that such an arrangement was in fact healthy for the orphans in each cottage. The girls would do well, she thought, under a woman who was herself an active mother—usually one who alone had had to care for her own children and would thereby be more sympathetic to the plight of needy children. Reminiscing in a 1934 letter to the Bordogna children, whose mother, Josephine, was the housemother at Tanglewood Cottage, Ueland wrote, "I remember so well when your mother and I first knew each other. You three were all little things then . . . and your mother so beautiful,—just on fire with high courage to give you every chance in the world. And I thought then that if it could be possible for Mrs. Bordogna to make a home for you children—and in doing this, to share the home with children who had no mother,—that this would be a very big thing."[27]

The orphan girls themselves ranged widely in age in each cottage—from as young as six to as old as eighteen—instead of being segregated into age groups as they typically were in orphanages, including Girard College and the Hershey Industrial School at Hershey, Pennsylvania.[28] They were so dispersed at Carson in order to simulate some conditions of the "normal family," where the children would in fact be at different levels of maturity. The children addressed their housemothers by a variety of names, depending upon the likes of each housemother. Some preferred "Mother," as with "Mother Jackson" at Orchard Cottage or "Mother Bordogna" at Tanglewood. At Lower Beech there was "Aunt Betty" Bettman, while "Mom" (Mrs. Bill) Goss presided over Upper Beech. Still other housemothers wished to be called "Miss" or "Mrs." along with their last names.[29]

The housemothers also varied in their styles of managing a house full of girls. Mother Jackson had a reputation as a strict disciplinarian, while Miss Hart at Thistle was more easygoing.[30] For the most part, housemothers disciplined the girls by withholding privileges, such as a trip to the circus or a hike in the woods, or certain treats, such as dessert after a meal or a snack in the evening.[31] Physical punishment, however, was not entirely absent. Alice (Steel) Wandel, who lived at Carson from 1929 to 1934, remembered that she received a spanking one night for defying the "lights-out" rule in her cottage.[32] Caroline (Conley) Vankouwenberg, who was a resident during the 1940s, recalled that her housemother slapped her across the face for talking back.[33]

Despite their differences in management styles, most housemothers seemed to find their situation at Carson acceptable, as attested by the considerable numbers of them who remained at Carson for many years, such as Josephine Bordogna and Salome Jackson. Relying on these women's own experiences and common sense, Ueland and other members of Carson's professional staff held what might be called in-service training and enrichment sessions with the housemothers, in addition to paying their expenses to attend educational and social work conferences off campus.[34] This arrangement was apparently satisfactory, since there is virtually no criticism of the system in any of Carson's voluminous records from the 1920s, or even in Ueland's extensive and often frank private correspondence.[35] Nor was the lack of professional training among the housemothers unusual, in that, for the tending of their children, virtually all other orphanages at the time hired men and women who had no formal education as child-care workers.[36]

Ueland herself did not play a significant role in the everyday lives of the children in the cottages. Although former residents interviewed by this author universally admired Ueland—many of them for her beauty and poise—she was something of a remote figure to them. Helen (Traiche) Heath remembered Ueland during the 1930s as a "handsome woman" who, upon running into a group of children, would commonly exclaim in a cheerful voice, "Hello, girls, how are we today?" Nor did Heath ever feel that Ueland came across as a "motherly type."[37] Alice Wandel, who was also at Carson during the 1930s, remembered Ueland as being "beautiful but stern."[38] Florence (Johnson) MacFarlane and Caroline Vankouwenberg experienced the same sort of distant attitude toward Ueland in the 1940s.[39] In a personal diary entry from January 5, 1940, Ueland herself admitted a lack of personal contact with the girls: "I realize that I do not know these children at all myself—have not talked to them."

On a day-to-day basis, then, it was the housemothers who gave direction to the girls' lives. As part of their regular chores at the cottages, the girls cleaned house and kept their bedrooms neat, cooked meals, washed dishes, raked leaves, pulled weeds, clipped shrubbery, pruned trees, and performed many other tasks. These activities were calculated to make

Fig. 26. Preparing a meal, kitchen of Orchard Cottage, 1922–23. CVS.

them feel that they were part of a family and that their work was valued, thus building self-confidence and self-esteem. By citing the educational reformer Maria Montessori as an authority on how such activities could be lifted from the mundane level to one of personal enlightenment, Ueland explained her views on such practical work to the Carson board as early as September 1918:

Madame Montessori has demonstrated the educational possibilities in ordinary household tasks. We are trying to realize her spirit [here at Carson], to avoid the usual institution[al] mistake of making housework only drudgery, and to make the most of the educational opportunities in each cottage. To this end, the children have all really *cooked.* The breakfast group, dinner group, and supper group have actually learned to prepare these meals and to put them on the table. There have been some crises, to be sure. Attempting to beat eggs with the shells on, and to cook rice in the tea kettle after the water had been poured out, are [just two examples]. . . . All have had thrilling[,] creative experiences in making certain dishes for the family and for company.

They are also learning something of food values and costs, and of the planning of meals. We want them to learn not only how to carry out a single recipe in a domestic science class, but how to put the meal on the table, everything hot at once, how to plan it within a certain money allowance, how to market intelligently at the ordinary grocery store.[40] (Emphasis is in the original.)

The girls also learned about the cost of clothing and how to make the best use of the $6 or $7 per month, depending upon their ages, allotted to each child for clothes. As Ueland explained in an interview for an article on Carson that appeared in the *Green Book Magazine,* "We take them shopping. . . . They know what we are after, what we intend to use it for. . . . It is surprising how quickly they learn thrift. One of the older girls wanted a new cape last winter. We told her she could have it, but pointed out that prices would surely be reduced after the first of the year. She repaired an old coat and went through the [early] winter with it, and finally got her cape at a great reduction, in January."[41]

Besides the everyday chores in and around the cottages, the girls participated in the work of the Carson farm, which produced a good deal of the food consumed at the college. At first, the farm was under the management of Miss Charlotte Passmore, who came from Minnesota at Ueland's recommendation in January 1917.[42] Having a woman preside over a farm was somewhat unusual for the times, and was doubtless another way in which Ueland wished to demonstrate that women were capable of doing many jobs hitherto associated with men. Ueland was delighted with Passmore at first, but by November 1917 she concluded that hiring her had been a terrible blunder. Ueland wrote to her mother, "May I be forgiven for having made so serious a mistake. She is losing ground and no one can work with her."[43] Ueland apparently could not bring herself to dismiss Passmore, or anyone else, as would be revealed in future years. Three years later, Passmore was still at Carson, with Ueland describing her as a serious "error."[44] Passmore was not only hard to get on with, but the farm had failed to pay for itself and was actually losing money.[45] Finally, in 1924 Passmore quit, and Ueland went through two more farmers before she engaged William "Bill" Goss, who had been in charge of maintenance at Carson since about 1922 and an employee at Carson since 1919.[46] Goss, "Mr. Bill"—or in later years "Pop Goss"—as the girls called him, would remain at Carson for more than three decades. Beginning in the early 1930s, he and his wife "Mom Goss" were houseparents at Upper Beech Cottage—though it was "Mom Goss" who clearly presided over the cottage, while "Pop Goss" tended to his extensive duties on the farm, grounds, and buildings. An all-around handyman with a blustery exterior but a genuinely kind heart, Bill Goss was a man who could fix anything, and he soon introduced new economies to the farm that reduced its expenses.

Albert Kelsey's original plans had called for an elaborate set of farm buildings, but soaring costs during and just after World War I led the Carson board in early 1918 to purchase, for about $12,000, the small Goss farm, which apparently had been rented by Carson for the past two years or so. It had belonged to Bill Goss's family, and Goss himself had grown up there. Containing some eleven acres, the Goss property faced Bethlehem Pike in Flourtown and backed directly onto the Carson grounds. It contained a modest house, along with a barn, several outbuildings, a pasture, and a mature orchard.[47] The house, which Ueland named Orchard Cottage, stood between two dwellings on the pike that were rented by Carson, Darwin Hall to the south and Tanglewood Cottage to the north. In later years, when the leases on these rental properties had been lost or given up, Orchard Cottage would assure Carson a continued presence along Flourtown's main thoroughfare. (It is also evident that Ueland saw the Goss property from the first as the ideal site for a large playground that Carson could share with the whole Flourtown community.)[48]

During the summer in particular, the girls had assigned groups for farmwork. They helped to till and harvest crops, feed the animals (horses, pigs, chickens, sheep, and cows), and process and preserve a variety of fruits and vegetables. Accounts of this work often appeared in the student newspaper, known as the *Jabberwock* in the late 1920s and early 1930s. In the issue for December 1930, Alice Mary Steiner recounted her recent experience digging potatoes after school: "One of the farm people would run the tractor with the potato digger hitched on to it. . . . Then everybody would run and try to get the most potatoes in her basket. . . . After almost all the potatoes . . . were picked up, Miss Ueland thought it would be nice to have a picnic. . . . [There were] two . . . bon fires with a table near, with hot dogs. We toasted our hot dogs and roasted our apples and had a good time."[49]

As in this student account, much of the children's farmwork included some mild form of competition, combined with companionship, cooperation, and a festive reward at the end. Work in the vegetable gardens at each of the cottages involved many of these same elements, with a display of

Fig. 27.   Orchard Cottage (former Goss farmhouse), 1922–23. CVS.

produce and an awarding of prizes in each category.[50] Yet none of the former residents interviewed by this author had enthusiastic memories about such work. Helen Heath disliked gardening as well as canning.[51] Florence MacFarlane, who was at Carson from 1945 to 1953, had similarly negative thoughts about the gardening and canning, though neither individual despised it with any great intensity. Rather, they seemed to regard the work as would any child who looks back upon required chores.

In order to coordinate the gardens and tend to the various fruit trees and other plantings on the grounds, Carson College created a Horticultural Department in the spring of 1922 under Miss Helen Ellefson, who had come to Carson in 1918 to teach "nature study." (Nature study was a somewhat informal exploration of the out-of-doors that, like so much about progressivism and progressive education, tried to reconnect individuals with the preindustrial world.)[52] Three years later, in 1925, Miss Ellefson began teaching horticulture to the Carson girls, with an emphasis upon practical work around the campus. The creation of a horticulture program eventually led to Carson's accepting student teachers from the School of Horticulture for Women at nearby Ambler, Pennsylvania (later a part of Temple University). As early as 1922, the Ambler school was also advising Carson on its orchards, gardens, and various plantings.[53]

In addition to studying horticulture and tending gardens, the girls had some responsibility for livestock. Beginning in 1924 several of the cottages possessed their own chickens. The girls collected the eggs, which then ended up on the breakfast table or as ingredients in various recipes. The girls even helped to build the chicken houses. They also raised pigs. When one of the sows gave birth to eight piglets, groups of girls went together to buy them—on credit—for five dollars each, built pig pens, and fed them all summer with garbage from the cottages. At the end of the season they sold the pigs for an average profit of $20.00 per animal.[54]

Fig. 28.   Nature study, 1925–26. CVS.

This activity, along with other work undertaken by the girls, had typi-cally been associated with farm boys. But Ueland believed that girls, as much as boys, should learn these tasks, including how to construct vari-ous objects, and accordingly chose workmen for Carson who loved chil-dren and did not "mind answering questions and explaining things."[55] In this spirit, the girls helped the men to build a wading pool near Orchard Cottage in the summer of 1919.[56]

Elaborating on this idea during an interview, Ueland stated:

> Now, I do not want to be carried away here with the idea that women will do everything that men do. There must, or should be, a physical limit somewhere. But it has been my idea always that the average woman is unnecessarily helpless. She has no knowl-edge of tools and mechanics. Whether or not she has any actual physical need for this knowledge, she should know [about it]. It is, to my mind, part of the foundation of a broad economic under-standing of how the world progresses and how cities and indus-tries are built. The lack of such simple, fundamental information explains why many women find it difficult to understand prob-lems of finance and industry and construction.[57]

Some of the jobs that the older girls did on campus were, in fact, part of Carson's program of vocational training, a feature that again had its roots partly in Ueland's prior experiences, most recently at Gary and before that in her work with the Vocational Guidance Association in New York City. The advancing ages of those girls who had been admitted to Carson in the early years also made vocational preparation imperative by 1923. In January of that year the management committee of the board reported that there were twenty-eight girls on campus between the ages of fourteen and sixteen, seven of whom were sixteen or nearly so. Just a year later, there were a dozen girls who were sixteen or over.[58] According to Ueland, vocational preparation was the greatest of all challenges for Carson: "To fit our girls for independence at eighteen, in the world as it is," she wrote, "is our greatest problem; and if we do it well, it will be our greatest contribution to educational thinking."[59]

Though Ueland was very much concerned about vocational guidance for her girls, and wrote or spoke on the subject with regularity, it was Frances W. Jones (1878–1958), Carson's first full-time social worker, who took charge of the vocational program. Jones came to Carson in July 1922 and, it would appear, assumed the functions that had been performed on a part-time basis by Virginia Robinson, who was now devoting more and more time to the University of Pennsylvania School of Social Work.[60]

There was a particular stress upon giving Carson girls vocational experiences during the summer months, when they were free from the demands of the regular school year. During the summer of 1922, two girls worked as assistants to the swimming teacher, two helped in school offices, and four worked in the laundry. Others had employment experiences off campus: four went to Philadelphia every day to work in offices; three went into the city for jobs at a children's hospital; two went to nearby Ambler, where they worked at the horticulture school; and two went to New York as apprentices in a school of weaving. In the summer of 1926 fifteen girls had summer jobs at Carson, while ten worked off campus.[61]

Ueland was adamant, however, that girls who worked during the summers as mother's helpers were not to be overburdened or treated as household servants. She therefore insisted that this and other work done by Carson girls off campus should be carefully monitored by the school. In addition to protecting the girls from misuse, such monitoring could provide a valuable record of experience for future placements.[62]

Nor would the working girls be allowed to squander their earnings, but had to contribute a portion of them for their room and board at Carson. Allowing the girls to spend their wages as they liked, Ueland feared, would make them "just as extravagant and irresponsible as . . . 'flappers' of the present time."[63] As evidence of this concern, Ueland advocated a "pretty strict parental control [by the Carson housemothers] . . . with regard to the expenditure of money, as well as the clothing worn, and the use of powder, paint, etc., by either our high school or working girls."[64]

Those who were too young to work, or who did not have jobs during the school year, received a weekly allowance from the housemothers, ranging from 15¢ for those beneath the ninth grade and 30¢ for the high school girls. The latter had to maintain a written account of their expenditures, which were supposed to go for such things as club dues at school, Sunday school and church collections, entertainment, gifts, and regular savings. The purpose of this strict regimen was to teach the girls something about the value of money and how to stay within a budget.[65]

Once the girls turned eighteen and left Carson, the school maintained its concern about their vocational prospects and kept careful track of where they lived and worked. Anticipating such concerns, Ueland wished as early as 1922 that Carson's care could be extended to age twenty-one so that the institution could "stand back of them with protection and 'follow-up' care even though we still expect them to earn their living at eighteen." Continuing with this line of thinking, she asked of the management committee, "Would it be feasible to organize a home within the city for girls who are trying themselves out in jobs?"[66] Although her projection of what would later be known as a halfway house did not materialize in the 1920s, Ueland's concern was unfailing, and girls who had difficulty finding positions were frequently invited to come back to Carson, where they might live and work in some capacity until they could stand on their own.

In an article about the Carson program in general, school director Phoebe Allnutt set down the many positive benefits of the girls' work experiences:

> It teaches them to be resourceful, . . . and resourcefulness means a trained intelligence. . . . There is something about work that fills a real need that is both stabilizing and satisfying. . . . Most important of all, perhaps, this type of program makes possible a far greater variety and richness of experience for children than can be had otherwise. Without variety of experience, children cannot learn to make choices. . . . A child whose school life is too closely directed does not have a chance to develop this power, and so, when face to face with a decision to be made, will probably follow the line of least resistance.[67]

In the same article Allnutt explained how an interest in one of these vocational experiences salvaged a girl who had been troubled both emotionally and academically. "Susan," as she was called in the article, had been a behavioral problem in both her cottage and at school, yet she demonstrated a marked kindness toward pets, children, and sick people. Katherine Tucker, Ueland's housemate and head of Philadelphia's Visiting Nurse Society, noticed these qualities and asked Susan to assist the school nurse. Realizing that she wanted to pursue a career in nursing, Susan now concluded that school was worthwhile, if only as a practical and necessary step for acceptance into a nurses' training program.[68]

As early as 1924, Carson College also decided to pay the tuition of girls who wished to pursue vocational education beyond high school. In that particular year Carson sent three girls on for further schooling: one to

Drexel Institute (later Drexel University), one to Philadelphia's School of Industrial Arts (later merged into the University of the Arts), and another to a local "business college." In 1927 Carson girls were attending Drexel, West Chester Normal School, Temple College (later Temple University), and the Sargent School of Physical Training in Cambridge, Massachusetts.[69]

Meanwhile Carson opened a new program that offered opportunities for vocational training on campus. This was a nursery school for children—both girls and boys—under the age of six. There was a trial run in the summer of 1924, and the following October the board of trustees approved a nursery school to operate from the Carson grounds. The stated purpose of the nursery school was to give the older girls on-site training in child care. Even for girls who did not pursue child care as a profession, this would be an invaluable experience for those who became mothers themselves, especially since they were not growing up in households with younger siblings.[70] As an extension of this idea, the board gave its approval in 1921 for Carson to adopt two infants so that the girls could have direct experiences with very young children.[71] This plan did not materialize, but a housemother at one of the cottages apparently came to campus with a baby, as Ueland indicated to her mother in the fall of 1921. "Did you know we [have] a baby at Red Gables Cottage," she asked, "that the older girls are learning to take care of?"[72]

As to the curriculum of Carson's nursery school, it was as progressive as the school program for the orphans themselves. Indeed, the whole idea of the nursery school, or "play school," as it was often called, had emerged out of the progressive-education movement. It emphasized a child-centered environment where small children could use their own creative imaginations to explore the world around them and make sense of it through play. In the words of Lawrence A. Cremin, the play school was "a child-sized community in which the inhabitants, through play, might grasp the essential truths of the universe."[73] According to Cremin, the first such school was opened in 1914 by Caroline Pratt in Greenwich Village, New York. Known at first as the Play School, it was later renamed the City and Country School.[74] Although there is no evidence that Carson's nursery school was inspired directly by Pratt's work in New York, it would be safe to assume that Ueland was well aware of this first play school: Pratt had taught for a number of years in Philadelphia before going to New York, and Pratt's close friend Helen Marot had lived and worked at Carson for a time in the early 1920s.[75] Ueland's own friend Lucy Mitchell had also worked closely with Caroline Pratt in New York

Fig. 29.   Carson College Nursery School, 1930s. CVS.

and subsequently opened her own much lauded nursery program at the Bank Street School, another possible source of inspiration for Carson's nursery school.[76]

One might also conclude that the first director of the Carson College Nursery School, C. Madeleine Dixon (1889-1945), likewise knew something of Pratt's work. Dixon's training was in physical education and dance, and her earliest experiences with children were in the Philadelphia playground system, in which Ueland as well as Carson board member Otto Mallery took great interest. Dixon taught dance at Carson and, at one point in her career, at Lucy Mitchell's Bank Street School.[77] Dixon herself became widely recognized as an expert on nursery and play schools, and authored several publications on the subject that drew upon her experiences at Carson. Her book *Children Are Like That* (1930) was based almost entirely on what she had observed at Carson.[78] In this way Carson College's nursery school participated in the wider dissemination of progressive ideas and methods in the teaching of small children. This could only have pleased Elsa Ueland, who wrote in 1926 that she wanted to make Carson's nursery school "the best 'model' . . . we can."[79]

Like Caroline Pratt, Lucy Mitchell, and other progressive educators, both Ueland and Dixon believed that even the smallest children should have the opportunity to explore the world in a safe and affirming environment and thereby to gain self-confidence and self-esteem by learning new skills and insights at their own pace. Thus, according to the report on the Carson nursery program drawn up by Dixon in September 1926, children would experience the "joy in finding out things" on their own. Though the children were well superintended, Dixon added, the staff was careful "not to superimpose learning." In Carson's country setting, Dixon was also happy to state, children could experience "the constant changes of out door things where, . . . [they] can know a little of the fundamental hardships through being in a world where speed and the use of machinery are not inevitable." Indeed, her report pointed out the various elements of a more traditional world that children might experience at the Carson College Nursery School: "In the country the barn yard with its bull, its horses, its sheep, its pigs, is near at hand. [There is] the creek with its source of pollywogs, crayfish, [and] frogs. . . . Gardens are possible. Tent life is experienced. Out door fire places are built. Small groves of half grown trees make mysterious forests. . . . The place is full of invitation and challenge rather than prohibition."[80]

The report went on to list some further activities of the nursery school. Under "individual chores," the children hung up their clothes, gathered and changed flowers on the tables, fetched wood for the stove, and helped to serve lunch. "Group pursuits" included feeding the chickens, cleaning the aquarium, and tending gardens. "Nature study" led them to explore the Wissahickon Creek, to care for pets, to hunt for dye stuffs on the Carson property, and to collect clay from stream banks. Like the girls in the primary division at Carson, the nursery school children tried their hands at construction. In 1927–28 they built a new playhouse. With considerable help from the teachers and workmen, one would suppose, the children mixed cement, laid up a stone fireplace (complete with spikes for hanging pots and pans), and pounded shingles onto the roof. They also sang songs, played percussion instruments, put on little plays, and shared their projects with the older children during assembly time.[81]

The nursery school operated at first from a renovated chicken house that stood just across the road from Mother Goose Cottage, and in 1926 it expanded into a small wooden building, one of two built on the same site as "temporary" structures, to serve until Carson might erect a more substantial and permanent school building on the premises.[82] This small and intimate space, well lighted by many windows and heated by a pot-bellied stove, provided just the right atmosphere for small children, according to Ueland—what she called an "informal 'child world' atmosphere of the little 'chicken house class rooms.' "[83]

Besides helping preschool children to discover themselves, yet another explicit purpose of opening the nursery school was to provide links between Carson College and the local community. By the spring of 1925, at the end of its first year of operation, the nursery school was drawing children (ages two and a half to six and a half) from Flourtown, Chestnut Hill, Germantown, and the Oak Lane section of Philadelphia.[84] The following year its enrollment reached approximately one hundred youngsters, and by 1929 the nursery school accepted children as young as eighteen months.[85] Parents paid only enough to cover the expenses of the program ($150 a year in 1928), for the main purpose of the nursery school was not to raise revenue for the institution.[86] Yet the nursery school would more than pay its way by putting Carson girls in touch with local parents and by providing them with an avenue to child-care positions in area homes. It would also be a way of Carson's maintaining a positive profile in the local community. (In a later period nursery school parents would become an important resource for fund-raising and other aspects of public relations.)

This use of the nursery school as a means of connecting Carson with the outside was probably one way that Ueland figured she could help to compensate for the local school board's refusal to run a cooperative elementary school. But she was far from content with just the nursery school connection to the community, and was constantly looking for other mechanisms to forge links with Carson's neighbors. These connections would not only help the girls to have as normal a life as possible—despite living in an orphanage—but they would give them a more realistic view of what they themselves could expect as adults, since Ueland believed that the vast majority of her young charges would grow up to have lives not unlike the average family in Flourtown. Such was the topic at a teachers' meeting held in June 1924. As recorded in the minutes:

> Miss Ueland gave some suggestions as to what sort of life our girls will have after they leave [Carson] College. From census reports, etc. we may infer ... that every one of them will for a period of time have to earn her own living; that nine out of ten will marry; not more than one in every 15 will have a servant; 75 out of 100 will at some time live in a small house with a piece of ground big enough for a garden. In fact, their interests and resources will not be very different from those of a typical Flourtown family. It was interesting to speculate on the possibility of our spoiling the children for this somewhat limited environment by letting them form pictures of themselves that can never be realized. *How can we do more with Flourtown,* in teaching the children to know the world as it is and to take their own part in it?[87] (Emphasis is in the original.)

In contrast to most orphanages, where the children were set apart from the surrounding community (in the case of Girard College, by a high stone wall), Carson was truly enlightened in trying to forge as many connections as possible with Flourtown.

Another of these connections, as it turned out, was through the local high school. In the spring of 1921 the Carson board decided that it would send its older girls to Ambler High School, located in the town of Ambler, some five miles further out Bethlehem Pike from Carson.[88] At the time, there was no high school in Springfield Township, and Ambler was the most convenient place to enroll the girls. Both Ueland and the Carson board were thus delighted to learn in 1923 of plans to build a Springfield

Township High School. It would not only mean less of a commute for the girls, but the new school might provide another chance for close cooperation between Carson and the local school district. Thus, in April 1923 the Carson board offered to donate a parcel of land to the school district for its new facility. The tract that they had in mind ran back from Bethlehem Pike, between Darwin Hall and Orchard Cottage, and continued on behind the Flourtown Elementary School, whose grounds directly adjoined the Carson College property. The Carson board also offered to erect a "shop building" behind the high school, which the district could share free of charge.[89]

In a letter to the Springfield authorities, Ueland conveyed her hopes for a fruitful collaboration, which again echoed the Gary Plan: "Carson College is obviously interested in the new high school because of the great part it will play (perhaps for the next fifty years) in the education and training of our girls. [Carson] is also interested indirectly in a school which will do so much to stimulate the life of the whole township."[90]

Once again the Springfield board declined the offer of cooperation from Carson. In its official response the school board asserted that it could not afford to wait until the trustees of the Carson estate approved such a plan and that they had already made a tentative agreement to buy the former Chestnut Hill Park property, located at the intersection of Bethlehem Pike and Montgomery Avenue and once the site of an amusement park (also known as White City).[91] Although the offer was rebuffed, the Carson girls who attended Springfield High after its opening in 1924 had an opportunity to participate in sports and other extracurricular activities, and to make friends among their schoolmates from the neighborhood. It is interesting, too, that Ueland took the principal-to-be of the new Springfield High School on a personal tour of the Gary schools in early 1923, following a meeting in Chicago of the National Education Association.[92] Like all her other attempts to interest the local schools in a cooperative system of progressive education, this was of no avail.

Yet another connection between the Carson girls and the community was attendance at local churches and Sunday schools. Ueland continued to list herself as a Unitarian, though she seldom attended religious services and doubtless continued to hold many of the freethinking views of her parents.[93] Nevertheless, she bowed to the wishes of both the Carson board and the Carson will that the girls receive religious instruction. Besides the prayers at weekday assemblies, there was a vesper service, at least in the early years, every Sunday evening at Stork Hill Cottage, where they said evening prayers and sang hymns.[94] Just who conducted these Sunday evening services is unknown. On Sunday mornings the girls were taken to whichever church their families had belonged to—or to a church that they themselves elected to attend. In reality this meant a choice among the First Presbyterian Church in Springfield (more commonly known as the Flourtown Presbyterian Church), Zion Lutheran Church, St. Thomas Episcopal Church (both a mile or two out Bethlehem Pike), and Our Mother of Consolation Roman Catholic Church in Chestnut Hill.[95] The girls were encouraged to make friends among these congregations, and in fact many of them became active in the various youth groups at church. Some of the Sunday school teachers took a special interest in the Carson girls and did whatever they could to help them along the way.[96]

While church, Sunday school, and high school took Carson girls into the community, Ueland tried hard to provide additional ways, beyond the nursery school and summer school, to bring the community into Carson. One of these, again reminiscent of the Gary Plan, was the community library that Carson operated along Bethlehem Pike in Darwin Hall. Since Flourtown had no library at the time, the facility was well received by the community after it opened in February 1919; it provided an informal meeting place for the Carson girls and the neighbors. (After Carson lost its lease, for unknown reasons, on Darwin Hall in 1926, the library moved across Bethlehem Pike to Marigold Cottage.)[97]

In 1920 Carson also provided space free of charge in Darwin Hall for the Visiting Nurse Association of Springfield and Whitemarsh Townships, an organization initiated with the help of Katherine Tucker, who still headed Philadelphia's visiting nurse organization. The director of the Springfield/Whitemarsh unit was Mary K. Willets, a woman who had worked at the Henry Street Settlement House in New York and was recruited for the position in Flourtown by Tucker herself. In addition to heading the local Visiting Nurse Association, Willets served as the nurse for Carson College. As part of this operation, Carson cooperated with the association to install a dentist's office in Darwin Hall. Providing further support, Carson opened its facilities for fund-raising events put on by the local Visiting Nurse Association, including dances, dinners, and "card parties."[98]

Even more significant was the community playground that Carson erected along Bethlehem Pike on the large vacant lot between Darwin Hall

Fig. 30.   Carson's community playground, 1922–23. CVS.

and Orchard Cottage.[99] It contained swings, seesaws, sliding boards, volleyball nets, basketball hoops, chin-up bars, climbing equipment, a baseball diamond, and a running track. In 1924 Carson even contemplated building a swimming pool on the playground, which would likewise be open to the entire Flourtown community. Though the pool project never materialized, a wading pool constructed in 1919 remained at the playground. In 1920 the board voted money to build an outdoor dance floor on the playground for both Carson girls and village youngsters. This dancing facility, with music provided by a Victrola, enabled Carson College to give in to the popular craze for dancing, but within a safe and well-supervised environment: "We would rather have our young people dance near home," Ueland reported to the management committee, "than seek all the high lights of recreation away [from campus]."[100] As an added attraction, Carson provided the playground with a refreshment stand, complete with card tables and folding "camp chairs." For years the playground was also the site of a Fourth of July celebration put on jointly by Carson and the village.[101] That the community playground and its attendant activities proved an immediate success seemed apparent from what Ueland wrote to her parents in August 1918: "We have a lot of big boys using the baseball field in the evening. . . . We also have a community sing on Wednesday evening under the orchard promoted by one of the local ministers and growing to be a great success."[102]

Still other programs held on the playground connected Carson girls with Flourtown. In the summer of 1929, for example, the older girls operated a "tea room and food shop" from Orchard Cottage. The project provided practical instruction in cooking, waiting on tables, and selling various items to the general public.[103]

During the winter months Carson offered "gymnasium instruction" in the Mother Goose playroom/gym to the older Flourtown boys. Village boys and girls in their teens regularly received invitations to dances and other parties at the school, which they apparently attended in substantial numbers. And Carson used every opportunity to lend its facilities to local organizations for meetings or activities, as it did to Flourtown's newly formed American Legion post in December 1919 (who were grateful but declined). Rehearsals for *HMS Pinafore* in the spring of 1926, billed as a "community operetta" put on by Carson students, staff, and village residents to benefit the Visiting Nurse Association, took place at Carson. As might be expected, there were no objections from Ueland or the board to allowing the local Whitemarsh Hunt Club to run over a portion of the Carson property during the 1920s.[104]

Ueland also opened Carson's facilities to the League of Women Voters of Springfield Township. Indeed, the group held its organizational meeting at Carson on May 25, 1925. Ueland was one of its organizers and thus a charter member, and would remain active in the group for the rest of her life. Her role in organizing the local chapter arose naturally from her earlier suffrage activities, in that the League of Women Voters was the direct successor of the national American Women's Suffrage Association, having been created at the last convention of the suffrage association in early 1920.[105]

In addition to all of this, Ueland organized a community swimming hole along the Wissahickon Creek just across West Mill Road from the campus. Swimming had been taking place for many years at this bend in the creek, where the water formed a wide pool of moderate depth. Because of drowning, other accidents, and some rowdyism at the site, Ueland decided soon after Carson opened to provide lifeguards and supervision at the creek during the summer months. Carson also cleared the pool of limbs and other debris each spring and built bathhouses for changing into and out of swimsuits. The creek became a major source of recreation for the Carson girls every summer and yet another point of contact between Carson and the village. Both the Carson girls and the village children learned to swim at the creek from Mrs. Bessie E. Lightcap, who would be a familiar face on campus for some four decades.[106]

Despite worries that Carson girls might form unreal images of what awaited them in later life, they enjoyed still other recreational and cultural opportunities that went well beyond the expectations of most children of the day. Each summer, beginning in 1925, they spent a week on the New Jersey shore at Ocean City, where Carson College rented a large house for the season.[107] They also went to a camp that Carson rented in 1924. Called Camp Hopewell, it was about twenty-five miles from the school, near Sumneytown, Pennsylvania.[108] Ueland clearly loved the camp, which reminded her in some ways, as she wrote to her father, of summers

Fig. 31.   The swimming hole, Wissahickon Creek, c. 1920. CVS.

Fig. 32.   Camp Hopewell, 1920s. CVS.

back home on Lake Calhoun:"Next Friday . . . I go up to the woods, 25 miles from here, to take charge of our camp—18 children [and] myself. This is fun for me. It is simple primitive life in some old army tents,— very good swimming—, and no grown-ups,—no organizing, administering, telephoning, typewriting, conferring. Just living." [109]

The girls, too, had pleasant memories of Camp Hopewell. Besides the swimming, hiking, and break from routine school and cottage life, several former Carson girls recalled with humor the names they used for the three tents erected on a sloping piece of ground. They dubbed the lowest of these Hell, the middle tent Earth, and the upper one Heaven. [110]

They also went into Philadelphia on occasion to the theater, the orchestra, and even the opera. And for several years Carson took its eighth-graders on a spring trip to Washington, D.C. On these occasions, as well as on a daily basis, the girls were very well dressed according to the conventions of the day, a fact that sometimes created envy among the village children who participated in events on the campus. How Carson could avoid raising the false expectations for later life to which such experiences might give rise apparently never received an answer from Ueland or her staff.[111]

During these early years at Carson, Ueland often reflected on her many challenges in presiding over an orphanage for girls. She shared these reflections in interviews for newspapers and magazines, in articles that she herself wrote for the periodical press, and in talks before professional meetings and before the Carson staff itself. A theme that runs through all these is a concern for what might be called the immaterial needs of each child. She was not arguing that physical beauty and ample shelter were unimportant in providing for the emotional development of children. Rather, she believed that too many child-care institutions emphasized their physical plants and other material requirements at the expense of less visible but very crucial elements for a healthy development. In a paper that she delivered in 1924 before a meeting of the Children's Division of the National Conference on Social Work, she declared, "We are more and more evaluating our work [today] in terms of non-material ... standards. We are thinking less of our front lawns and bronze gateways,—thinking even less of our infirmary equipment,—and more of the subtler, non-material, emotional needs of children."[112]

In an article entitled "Celery Child or Strawberry Child," published by the *Survey* magazine, Ueland elaborated on what she considered to be the five most important emotional needs of all children, including those in an institution like Carson.[113] The first was "a need for 'mother,' or for some person who feels like mother." Carson College attempted to meet this need through its cottage housemothers. Second, the child required "a place that feels like home." At Carson children had the freedom to decorate their own bedrooms, to rearrange the furniture "until they finally feel that the room and everything in it fits them better." A third necessity, "economic experience," was closely related to this sense of belonging in a homelike atmosphere. Helping to make choices about the cottage budget reinforced a child's sense of attachment to a household at the same time that it helped her to learn about limited means and economic choices.

The fourth need, that for "freedom," and the fifth, that for "adventure," were likewise connected. In speaking of freedom, Ueland actually meant an autonomy and independence, combined with a sense of civic responsibility, that should belong to every family unit. Carson provided for this by allowing each cottage "family" a measure of flexibility in planning its activities at home as well as with the Flourtown community. The child's need for adventure, on the other hand, had much to do with individual freedom and self-initiative. There was thus a conscious effort not to be too protective, to allow the Carson children to explore the world on their own. In her concluding remarks about such adventures, Ueland summed up the entire article by comparing child rearing with the cultivation of two very different kinds of plants. The choice was between what she called the "celery child" and the "strawberry child": "The celery type of young girl may be very attractive (made tender and delicate by being shut away from contact with the elements), she cannot fight her way alone in a stormy world at the age of eighteen. The strawberry grower hardens his plants by exposing them to the cold before the final transplanting from the hot bed to the garden. It takes more courage to expose growing children to the blasts of outside experience than to expose strawberry plants. But such a course may be the best assurance for a strong and hardy future."[114]

In emphasizing the emotional and developmental needs of her Carson girls, Ueland again showed herself to be in the forefront of the progressive-education movement, which in the early 1920s was just beginning to stress what was called "mental hygiene."[115] One might conjecture that Ueland was influenced in this regard by the psychological orientation toward child care and social work being emphasized by her close friends and Flourtown neighbors Jessie Taft and Virginia Robinson.

Other articles published by Ueland during this period included "Every Child—Where and How He Plays" (1925) and "The Rights of the Child" (1925).[116] She also participated in a number of professional meetings, where she was in great demand as a speaker. She spoke before the Milwaukee Conference on Social Work in 1924 and before the National Conference of Social Work in 1924 and 1926. In addition, Ueland and other members of the staff put together a photographic exhibit about Carson for the Progressive Education Conference in 1926. (At that same time Ueland began serving on the executive committee of the Progressive Education Association, a position that she held until 1928.) In the spring of 1925 Ueland gave a talk before the Alumnae Conference at Vassar College.[117]

Other meetings and conferences took place at Carson—at Ueland's invitation. For example, in December 1924, Stanwood Cobb, the president of the Progressive Education Association, gave a talk at Carson, and the Institute of the Pennsylvania Department of Public Welfare came for three days in July 1925. Welcome too were visits from college and university students. Education classes from Swarthmore College came to tour and observe in March 1925, and that May students from the University of Pennsylvania School of Social Work did likewise.[118]

Students, educators, and the general public could learn about Carson from a number of positive stories that appeared in newspapers and magazines during the decade after its opening. These included the *Public Ledger* magazine section (February 9, 1919), the *Architectural Record* (July 1921), the *Green Book* (March 1921), the *Philadelphia Inquirer* magazine section (February 14, 1926), the *Christian Science Monitor* (December 21, 1928), and the *Survey* (April 1, 1924). The latter carried an article entitled "The New Pied Pipers," in which author Neva R. Deardorff compared Carson with several other well-known orphanages of the day, including Philadelphia's Girard College and the Hershey Industrial School. In her opinion Carson was by far the most impressive, "one of the pace makers in the field of institutional care of children."[119] Yet Deardorff observed, in a mild criticism, that a Carson cottage was not comparable to a real family home. While it was a great improvement over the traditional practice of housing children in dormitories and feeding them in common dining halls, "the number of children in a [Carson] cottage [was] three or four times as many as any mother, real or foster, [could] actually look after."[120]

Finally, Carson received high praise from Pennsylvania's secretary of welfare, Ellen C. Potter, who headed the department that inspected institutions like Carson. In a letter dated January 10, 1926, the secretary had nothing but congratulations to shower upon Carson College: "We visit this institution, as we have written [to] you before, not to 'inspect' it in the sense that we must supervise a very large number of institutions throughout the State, but rather to learn what new and interesting things have been done since the time of our last visit, as well as to get concrete examples that we may take to other institutions. Needless to say, we have always succeeded in our quest, through the generous cooperation of Miss Ueland and her devoted assistants."[121]

By the middle 1920s Carson College had thus become a model orphanage and a model progressive school, despite its unpropitious beginnings and the many expectations that it would never succeed. Thus it is not surprising that Ueland became more and more respected as an educator and an expert on institutional child care, and was rewarded with inclusion in the 1928 edition of *Who's Who in America*. Nor is it any wonder that she received a number of other job offers during the 1920s, including positions as principal or superintendent of schools in several widely scattered communities around the United States.[122] In each instance she felt torn between her affection for and sense of duty toward Carson and the feeling that she was confining herself unduly to one place and set of circumstances. As she confided to her father in the summer of 1929, "I have come back [after a vacation in the West], increasingly unsure whether or not *to stay here*. I love the place, and yet often feel *bound down* by it"[123] (emphasis is in the original).

Neither Elsa Ueland nor anyone else in the United States could know that the greatest economic disaster in the nation's history lay just ahead. That event and Ueland's own entrance into middle age would foreclose any realistic possibility of her leaving Carson College.

CHAPTER FIVE

TRYING
TIMES

During the late 1920s Carson College continued to flourish. The progressive programs put in place earlier in the decade were maintained and extended, while income also increased year by year. With such progress in mind, the board authorized a second round of building construction. Only part of these plans was realized when the economic depression of the 1930s hit Carson especially hard. In addition to the more general deprivations experienced by many individuals and institutions across the nation, Carson suffered from particularly bad investments made by the trustees of the Robert Carson estate. At the same time, a decline in the numbers of children eligible for admission under the Carson will posed yet another serious threat to the existence of the Carson College for Orphan Girls.

By the late 1930s Carson's continuing crises began to wear away at Elsa Ueland herself. Now in middle age, she feared that her own professional fortunes were declining as rapidly as the institution that she headed, and she suffered from a serious episode of depression. Yet she managed to rally, and with the help of several board members obtained changes in admissions policy just as the American economy and Carson's own finances began to improve with the outbreak of World War II. Although Carson did not return to the golden years of the 1920s, it achieved a stability that would allow it to survive into the postwar period. Unfortunately, Carson College was forced to close its own elementary school during the late 1930s and thus lost a major component of its progressive program. However, the progressive spirit survived in various aspects of cottage life as well as in the many recreational and extracurricular activities offered at the college.

One measure of Carson's success during its first decade had been a dramatic increase in enrollment, from 37 in the fall of 1918 to 112 in 1928.[1] Just as impressive was the rise in income paid to the college from the Carson estate—from just under $80,000 in 1918–19 to $175,000 in 1928.[2] During the preceding half dozen years or so the board, as well as the estate trustees, had taken certain measures that they hoped would provide for greater financial security in the future. In 1922, for example, the board voted to create a depreciation fund, setting aside $40,000 to $50,000 annually for future replacements and repairs. It also authorized a fund for "accumulated income," a portion of income that was not spent each year and accumulated for future contingencies.[3] Four years later, in 1926, the estate trustees, in concert with the board, decided to sell its large block of securities in the Interstate Railways Company, with a face value of about $2.3 million. This was a company established by Robert Carson, and the stock had come to Carson College as part of the Carson bequest. But because of a decline in the profits of the street railways and interurban lines owned by this company, doubtless due to the proliferation of automobiles and motor buses during the 1920s, the trustees and board thought it best to sell these securities. The divestiture process took about four years, and the securities were sold, on average, at about 50 percent of face value.[4] The proceeds were invested for the most part in real estate mortgages, which at the time seemed to promise higher income.[5]

With enrollments and income apparently on a sure footing, the board decided that it was time to recommence Carson's building program. The most immediate needs were two new permanent cottages on the college grounds (as opposed to the rentals in Flourtown), maintenance and storage facilities, a new and larger barn for the farm, a new residence for Elsa Ueland (that was owned, rather than rented, by Carson), and, most especially, a permanent school building on the Carson grounds. The decision to construct a residence for Ueland stemmed from the fact that the lease on the Maples, where she had been living since 1917, was due to expire in 1927 and the owner did not wish to renew it. The desire for a genuine school building at Carson was intensified by a loss of the lease, in 1926, on Darwin Hall, which contained the community library, the health office, and several classrooms. Inadequate maintenance and storage space called for more suitable facilities. And a new barn was needed to alleviate the cramped conditions hampering the farm operation, which still had to rely on a small barn and several outbuildings on the old Goss Farm, which stood just north of Orchard Cottage.[6]

Ueland and the board began to consider these projects seriously in the spring of 1925 and opened tentative discussions with architect Albert Kelsey, who had designed the original campus structures a decade before.[7] While these explorations were going forward, the Carson board discovered potential legal problems with funding the projects. Although some $380,000 remained from the $1 million that had been provided in the Carson will for the erection of the physical plant, the board preferred to have this sum stay as part of the estate's corpus (or principal) so as to continue deriving income from it. Instead, it wished to pay for the new building projects out of the accumulated-income fund, which in April 1929 amounted to nearly $730,000.[8] Unfortunately, the laws of Pennsylvania governing charitable trusts at that time forbade institutions to use accumulated income for capital projects such as erecting new buildings. Carson's first step was to have legislation drawn up and proposed to the state legislature that would amend the law. In pursuing this effort, the college engaged the legal firm of Hepburn and Norris to formulate the necessary documents and to serve as liaison with the legislature in Harrisburg.[9] After the requisite amendments passed in the spring of 1929, Carson College's attorneys still had to approach the Montgomery County Orphans Court in order to obtain permission to go beyond the Carson will, which had directed that all building funds be taken from the principal of the estate (rather than from accumulated income). The argument presented before the court asserted that Carson College had inadvertently (but improperly) spent about $146,000 of the original building fund for such items as furnishings and landscaping. Carson College now wanted the courts to allow them to transfer $146,000 from accumulated income to principal, and then to use it for financing the new buildings. In May of 1930 the court allowed the transfer to be made.[10]

Although Carson was now free to go forward with its plans, five years had been lost in the legal and legislative process. This lapse of time gave Ueland and the board much opportunity to think about just what kinds of buildings they wanted. In the process, they decided to dismiss Albert Kelsey as their architect and to turn elsewhere for a designer who was more sympathetic to their needs.

For example, in thinking about the new cottages they might erect, Ueland had as a conceptual model the sorts of residences that Carson was renting in the village of Flourtown itself, rather than the elaborate buildings that Kelsey had originally designed on campus. Thus she wrote in her annual report for 1925:

> The rented cottages have brought plenty of difficulties. But they have shown certain advantages which need not necessarily be lost with the expiration of our present leases. They have . . . shown the advantages of houses built for *ordinary family use.* . . . There may be an aesthetic or institutional advantage in having the kitchen far away from the other main living quarters of the house [as at Mother Goose and Red Gables]. But where the kitchen is the house-mother's headquarters for a large part of the day, the ordinary compact type of house construction serves very importantly to unify the family group. And the ordinary attics, the ordinary bath rooms, the ordinary back yards, of the houses built for ordinary family life [in Flourtown] have really served our family needs better than [Mother Goose and Red Gables].[11] (Emphasis is in the original.)

Ueland's thinking about what constituted an appropriate family home for persons of modest means had probably been influenced by a great deal of writing over the past three decades, by progressive-minded women in particular, about domestic architecture and household appointments. In a revolt against the complex and often time-consuming designs of Victorian dwellings, women reformers had advocated housing that was compact, efficient, and easy to clean, housing that was designed along simple lines, that lacked the ostentation of so many Victorian structures. Such progressive housing offered women and their families more hours of recreation, it was asserted, more time to spend on creative activities with their children. Kelsey's expensive and elaborate designs clearly contradicted the latest advice of housing reformers.[12]

Thus, if Carson were going to build new cottages, Ueland reasoned that they should be as much like common family homes in the vicinity as was possible, the types of homes that would be easy to maintain for future housewives of modest means. Specifically, what she had in mind was the two-family dwelling that had evolved in eastern Pennsylvania, "each half of which is designed to serve admirably a family group." Carson could modify this design slightly so as to accommodate "the usual College family group of eight to sixteen persons." And if for some reason Carson College were not needed in the future as a residential orphanage, these homes could easily be sold or rented to local families.[13] Above all, Carson College should realize that it was more important to mold young lives correctly than to erect magnificent structures. In Ueland's words, "The task of the College will always be *to build:* primarily to build lives, secondarily to build physical surroundings.... We wish to build for a *fine home life,* where there is simplicity and affection and cheerful activity"[14] (emphasis is in the original).

Under the circumstances, serious sparring between Ueland and Albert Kelsey commenced in June of 1925 when she submitted her own written specifications for two new cottages, along with fairly detailed floor plans drawn by herself.[15] Although Ueland wanted the new cottages to be attractive, she intended them to look like real residences rather than small-scale university buildings. She also wanted the design to arise from actual use rather than from some fanciful notion of a children's medieval village. Thus she began her recommendations by stating, "A *compact* house is advantageous from the point of view of management. When the housemother stands in her kitchen, or sits in her living room, or rests in her bedroom, she should be able to hear where her children are and know from what she hears, what they are doing"[16] (emphasis is in the original).

Continuing in the same vein, Ueland advised that the housemother's bedroom be placed near the top of the stairs to the second floor in such a way that she could easily tell what was transpiring on both floors.[17] As to the living room, it should be spacious enough for the whole cottage family to "gather around the fire for stories, the children sitting on the floor."[18] Across the hall from the large living room, Ueland wanted a smaller reception area where a girl might visit with relatives or receive a caller. This room should have a fireplace, a desk for letter writing, reading lights, and bookshelves. The entire house ought to be well lighted by windows, which would allow for generous breezes in the summertime.[19] Ueland likewise had plenty of advice regarding the grounds around each of the new cottages: These should allow for tennis courts, swings, play houses, a dog kennel, wading pool, tool shed, vegetable garden, a few fruit trees, and a grape arbor.[20]

Ueland's experience and self-confidence came through in every line of her remarks. Albert Kelsey was just as firm in his own views, however, and in the preliminary drawings that he submitted in October 1925, it was clear that he had not abandoned the idea of adding to his little Gothic kingdom. His idea was to design a pair of cottages, which were joined so as to present a massive facade of stone, half-timbered gables, and fanciful chimneys that were very similar to what he had designed for Carson in its first set of buildings. In the accompanying letter he made an observation that could only have confirmed Ueland's belief that the architect was unsympathetic to her own ideas: Surmising that Carson might not be ready to start building for some time, Kelsey nevertheless wanted authorization to begin on the project, writing, "[T]his kind of work has to be dreamed over, studied, and re-studied in a leisurely manner and when I am in the mood for it."[21]

Kelsey's preliminary front elevation and floor plans arrived at Carson on October 15. The very next day, Theron I. Crane, who was chairman of the board's building committee, sent a brief note to Kelsey expressing his dislike for the steeply pitched roofs, believing that they would not allow enough space in the third story, where Ueland had projected several small bedrooms.[22] On the seventeenth Kelsey responded to Crane, arguing that the roof was "no steeper or higher" than those of the earlier buildings, and that changing them "would throw everything out of scale." Ueland then wrote to Kelsey on the nineteenth to explain that the board meeting scheduled for the sixteenth of October had been postponed for lack of a quorum, adding that she herself had "a score of questions and suggestions and inquiries" about the cottage proposal.

When the board did finally meet, on October 23, the group concluded that attendance, although sufficient to make a quorum, was not substantial enough for them to render a firm decision about Kelsey's design. In her letter explaining the situation to Kelsey, Ueland added that those present had objected to the massive design, and asked, "Would it not be less imposing and institutional; and more homelike and intimate to have separate smaller units [as opposed to twin houses]"?[23] The board members further agreed that the steep roof lines would militate against space for bedrooms on the third floors. Various staff members, to whom Ueland had shown the drawings, wanted to know if the new cottages could have at least one sleeping porch each.[24] It was also evident at this point that the board had no intention of allowing Kelsey to go ahead with the administration building, with its soaring Gothic tower and romantic allegories, that he had projected a decade before as part of his original campus plan.[25]

By May of 1926 Ueland was clearly exasperated with Kelsey, who was agonizingly slow in providing any detailed answers regarding how he would meet the specifications set down by Ueland and agreed upon by the board. On May 18 she wrote him the strongest letter to date. She again stated her objections to building the two cottages together, despite her earlier preference for a double house, and warned him that she would rather put up with all the inconveniences of the rented cottages than have a "permanent lack of comfort fastened upon us." Later, in a diary entry, Ueland would describe Kelsey's work at Carson as a "monument to [his] vanity."[26]

In fact, Ueland's displeasure with Kelsey had begun soon after her arrival in Philadelphia. As early as July 1916, before she had officially taken up her duties at Carson, Ueland wrote to her mother of "an impending conflict" with Kelsey.[27] In October she wrote home that she much preferred "a village of bungalows" on the campus to Kelsey's grandiose scheme, but that board member James Carson was insistent on a "monument" to his uncle, Robert Carson. Unfortunately, none of the other board members was willing to oppose James Carson at the time, an attitude that struck Ueland as irresponsible, especially in light of the fact that construction costs were escalating because of the war in Europe.[28] Fortunately for Ueland, James Carson was, in 1926, no longer in the picture, and she now had the sympathies of the board when it came to Kelsey's continuing extravagances.[29]

Although Ueland and the board were unhappy over Kelsey's plans for the cottages, it was his design of a new residence for Ueland herself that actually brought matters to a head. Told that he must keep the price below $18,000, he continued to submit plans that would cost far more.[30] Thus, in February 1927, Carson board member Leo Nelson Sharpe, who was also a lawyer, proposed to investigate whether the institution was under any obligation to continue with Kelsey's services, even though he had won the original competition.[31] After some legal consultation, Sharpe informed the board that they were free to dispense with Kelsey and to choose whatever architect they wished to design the new president's house and the other projected buildings on campus.[32]

As architect for Ueland's new residence, the board selected S. Arthur Love, who submitted a design that fell within the $18,000 budget. At the time, Love was in the process of developing an "English Village" in the Wynnewood section of the Philadelphia Main Line, in partnership with his brother Donald, who was a builder. Arthur Love had become enamored with English vernacular-style dwellings during World War I and, after returning home, specialized in English cottage motifs.[33]

Ueland named her new residence South Fields, which, like the Maples, she shared with her friend Katherine Tucker. The name of the new house came from its location on a plot of land just south of the Wissahickon Avenue entrance to Carson College, which the institution had purchased back in 1917 in order to protect its view.[34] And in fact the house provided Ueland and Tucker with a fine prospect over rolling fields that were part of a farm operated by the Sisters of St. Joseph, who resided just across the city line at Chestnut Hill College, which they had founded in 1924.[35] Further in the distance, the residents of South Fields could see the gigantic Trianon-style mansion, Whitemarsh Hall, designed by Horace Trumbauer for the multimillionaire Edward T. Stotesbury.[36]

Completed in 1928, South Fields was a stucco house in what one might loosely call the English Cotswold style (then much in vogue in prosperous suburban communities like the Loves' development in Wynnewood— or in neighboring Chestnut Hill, where Dr. George Woodward had just fashioned an entire Cotswold Village).[37] True to the Cotswold style, South Fields had steeply pitched roofs, half-timbered dormer windows, and banks of small-paned casement windows in all the main rooms. The interior was very plain, with trim provided only by unmilled lumber. In this regard, at least, the house comported with progressive ideas about simple, unadorned housing design.

For its two new cottages Carson selected William Pope Barney (1890–1970) as architect. Why Love was not retained is unknown, though there seems to have been a low-key competition of some sort during the spring or summer of 1930, with several architects (whose names have not survived) being invited to submit proposals.[38]

Whoever the others might have been, Barney himself was an accomplished Philadelphia architect by the early 1930s. After receiving bachelor's and master's degrees in architecture from the University of

Pennsylvania in 1912 and 1913, respectively, he entered the office of Paul Cret, with whom, ironically, Kelsey had also worked in his early days. Barney was later associated with several other well-known architectural firms in Philadelphia, including Zantzinger, Borie, and Medary, who were known for a number of important residential commissions in Chestnut Hill, many of them executed in American colonial or English vernacular styles. A scholarship in 1922-23 allowed Barney to travel in England, France, and Italy. He established his own firm in 1912, in partnership with Roy Banwell (1893-1973).[39]

In September 1930 the Carson board approved a contract with Barney for two separate cottages, at a cost of $50,000 each.[40] In November of the same year, the board amended the agreement to include an infirmary wing on one of the cottages for an additional $10,000. The contractor selected to do the work was John P. Hallahan.[41] Completed by the fall of 1931, the two cottages were called Upper Beech and Lower Beech, in reference to the prominent beech trees on both sites. The infirmary, attached to Lower Beech, was dubbed Beech Branch and apparently provided an office for the local Visiting Nurse Association as well as sick beds for Carson children. Both cottages blended well with Kelsey's earlier structures in that they were built of Chestnut Hill stone and contained certain features associated with late medieval English architecture, including multiple chimney flues, peaked gable ends, and casement windows. But the massing was much simpler than in Kelsey's designs, and the cottages exuded much more of a residential look than the earlier structures on campus. Indeed, in their open and free adaptations of English vernacular designs, Barney's two cottages are reminiscent of the work done in Britain over the preceding three decades by C.F.A. Voysey, though there is no direct evidence that Barney owed a debt to the English architect.[42]

Throughout the project, Ueland worked well with Barney, who was more than happy to accommodate her ideas and requirements. That Ueland was pleased with the architect is evident from the article that she wrote for the school newspaper, the *Jabberwock,* in December 1930, just as the construction was beginning: "Two old favorite places have been chosen; one cottage will be back from the road near the upper beech tree; and the other near the [Widener] race track; by the lower beech tree and the orchard. Favorite places, because here are the breezes in summer, the south sun all the year, and long vistas over the valley. . . . There will be great 'flights of windows,'—metal casement windows along nearly the whole south side of every room, letting in floods of sunlight."[43]

Fig. 33.   Upper Beech Cottage, designed by William Pope Barney and completed in 1931. Photo by Graydon Wood, April 8, 1986. CVS.

In fact, there were so many banks of casement windows on both the first and second floors of these cottages that some of the facades looked like curtain walls of glass, especially from the distance. Lots of fresh air and sunlight were central to Ueland's concept of cheerfulness and good health, ideas that doubtless stemmed from her childhood on Lake Calhoun back in Minnesota. (Sealing these windows against the cold in later decades when fuel was much more expensive would provide an ongoing challenge, as would the installation of air conditioners—necessary, in part, because of all the summer sunlight pouring into the cottages—in the odd-sized window openings.) The grounds of both cottages also met Ueland's other expectations, with tennis courts, wading pools, swing sets, garden plots, tool sheds, and the like at both Upper Beech and Lower Beech.

In addition to the two cottages, Carson commissioned Barney to design a maintenance shop and storehouse building (later commonly known as the storeroom), which extended, on a ninety-degree angle, as a wing from the garages adjacent to Thistle Cottage. Built in 1932 of Chestnut Hill stone, this two-and-one-half-story structure likewise contained ranks of casement windows, especially on the south and west sides. Although much plainer than either Upper or Lower Beech, the stone facade and small-paned casement windows have a Voyseyesque quality to them as well. When approached from the east, the storeroom building reminds one of a small English railroad station from the 1930s.[44]

In early 1932, as the plans for the storeroom were being completed, Carson College was still contemplating another structure, a separate school building that would allow it to move classes out of the "temporary" wooden school rooms and other assorted buildings and to hold them in one central location. Plans for a separate schoolhouse had been part of the original conception back in 1915, but it had been put on hold because of higher-than-expected building costs and uncertainties about enrollments in the early years. The idea of a school had been revived in 1926, when the board asked Albert Kelsey to draw preliminary plans for such a structure, to be located on Bethlehem Pike just south of Orchard Cottage. But the same legal difficulties that had held up funds for the two new cottages forced postponement of the school.[45] By the time that the cottages were finished and Carson was ready to go ahead with the school, a deepening nationwide depression, combined with some very unwise investments made by the Carson trustees, brought this and any other building projects to a complete halt.

Like most Americans, Ueland and the Carson board must have believed that the economic slowdown, which was announced by the stock market crash of October 1929, would last for a year or two and then be followed by the usual recovery. What they could not know was that the Great Depression would become the worst economic disaster in the nation's history and last for the better part of a decade. Thus Carson went ahead with building plans in the early 1930s, only to discover in 1932 that their investments were at risk and that the college's income was seriously compromised.

In 1932 the principal of the Carson estate stood, in round numbers, at $2,163,000. The accumulated-income account was approximately $699,000. The income for 1932 amounted to $141,000, about $38,000 less than in 1931. In 1933 income fell to $80,000, in 1934 to $41,600, and in 1935 to $33,600. This last figure, which turned out to be the low point of the depression—at least in income for Carson—was only one-sixth of the sum produced by the estate in 1928.[46]

Especially alarming was the fact that the bulk of Carson College's funds were now invested in real estate. As homeowners lost their jobs, they began to default on mortgage payments in record numbers, and the Carson estate had to foreclose a number of mortgages beginning in 1931. That year alone they took back property worth $65,000. In 1932 the amount was $239,000, and in 1933 it was $191,000.[47]

By early 1935 the Carson board began to grow suspicious over the large numbers of defaults on mortgages held by the Carson estate, and decided to investigate the matter themselves. In April the board learned that the trustees had purchased, on January 5, 1929, a total of 120 mortgages with an aggregate value of $520,000. It had bought these mortgages from the Real Estate Land Title and Trust Company, which was itself one of the trustees of the Carson estate. Not only did this transaction raise questions about a possible conflict of interest; it appeared that a large portion of these mortgages "were of questionable value as investments." According to the board minutes of April 24, 1935, an investigation had shown that there were unpaid real estate taxes on a number of these properties when the mortgages were purchased back in 1929, and that many of the properties had been in poor repair at the time they were added to the Carson portfolio. Under the circumstances, the board voted to conduct a fuller examination of the entire matter. A special board committee made up of Lewis N. Lukens Jr., Leo Nelson Sharpe, and Shippen Lewis, the latter two being lawyers, undertook the inquiry.[48]

On October 18, 1935, this committee reported its findings to the full board. Its revelations were alarming and led the board to adopt a strongly worded resolution to the trustees of the Carson estate. Included in the resolution was the charge that "a substantial part of the funds of the Estate have been *unlawfully and negligently* invested in mortgages purchased from one or both of the Trustees of the Estate" (emphasis is added). The resolution went on to demand "that any and all unlawful investments made by said Trustees shall be properly accounted for and that restitution be made for any losses suffered by the Estate on account thereof."[49] The resolution contained a thinly veiled threat to sue the trustees unless they made full restitution. Almost exactly a year later, on October 1, 1936, the Real Estate Land Title and Trust Company agreed to pay the Carson estate $441,771 in settlement of the claim.[50] In order to avoid any further risks, most of this money was invested in U.S. government bonds, which were then yielding about 2 percent.[51]

In addition to the $442,000 that had been put into questionable properties by the trust company, nearly all the rest of the Carson estate had been tied up in real estate of one sort or another following the divestiture of traction and street railway stocks in the late twenties and early thirties. As of May 1933, $2,434,086, or nearly 80 percent of the total Carson estate funds of $2,862,948 (presumably including the principal and the accumulated-income fund) had been invested in real estate.[52] Given the precarious nature of the entire real estate market at the time, these figures were truly alarming.

Although the most threatened portion of Carson College's funds had been salvaged in the agreement with the Real Estate Land Title and Trust Company, declining income forced the college into a series of severe retrenchments and into a constant search for alternative ways of raising revenues. One emergency source of revenue was the accumulated-income account: Between 1933 and 1936 the college borrowed approximately $131,000 from accumulated income.[53] In May of 1934 the board attempted to raise funds by selling 17.44 acres of land bounded by Wissahickon Avenue and the Widener race track on the Widener estate, but were unsuccessful.[54]

In 1934 the board ordered the first round of severe cutbacks for Carson College. These included the closing of Tanglewood Cottage on Bethlehem Pike and Ninth House on West Mill Road—both of them residences in Flourtown that had been rented by Carson. (Marigold Cottage on Bethlehem Pike and the cottage known as Mill Road, likewise rentals in Flourtown, had presumably been vacated upon the completion of Upper Beech and Lower Beech.)[55] At the same time, Mother Goose was closed as a cottage for children and given over completely to administrative offices and staff housing.[56] Employee wages were also slashed in 1934, between 20 and 50 percent, depending upon the position. Ueland's salary, which had reached $5,250 in 1929, was cut back to $3,500.[57] The following year, 1935, the board successfully pressed the trustees of the Carson estate to lower their fees from $14,000 to $8,500 per year, especially in light of the precipitous decline in income.[58]

The most serious of the financial retrenchments was Carson's reluctant decision to close its own elementary school and to put all its girls into the public school system of Springfield Township. Financial difficulties over schooling had actually begun back in 1931. In June of that year the local school district, which was probably feeling a loss of funds through property-tax delinquencies, demanded that Carson pay "back tuition" for its children who had attended Springfield High School since its opening in 1924. Since all of them had originally come from communities outside the Springfield district, the school board argued that it was not required to educate them tuition-free. The total amount requested was $19,561.96. Carson refused to pay such arrears, arguing that state law gave school districts discretion over whether to charge tuition for nonresident students and arguing further that any decision to charge Carson tuition should have been made *before,* rather than after, the fact. In the fall of 1932 Carson did agree to pay tuition in the future, but would pass along the bill for each child to the district of origin.[59]

Although Carson College had settled the problem of paying for high school, its on-site elementary program was proving more and more difficult to finance as institutional income dwindled and showed no signs of substantial recovery. Thus, during the summer of 1937, the college decided to close the elementary school and to place all its students in the Springfield system.[60] The very successful nursery school also closed and would not reopen for over a decade.[61] Not until the 1980s would Carson again operate its own, on-grounds school for residents. In the process, Carson's much renowned progressive school became one more victim of the Great Depression.

With the nursery school closed, Carson girls lost an important opportunity for vocational training. Meanwhile, the paucity of jobs during the depression made it difficult to place Carson girls in summer or after-school employment. About the only jobs available were positions in Chestnut Hill—and other wealthy neighborhoods—as "mother's helpers" or "household assistants."[62] Some Carson girls who had found jobs just before the depression set in were thrown out of work and, as orphans, had nowhere else to turn but to their Carson family. Thus, in December 1931, the board voted to assist such girls financially until they could find employment.[63]

Ueland anticipated the wider implications of budget cuts at Carson as early as May 1934, when she composed a memorandum on the budget. Recalling that even members of the Carson board had originally believed that the "day of building orphanages was over," she explained that they had nevertheless decided to go ahead with the provisions of the Carson will in the belief that they might accomplish something very special for their orphaned girls, as well as for families in the Flourtown community. Now that its income had fallen so disastrously, Carson College faced the possibility of becoming just another mediocre child-care institution.[64]

That such vicissitudes were difficult for Elsa Ueland personally was only to be expected. For at the very pinnacle of her success at Carson, just as Upper Beech and Lower Beech were completed and as she turned to the prospect of finally building a permanent school on campus, everything collapsed through no fault of her own. After three years of crisis and worry, Ueland sought relief by joining her old friend Lucy Mitchell and her student teachers of the Bank Street School for a bus trip to West Virginia and back via Washington, D.C., in the spring of 1935. (By then Mitchell was using geography, broadly conceived, as a way of training her students and as the basis for curriculum materials that they could use in the schools.)[65] They traveled aboard the green bus that Carson had purchased back in 1931 and were driven by the ever faithful Bill Goss. As part of their itinerary they visited the new community of Arthurdale, one of the centerpieces of the New Deal's Resettlement Administration.[66]

As both a Democrat and a liberal, Ueland greatly admired Franklin Roosevelt's New Deal and was excited by the Arthurdale undertaking, which was a favorite project of First Lady Eleanor Roosevelt, whom Ueland frequently praised to family and friends.[67] Unlike older or more conservative progressives, who had wanted to rely mainly on fact-finding and private solutions to modern problems, Elsa had no trouble in continuing to hope for social and economic reform through New Deal programs.[68] Doubtless her youth in Minnesota and her continuing contacts with that state through visits back home reinforced such attitudes. For Minnesotans had long believed that government action was appropriate for confronting both social and economic problems, an attitude that some historians have attributed to the large numbers of Germans and Scandinavians who settled in the state and brought from their home countries a tradition of vigorous governmental action.[69]

In a mood of continuing admiration for Roosevelt and the New Deal, Ueland returned to Carson from West Virginia and sought a partial leave of absence from the school, which would allow her to spend about half of each year working for the Resettlement Administration in West Virginia and the other half at Carson. Since Carson's program was in the process of serious retrenchment, the board agreed that she did not, in fact, have enough to do on the Flourtown campus. The savings of half her salary for the year was also attractive to the board.[70] (Directing Carson College during Ueland's absence was Margaret E. Roberts, a longtime member of the staff, who took the title of acting president.)[71] Ueland went on to serve for two years (1935 and 1936) as a supervisor of the schools run by the Resettlement Administration at the Tygart Valley Homestead at Elkins, West Virginia.[72] She may have thought of remaining there even longer, for she wrote a resignation to the Carson board in October 1936.[73] Since the board minutes contain no official notice of the resignation, it may be that she did not submit it at all, or that the board dissuaded her from leaving at an informal meeting. It is also possible that the resignation followed an outburst of anger from Ueland at the board. Although she usually kept her feelings under control, she was known to explode on occasion over issues of great importance to her, according to those who knew her well.[74]

Whatever the reasons for the letter of resignation, Ueland sought another respite from her worries at Carson by taking a five-month trip, in the summer and fall of 1938, to the Netherlands, North Africa (including Egypt), Singapore, Java, India, and Palestine with her old friend Lucy Mitchell and Lucy's husband Wesley "Robin" Mitchell, a well-known economist of the day and professor at Columbia University.[75] This was by no means Ueland's first trip abroad. In 1913 she had gone to Norway with her father, and in 1923 she had spent twelve weeks touring Europe. The 1938 journey turned out to be unexpectedly exciting when an armed band attacked the taxi in which Ueland was traveling on the Jerusalem–Jericho road on November 24. Though bullets ripped through the vehicle, no one was hurt, according to the Philadelphia newspapers, which picked up the story and reported it in some detail.[76]

Despite the continuing hard times, Ueland could well afford to make such an extensive trip. Her salary of $3,500 (which was restored to the $5,000 level in 1939) went very far in a world where prices still had not recovered from their steep declines earlier in the 1930s. Besides her salary, Ueland had inherited an unknown amount of money when her father died in 1933. She had further saved and invested modest amounts of money over the years.[77] In any case, she felt prosperous enough in December 1938, just after her return from the Holy Land, to buy a green 1939 "Deluxe Ford Tudor Sedan" for $793.[78]

Not having to pay for housing was an additional savings for Ueland, who remained at South Fields until May of 1938. At that point she moved into a new house called Oak Run that Katherine Tucker had built on East Mill Road in Flourtown. (South Fields then became a residence for Carson staff.) The cost of building and landscaping the new house, about $34,000, was a considerable sum of money in those depression days, and represented either a gift—or an inheritance—from Tucker's wealthy father. Kate and Elsa called the place Oak Run because of its location near a small creek that fed into the Wissahickon, and for a number of beautiful oak trees on the property.[79]

Designed by Pope Barney and completed in the spring of 1938, the house at Oak Run was originally surrounded by about fifteen acres of partly wooded land. Built of stucco and Chestnut Hill stone, it might be described as being in a rural Pennsylvania colonial style—at least overall. However, its banks of casement windows, so admired by Ueland, exude something of a Voyseyesque look, and particularly on the southwest side, where this fenestration is most prominent. It was on this same side of the house that Barney designed a large rectangular room that extended almost the entire length of the house. Functioning as a combination living room, library, dining room, and music room, it was flooded with light throughout most of the day. In the wall opposite the windows there was a large slate fireplace and beside it, in the corner, a Steinway grand piano

Fig. 34.   Oak Run, on East Mill Road in Flourtown, home of Elsa Ueland from 1938 to 1980. Designed by William Pope Barney and completed in 1938. Photo by the author, 1996.

that Elsa gave to Kate as a housewarming present. The house also contained a kitchen, a small study (lined with bookshelves), and a bedroom on the first floor. Upstairs were three more bedrooms and a long well-lighted studio/loft over a three-bay garage. Caring for the house and its extensive grounds were a husband and wife, who served as housekeeper and gardener.[80] Nearly sixty years later, the house and its surroundings present an atmosphere of warmth, ease, and exceeding charm.[81] Far larger than the dwellings touted by progressive reformers earlier in the century, its massing was nevertheless simple and its interior walls bereft of fancy woodwork or other expensive details.

Although she was now living at Oak Run, Ueland continued to keep a suite of rooms on the far south end of the second floor of Mother Goose Cottage, as she had during the years when she lived at the Maples and at South Fields. She could spend the night at Mother Goose in case of emergencies or at times when she simply felt the need to have a few days away from the daily routine at home.[82]

Yet even the comforts of Oak Run could not save Ueland from what was clearly a deep and protracted bout of depression. This emotional crisis seemed to envelop her in late March of 1939 as she was returning to Carson on the train from a visit to the family back in Minnesota. In order to come to grips with herself, she began keeping a diary on the train, which she continued, with almost daily entries, until the late summer of 1940. As such, it is the most extensive of any of Ueland's surviving diaries. In addition to providing valuable insights into her own state of mind, it offers fascinating details into the life of Carson College—and into the larger community that surrounded it.

The magnitude of Ueland's depression comes through powerfully in entry after entry of her diary. On May 3, 1939, she wrote, "Worn down—a deep deep sinking. Like an illness. . . . Tears, inadequacy, helplessness, humiliation. . . . Too little bounce: No hour of wealth of joy, of beauty. . . . In an office,—by an office table. Papers, Papers, Papers." On June 27 she felt a "lump of lead in the diaphragm." "Ears buzzing—I can't hear."

Other entries make clear that both internal and external forces had come together to produce such a terrible state. The never-ending economic depression, coupled with its depredations at Carson, was clearly one of the forces bearing down upon her. Thus, on December 19, 1939, she wrote, "Money and budget control is an empty shell and not a very beautiful shell either." She also felt hopeless and beaten down by the conservatism and lack of imagination that she perceived in the local community,

Philadelphia, and Pennsylvania as a whole. Thus she told her diary after attending several civic meetings in Springfield Township during April 1939:"What do these meetings mean to me? Certainly I see more clearly the actual stuff that makes up our township and county and our state of Pennsylvania—The roots in the past—property long owned—Wealth and poverty—[Edward T.] Stotesbury and community. Slums—Comparable to *India*—and very different from [progressive] Minnesota—Norway—Montgomery County will be one of the slowest to change and one of the most conservative strongholds in these present currents of change" [83] (emphasis is in the original). At the end of the year, on December 18, she again complained in her diary about the closed society that typified the entire region:"We realize that the British caste system—servants and the servant class—and their acceptance of this dependence—is a part of Philadelphia—Chestnut Hill—the Whitemarsh Valley." [84] In her rage against conspicuous consumption and privileged wealth, Ueland sounded much like Thorstein Veblen, whose writings she had admired since early adulthood. [85]

The troubled world scene, with the Germans constantly threatening to upset the peace and finally plunging the world into war in September 1939, also wore away at Ueland and only added to her feelings of sadness. On September 19, 1939, a little more than two weeks after war had broken out in Europe, she recorded in her diary:"A heavy heart—Hard to get up—to wake up. The war. Destruction. Break up. That insistent, hammering, inevitable German drive. Destruction. Destruction. Those iron tanks like the years of change. Rolling over all we know of greenness. Beating force. Unfeeling hardness. And this rolls over me—I know it—things as they are. This little orphanage as it is." For a progressive and now a New Dealer like Ueland, this second great war in just a quarter century could not help but be depressing and disillusioning.

The outbreak of war also coincided with a realization that the mounting success she had known just a few years before was slipping from her grasp, and that at age fifty-one it was too late to start over again. If she needed any confirmation of this fact, she only had to look at the 1940 edition of *Who's Who in America,* which had dropped her entry from its pages, never to reappear. What she may have thought about this is unknown, but the omission could only have fueled her sense that fame was ebbing. As she confided to her diary on December 29, 1939,"I do not seem to get over the feeling that I might be great—do great things—distinguished things." At the same time, she must have regretted turning down several other positions—of not leaving Carson College when she had the chance.[86] (Yet it would seem that she managed to conceal these feelings from her staff, as well as from most of her friends. Julia E. "Judy" Moore, who first came to Carson in the middle 1930s, who served in a variety of capacities, and who became a lifelong friend of Ueland, reported to this author that she knew nothing of Elsa's anguish.)[87]

Meanwhile, Ueland complained that her staff was growing old and tired, though she admitted that this sensation was partly a projection of her own consciousness of aging and of the inexorable passage of time: "Yes—I complain of the age of the staff," she reflected in her diary entry for April 3, 1940. "[But] it is my own age I am complaining of.... It is my own lack of time sense. Pressure!" Reeling from such pressures, she again had gone so far as to write a letter of resignation, and even to discuss it with various board members, but once more did not go through with it, for reasons that have not been recorded.[88]

It is also clear that Ueland was prone to depression and that she had suffered serious bouts of it in the past. Her mother's death in 1927 had sent her into a prolonged period of anxiety and despair and had finally led her to reveal to her father and other members of the family that she had known episodes of depression since early adulthood. To her father she wrote in December 1928, "I have had periods of depression almost all my life,—certainly ever since I was in the University.... It is true that [these] despondences have been more difficult since Mother's death,— harder to get on top of."[89]

Ueland managed to shake off her latest depression only gradually. In April 1939 she went to see the psychologist Otto Rank (1884–1939), her friend Jessie Taft's mentor for the past dozen years or so. Elsa had gone into therapy with Rank in 1927 during a siege of depression following her mother's death, and she may have consulted him at various times in the years since.[90] Rank's unexpected death during the summer of 1939, while Elsa was still in therapy, added to her sense of panic, but she tried to hold on to what Rank had told her and continued to consult his many articles and books. From reading Rank, she concluded, "One must make a center where one IS—and build from that.... Yes—one's own creation ...! Certainly for me the solution must be a degree of separation, and a degree of schedule—setting these limits,—practical personal limits as well as practical job limits, within which to LIVE."[91]

Ueland's summary of what she took to be Rank's advice reflected the increasing Rankian emphasis upon conscious will, as opposed to Sigmund

Freud's great reliance upon the unconscious and subconscious, in explaining many, if not most, aspects of human behavior. Rank had been one of Freud's most accomplished and beloved disciples in Vienna, but in the late 1920s he had broken with orthodox psychoanalysis, much to Freud's dismay.[92] It was at this same time that Jessie Taft met Rank and became his principal advocate in the United States, translating his major works into English and organizing lectures and discussion groups for Rank on this side of the Atlantic. In 1958 Taft would publish a biography of Rank that remains the most noteworthy study of him in the English language.[93] Taft herself became a leading member of the "Rankian school" and made Rank's will philosophy an integral part of the educational program at the University of Pennsylvania School of Social Work in Philadelphia. It is impossible to know from the vantage of the 1990s if Rank's insights were used with the orphans at Carson College, though a Rankian influence at Carson cannot be ruled out.

In addition to her consultations with Rank, Ueland turned to religion for relief from her anguish. She attended the Flourtown Presbyterian Church during several Sundays in May of 1939, and tried to find some solace in the Calvinist doctrine of "undeserving grace." Yet her religious quest was a synthetic one, inasmuch as she also read Roman Catholic literature on personal devotions, quoted Buddha, and wished that she could achieve the Buddhist escape from worldly desire.[94] Thus, on December 19, 1939, she exclaimed in her diary, "Yes, one needs the PRESENCE OF GOD, and seeks it."

Also helpful were continued trips back to Minnesota, which she appeared to make each year in late winter (around the time of her birthday, on March 10) and midautumn.[95] Her family looked forward to these visits and, according to her niece Clara Ueland, seemed to look upon Elsa as something of a family "patriarch," despite her gender. She was older than any of her brothers and was respected for her intelligence and successful career. The fact that she was more liberal than her brothers led to a lot of good-natured kidding, but never any rancorous arguments over politics. Typically, Elsa brought along materials for some sort of creative project, such as landscape painting or sculpting, which she organized for her nieces and nephews, as well as any interested adults in the family. They often joked at home that Elsa "never married but had hundreds of children" back in Pennsylvania.[96]

Then there was the strong sense of family that Elsa felt for her many friends in Flourtown. As Christmas 1939 neared, she remarked in her diary how Kate had made Oak Run "a family house center" for their little circle.[97] Besides Jessie Taft, Virginia Robinson, and Kate and Elsa themselves, the group included Gratia Balsh, who had been the music teacher at Carson since 1923, and Phoebe Allnutt, until recently the principal of Carson's school, who still lived at the Crow's Nest on East Mill Road, just down from Kate and Elsa's place and nearly next door to Jessie and Virginia's house. Out-of-town friends dropped in from time to time, among them Lucy Mitchell from the Bank Street School in New York and Alice Barrows, who since 1918 had worked as an agent for the City Schools Division of the U.S. Bureau of Education, from which she had tirelessly promoted progressive education in the public schools.[98]

Several of these women played with Elsa and Kate in a musical quartet, whose membership shifted according to who was available to perform. Elsa invariably played violin and Kate the Steinway piano. Performing together in the evenings at Oak Run was a healing balm for Ueland, helping her to relax and to forget her problems at least for a little while, as is evident from her description of one such evening in early spring 1939: "We all let go and hear the unbelievable color and grandeur of the Universe itself—clarified so that it can be heard—and with unimaginable beauty and intricate wonder . . . through the passion of Bach."[99] Elsa's niece, Clara, remembered that they played these pieces at a slow tempo.[100] Ueland's longtime friend Judy Moore described Elsa as a "good amateur" musician.[101]

And beyond Oak Run Elsa could find numerous entertainments, such as dinners at Jessie and Virginia's home, known as the Pocket.[102] In June, Elsa and Kate went to see the New York World's Fair, though Ueland left no record of her impressions. There were also trips to the theater in New York, as in January 1940, when Elsa joined Lucy Mitchell to see *The Time of Your Life*.[103]

An additional but unlikely source of emotional support came in the person of Carson board member Shippen Lewis (1888–1952). Lewis had joined the board in February 1928, became chairman of the management committee in January 1937, and in 1941 would become chairman of the entire board. A member of an old Philadelphia family (and a collateral descendant of Peggy Shippen, the wife of Benedict Arnold), Lewis was a successful lawyer, as well as a prominent civic leader, who then was living in Chestnut Hill. Although a Republican, he belonged to the progressive wing of the party and was involved in many reform causes. (In early 1952, under Philadelphia's Democratic reform mayor, Joseph S. Clark, Lewis would become chairman of a new civil service commission with sweeping authority to clean out the worst abuses of patronage and corruption.) Having lost his first wife, Esther Emlen, in 1927, Lewis married Mary F. W. Porcher in 1930. (Following Lewis's death, Mary would wed James Bond. It was this James Bond from whom Ian Fleming would later borrow the name for his fictional hero, Agent 007.)[104]

According to those who knew him, Lewis had an uncanny ability to size up a situation and offer practical solutions in a way that often brought comfort or reconciliation to all parties concerned.[105] In any case, during 1939 and 1940 Lewis typically visited Ueland about once a month, usually on a Saturday morning, in his capacity as head of the management committee. But it is clear that Ueland, who was exactly the same age as Lewis, shared some of her sorrows with him and that he offered sympathetic advice. On June 3, 1939, for example, he urged her to let go of the insistence that everything be perfect for Carson College and its girls, and to try to be satisfied with doing the best she could in light of difficult circumstances.[106] Later that month she remarked in her diary on Lewis's "fine spirit and intelligence," and soon came to see him as an indispensable ally on the Carson board.[107]

That Ueland had such a capable and sympathetic friend as Shippen Lewis was indeed fortunate, for despite her depression she continued to make plans for raising Carson out of its difficulties. And although frustration with these plans sometimes exacerbated her low moods, a determination to work faithfully for the school had ultimately beneficial results for Carson, as well as for Ueland herself.

As early as 1937 Ueland and the board had discussed how they might make the best financial use of Carson's assets, much of which were tied up in buildings and land. At that time they considered erecting rental properties near the community playground (in the area around Orchard Cottage), and even purchasing a strip of land between this property and West Mill Road in order to gain more space for their development. Because of the uncertain times, the board took no action, and in the meantime a developer bought the adjoining parcel and began putting up some sixty-five houses in the spring of 1939 along the present College Avenue, in a development called College Park (named for its close proximity to the Carson College grounds). Mortgages subsidized by the federal government, in addition to some easing in unemployment, were making such projects possible as the 1930s came to an end.

The houses in College Park were conventional red brick dwellings in vague colonial styles, arranged in rows on both sides of the street, with no thought for parks, open spaces, or recreational facilities—a lack of planning and foresight that appalled Ueland. She may have had in mind instead the modest-sized but attractive houses that Dr. George Woodward had built around Pastorius Park on the west side of Chestnut Hill.[108] But it is more likely that Ueland was drawing on her views of progressive housing, on her recent experiences with the Resettlement Administration in West Virginia, and especially on what she knew about the Greenbelt towns that were also built by the Resettlement Administration and that were hailed by reformers of the day as models of community planning. Although twenty-five such towns were originally projected, only three were actually constructed: Greenbelt, Maryland (near Washington, D.C.); Green Hills, Ohio (near Cincinnati); and Greendale, Wisconsin (near Milwaukee). Each of these towns arose in a somewhat rural area, surrounded by woodlands and farms, with an emphasis upon open space, fresh air, gardens, parks, and playgrounds.[109]

In contrast, the lack of planning in and around Flourtown, even as new housing appeared, was of great concern to Ueland and—she believed—to Carson College. Accordingly, on April 11, 1939, she wrote a long letter to Shippen Lewis about the whole situation and about her belief that the time had come for Carson to act as an agent of residential construction and community planning:

> Building is coming fast in Flourtown. . . . The schools must act promptly to care at all for this influx of new families and children. Still there is no public playground, and no public recreation planned for in the whole Whitemarsh Valley (to say nothing of opportunities for the under privileged in Chestnut Hill!).[110] I note this because we are now fairly seeing the metropolitan area of Philadelphia beginning to spread over us and beyond us, row on row:—and still there is little community planning. . . . Perhaps this spring . . . these community changes should again be considered with reference to the future policy of the College.[111]

The Carson board thought enough of Ueland's ideas to embrace the possibility of a planned residential community on the Carson College grounds. Board member Otto Mallery, who had used architect Frank Lloyd Wright to design modestly priced multiunit dwellings at what was called the Suntop development in Ardmore, Pennsylvania (on the Philadelphia Main Line), invited fellow board members to dine with him and Wright at the Franklin Inn Club in Philadelphia in the spring of 1938. A year later, in May of 1939, Mallery took Wright on a tour of the Carson grounds. Wright envisioned a community that would combine new Carson cottages with rental properties and a recreational area that would bring Ueland's concept of cooperative living and community relations to new heights. According to Ueland, Wright's preliminary plans for the cottages would place the kitchen on a sort of bridge, or balcony, that looked down on the rest of the house so that the housemother could view all that transpired above and below, an arrangement that would answer an ongoing concern of Ueland's that Kelsey's original cottages had not addressed.[112]

Ueland was enthusiastic about creating this new village on Carson property, to be located along Bethlehem Pike near Orchard Cottage. If all went well, the project would bring badly needed income to Carson, would renew Ueland's dream of cooperation and sharing with the surrounding community (with attendant benefits to her orphans), would provide affordable, decent housing to working-class families, and, as a model of institutional planning, would perhaps restore Ueland's own reputation as a preeminent reformer. Thus she was angered and depressed to learn in June or July of 1939 that the trustees of the Carson estate would not allow any funds to be used for building residential units on the property of Carson College (perhaps because of the trouble that they had had with unwise real estate investments only a few years before).[113] Learning of the defeat, Elsa wrote, "I feel like a hopeful fool. . . . Sold down the river."[114]

Ueland was far more successful in obtaining approval to change Carson's admissions rules so as to enlarge the pool of potential entrants. In fact, enrollment problems had begun to materialize at Carson as early as 1928, when ten girls reached eighteen and left the institution and no new applications were pending. In response Ueland and her staff prepared a new pamphlet describing Carson's facilities and programs and circulated it among various child-welfare agencies and juvenile-court officers. This initiative, combined with family hardships due to the onset of the Great Depression, yielded a number of new admissions for the next several years: 24 in 1930, 11 in 1931, and 15 in both 1932 and 1933. By the mid-1930s, however, admissions began to fall off precipitously, with no additions in 1935 and only 3 in 1936. Large numbers of "graduates" from the institution during this period only compounded the problem.[115]

Alarmed at these numbers, Ueland began to research the college's admissions policies in December 1936, and in early 1937 Carson College sent out some nine thousand leaflets about the school, only to receive ten inquiries in response.[116] In November 1937, in a long memorandum to the board entitled "The Dilemma," Ueland offered a detailed analysis of the admissions problem. "The present dilemma of Carson College," she began, could be traced directly to the will of Robert Carson. She as well as many others had realized for years that the will had unduly shackled the institution. But by 1937 its restraints were more crippling than ever. As Ueland put it, "The admission gate has always been extremely narrow; but as conditions have changed, and are changing now almost visibly, from one year to the next,—this gate is not only narrower than ever;—it is *in the wrong place*"[117] (emphasis is in the original).

Although the early and middle years of the Great Depression had made tremendous demands on orphanages like Carson, conditions by the latter part of the 1930s were leading to a decline in the numbers of children requiring institutional care.[118] The reasons for this were abundantly clear according to Ueland: Increases in average life expectancy resulted in fewer and fewer children under the age of ten (the upper limit for admission to Carson) who were left without parents. (For example, while 35 percent of the parents of Carson girls had died of either influenza, pneumonia, or tuberculosis during the early years of Carson's operation, only 2.5 percent died from similar diseases in the seventeen years after 1940.)[119] Mothers' aid laws passed by forty-five states (including Pennsylvania) also meant that mothers could afford to keep their children at home despite the death of a father. Most important, in 1935 the national Social Security Act had provided for aid to dependent children, who might live with any of a wide variety of adult family members (including aunts, uncles, brothers, sisters, and grandparents), all of whom could qualify for the new federal aid.[120] Thus, after reaching an all-time high of 124 in March 1931, Carson's enrollment dropped to 98 by the end of 1936 and to 92 by the end of 1939. It is probable, however, that not all these children were living on campus, since Carson had decided back in 1934, when it closed Tanglewood and Ninth House, that it was cheaper to board most of the older girls with local families. As late as 1945, for example, only 61 of the 83 girls listed on the Carson rolls actually resided on the grounds, a practice that continued, at least to some degree, into the early 1960s.[121]

With few new applications, it was only a matter of time until the "graduations" of those already in the institution would make enrollment matters far worse. Ironically, it had been continuing campaigns by progressive reformers for mothers' aid laws, culminating in federal aid to dependent children through the Social Security Act, that had done more than anything else to implement the progressive principle of keeping as many children as possible out of institutions. Thus the success of this progressive program on behalf of children had helped to undermine Carson College's own progressive school, and ultimately to threaten the institution's very existence.

Ueland could only conclude that it was not orphans who were in need of places like Carson, but "children in need because of broken homes," or "dependent and neglected children," as the matter was phrased later in her report.[122] Thus, Ueland observed, "Carson College can be of almost no service whatever to children of Philadelphia and Montgomery and neighboring counties, unless the admissions requirements can be interpreted in terms of present day conditions."[123] She further proposed that Robert Carson, if he had been alive in 1937, would want the institution to take cognizance of changing times and to make adjustments that would allow the general intent of the will, that is, assistance for "needing children," to be carried out in the most practical manner.[124]

The Carson board agreed with Ueland that changes would have to be made in admissions if the institution was to survive.[125] After considerable research, the Carson board approved a legal brief, later accepted by the Montgomery County Court of Orphans, that allowed Carson College to accept half orphans (that is, girls who had just one living parent), as well as girls who might be younger than six or older than ten.[126] The brief, composed largely by Shippen Lewis in his capacity as an attorney as well as chairman of the management committee, made three main arguments: (1) Robert Carson, as a practical and successful businessman, would have understood more than most individuals that one must adapt to changing times. (2) Benefactor Carson had specifically used the word "suggestions" in the seventh clause of the will, where he set forth conditions for admission. Since these were "suggestions" rather than firm and absolute directives, the board was free to implement those that were practical and to amend or disregard those that were not. (3) A decision handed down by the Supreme Court of Pennsylvania in 1859 (*Soohan v. The City of Philadelphia*) had held that fatherless boys could be defined as orphans and therefore admitted to Philadelphia's Girard College. Since Robert Carson had modeled his will partly on Girard's, and since there was no essential difference between fatherless or motherless children in their standing as half orphans, girls without either a mother or a father should be admitted to Carson College.[127]

In fact, Carson had been accepting some half orphans for a number of years already, though this was not mentioned in the legal brief. Back in 1918, the official opening year, the institution had begun admitting girls whose mothers had died and whose fathers' whereabouts were unknown.[128] As early as December 1929, Carson had admitted girls who were half orphans but whose mothers had been committed to institutions for the insane, leaving their daughters full orphans for all practical purposes.[129] But beyond such justifiable exceptions, Carson could not admit most half orphans until it received official permission from the court in 1939.

In yet another departure from the will, this time without formally approaching the court, the board voted in June 1940 to invite the brothers of Carson girls to visit for one week during the summer. In the summer of 1942, some twenty-nine brothers came for short stays.[130] Ueland had long opposed the restriction to girls alone, and it is more than likely that these summer visits by brothers were intended to pave the way for admitting brothers full-time and then for opening Carson completely to both boys and girls—whether they were related or not. If such were her expectations, they would meet with success, though it would take many years to realize them. (In fact, brothers who were having a particularly hard time adjusting in their own placements had been allowed as early as 1927 to stay at Carson for varying amounts of time in the same cottages as their sisters.)[131]

While all these changes in admissions were being contemplated or were in progress, Carson took another step that would have great implications for the future. This was a decision to accept children as wards of the court from the various counties, including Philadelphia, with board to be paid by the counties or municipalities in question. Carson appears to have accepted its first such ward from the Juvenile Court of Montgomery County in the fall of 1935. In November 1937 the board formally voted to accept payments from the counties and reiterated this decision three years later in November 1940.[132] Carson's financial difficulties during the depression doubtless made such revenues attractive, as they would continue to be in the future.

These changes in admissions policies had a salutary effect on Carson. In September 1939, Ueland reported to the board that 11 new children had come to the college over the summer. In May 1941 she could say that there had been 30 applications in recent months, though she did not give any figures for total enrollment that year.[133] The admissions report for the period June 1939–May 1940 also reflected the new policies and their success. Of the 39 children whose names were put in application, only 12 of them were full orphans, while 27 were half orphans. Their ages ranged from four and a half to fifteen.[134] The reasons given for placement were also revealing in that most of the children were neglected, unwanted, or not adequately supported. The following are four examples:

> —Relatives working or on relief,—large families of their own and have neither interest nor money to care for girls.
> —Grandmother too old to care for such a large family—has two of Lorraine's sisters....
> —Unwanted by sister who is guardian—incompatible home situation.
> —Mother unable to get along on aid to dependent children grant according to customary standards—also does not want to be tied to children.[135]

In November 1940, the year after Carson moved to admit half-orphans, the board of trustees adopted new bylaws that expanded the size of the board and allowed women to sit as members for the first time. Drawn up by Shippen Lewis, the bylaws did not directly challenge the mandate set down in the Carson will, which established a board of seven men, but the new provisions once again allowed the institution to work around the will. There were now to be eleven members of the board, the seven men appointed by the court under the Carson will plus four others who were elected by the board at its first meeting each year. So as not to run afoul of the will, the bylaws held that the "recorded decisions" of the board should be understood to be those of the seven male board members who were officially appointed by the court.[136]

Although Lewis had crafted the new bylaws, Ueland had probably been pressing for a change that would open the board to women, as well as to trustees who were less socially prominent and thus more broadly representative of the region. Indeed, her irritation with what she saw as the false pretensions of at least one Carson board member came through in a diary entry from July 1939, just after she had had dinner at his home in Chestnut Hill. In the entry she complained of the family's "careful good manners," adding, "To me it is a game.... The Chestnut Hill social manner and tricks I do not like."[137]

Whether or not such discontent was partly behind the expansion of the Carson board, there was only a modest change in the percentage of members of the enlarged board (elected in January 1941) who appeared in the Philadelphia *Social Register.* Five of the eleven, or 45 percent, were in the register, as opposed to four of the original seven members, or 57 percent, who were listed in the *Social Register* back in 1914. Three of the new board members were women, including Ueland herself, who was elected by the trustees despite the possible conflicts of interest arising from her position as president of Carson College.[138] Another new member was the minister of the Flourtown Presbyterian Church, the Reverend George T. Jamieson. (In 1945 Jamieson's successor at the local church, the Reverend Frank H. Stroup, would replace him on the board and become a central figure there, and would remain so for several decades.)[139] These changes certainly did not represent a social revolution on the board, but the new arrangement, combined with future amendments to the bylaws, would in time produce a board that was less dominated by the social elite and more broadly representative of the region.

Although Carson had passed through many changes during the past decade, Ueland and her staff tried to keep as much of their progressive program intact as they could. But with much less money and the closure of their own school in 1937, this was often difficult to achieve. Before the school closed, however, the teachers continued to take advantage of every opportunity to break down barriers between the classroom and the world outside. For example, the teachers made an imaginative project out of the

Fig. 35.   A visit to the lumberyard, c. 1930. CVS.

Fig. 36.   A trip to the stone quarry, c. 1930. CVS.

construction of the Upper and Lower Beech cottages in the early 1930s. The girls visited the docks on the Delaware River to see the raw lumber come in from the Pacific Northwest and then went to the lumberyard to watch it be sawed into boards for the new cottages. They also visited the quarry that supplied the stone. Once the buildings were started, the girls walked over to the sites regularly, where they talked with the workmen, made notes, took photographs, and put together their own project booklet on the construction.[140] In this way they learned about the elements of construction and the geography of the places that had supplied the materials, at the same time practicing their writing and photographic skills. By experiencing the whole building process, they gradually made the new cottages a part of their own lives. Meanwhile, they learned to appreciate all the planning, labor, and skills that went into making new homes.

Throughout the 1930s the farm continued to be an integral part of the girls' lives, with corn-hoeing sessions on summer evenings and corn husking in the fall. In late October of 1932, for instance, the girls gathered in the fields after school and worked together in small groups. As the autumn light began to dim, they built a fire and roasted "hot dogs" there in the field. Afterward they made a circle around the fire, and with shadows flickering against the shocks of corn, they sang songs before retiring to the cottages for homework and bed.[141]

Fig. 37.   Cornhusking, autumn 1931. CVS.

Summer activities were much truncated, as might be expected, because of the ongoing economic emergency. The week at the New Jersey shore ceased, no doubt because the rent was too much of a burden. The week-long stays at Camp Hopewell came to an end because the owner of the site put the land up for sale in 1937 and the Carson board declined to buy it, in deference to another bidder, the University Camp, which had for many years run a facility for underprivileged urban children directly adja-cent to the Carson camp. In 1938 the board investigated other possible campsites, but nothing came of these explorations, for reasons that are now lost.[142] Instead of the week at the shore and camp, the girls took day trips on the Carson bus to the New Jersey beaches and various sight-seeing trips. Between August 30 and September 1, 1938, for example, a number of the older girls took a bus trip to Washington, D.C., and returned through northern Virginia and eastern Maryland.[143]

Back home the girls enjoyed swimming at the creek and romping on the Carson playground next to Orchard Cottage. In the summer of 1941 Carson managed to enlist community help in supporting the playground activities by getting together with others in the village to form the Flour-town Recreation Association, an accomplishment that showed Ueland's continuing determination to find avenues of cooperation and sharing with Carson's neighbors.[144] On summer evenings there was a full schedule of recreation. During the 1933 season activities ranged from cards and various board games on Mondays to dancing in the gym on Wednesdays and baseball and tumbling on Thursdays.[145] All was not play, however. In addition to hoeing corn, gardening and canning "squads" were organized every morning, and cleaning and painting groups in the early afternoons. In order to mark the end of the summer program, the college continued to have its annual gardening and canning contests, with prizes awarded for the best items in each category. The day ended with swimming performances and races down at the creek, followed by a corn roast that featured Carson's own home-grown sweet corn.[146]

As in the past, Ueland and her staff believed that asking the girls to help with the harvest and to process and cook their own food would help to build self-confidence and make the world a less puzzling place. Although one could assume that the girls' assistance on the farm was of some financial help during the depression, evidence suggests that the farm operation was again costing the college more than it provided in

Fig. 38.   Hot-dog roast, c. 1940. CVS.

food stuffs or in income from surplus crops, a factor that would eventually lead to disbanding the farm altogether.[147]

A new social event at Carson, started in 1930, signaled the beginning of the summer months at the same time that it marked the conclusion of the Carson experience for those girls who had reached eighteen and were now free to make their own way. This event was the Eighteenth-Birthday Party. Held in late May (and, later, in mid-June) it was, according to Ueland, a sort of graduation from the Carson family.[148] In many ways the Eighteenth-Birthday Party was like a coming-out event. Although the details varied somewhat from year to year, there was generally a six o'clock supper "under the trees near Mother Goose," followed by a dance in the evening, to which the girls wore long white gowns. Invited to the gala event were the Carson board, faculty, housemothers, and special friends of the celebrants. The climax of the evening was the cutting of a large birthday cake.[149]

As with any children, keeping Carson's youngsters busy during the cooler months sometimes presented a real challenge. With limited funds for recreation during the depression, the task required great resourcefulness. Reflecting such realities, a memorandum dated winter 1935 listed "Possibilities for Good Times, that Cost Very Little Money." Among these

Fig. 39.   "Eighteenth-Birthday Party," 1940s, Elsa Ueland in center. CVS.

possibilities, depending upon age, were basketball, impromptu dancing, sledding, storytelling, reading aloud, "stunt parties," candy pulling, making paper dolls, dramatics, knitting, playing dress-up, evening sings, discussions around the fireplace, cards and board games, listening to the Victrola, baking cookies, wiener roasts, campfires, going to the library, roller-skating on the tennis courts (illuminated by kerosene lanterns), and hikes along the many country roads and woodland trails that surrounded Carson. A typical hike took place on Saturday, January 18, 1941. The Carson bus took a group of older girls to Wissahickon Avenue and Allen's Lane (in the West Mt. Airy section of Philadelphia), and from there they walked the four or so miles back home along the Wissahickon Creek and Northwestern Avenue.[150]

In the late 1930s the girls began participating in what were called "rhythmics," a combination of dance and exercise with music, taught by a visiting teacher named Miss Alice Kraft, who would offer her classes at Carson for over thirty years.[151] Kraft (1895–1973) had studied modern dance under the famed Isadora Duncan, who had associated free-form dancing with the advancement of democracy and the preparation of women for self-confident lives.[152] In Duncan's words, such dancing was "like the vibration of the American soul striving upward, through labour to harmonious life."[153] According to Duncan, dance would help young women in particular "to a new knowledge of the possible strength and beauty of their bodies, and the relation of their bodies to the earth nature and to the children of the future."[154] Although somewhat less mystical than Duncan, Alice Kraft claimed that in "the rhythmic motion [of the dance] confidence blossoms, inhibitions [and] self-confidence vanish."[155] Kraft gave separate lessons to Elsa Ueland and her Flourtown friends, and would continue to visit Ueland into the early 1970s.[156]

While teaching at Carson, Kraft had the girls swirling and leaping about, dressed in flowing chiffon gowns. From what can be gathered through interviews with former Carson residents, most of the girls thoroughly enjoyed their classes with Kraft.[157] In any case, Kraft (like Duncan) represented yet another connection to the broader progressive movement, in this case with art as a vehicle for liberation and reform.

As each winter began, the Carson girls could depend on the Christmas tableau, an annual celebration that continued into the depression years and usually took place on the Sunday before Christmas.[158] On Christmas Eve the children, faculty, staff, and of course "Miss Ueland" went caroling through Flourtown. In 1939 they carried little lanterns, though the moon was "nearly full and the night clear"—as Ueland remarked in her diary for December 24—ending up at Oak Run for hot chocolate (a tradition that would last almost to the end of Ueland's life). A week later, on New Year's Eve, Ueland joined some eighteen of the older Carson girls for a sledding party. "The whole valley in snow and starlight," she wrote. "How beautiful. And safe . . . Soft snow. The stars are *brilliant.* And not a soul in sight"[159] (emphasis is in the original).

With the world recently plunged into war, the soft blanket of snow and the clear, starry sky covering the Carson campus like a protective dome helped Elsa Ueland to feel safe and calm again. As the next summer rolled around, she was even proud of saying that she was now of an age (in her case, fifty-two) when many women had become grandmothers. Thus, in a memorandum to her senior staff in June 1940 she wrote, "NO ONE OF US IS ANY YOUNGER than we were ten years ago. Most of us [are] now of the grandmother age. . . . And still here are big families, immense gardens, [and] hundreds of quarts of food to be canned. . . . But grandmothers . . . have experience, and so have we."[160]

There would certainly be new challenges ahead, but Ueland seemed to sense that Carson College had weathered the worst of its depression storms and would survive into another day. Despite the ravages of the Great Depression and the war in Europe, she had also managed to save something of Carson's progressive program.

CHAPTER SIX

A
WAY
THROUGH

During the difficult days of the 1930s, Elsa Ueland had often written in her diary about the need to find "a way through." Both for herself and for the institution, this meant facing limitations and searching for realistic ways of working through or around various impediments. Changing Carson's admissions policies in 1939 to allow half orphans, as well as children who were younger than six or older than ten at the time of entry, had proved beneficial. So had the decision to accept board payments from various public agencies. Soon after World War II the institution would go still further by admitting boys, so long as they were the brothers of Carson girls. It was also in this early postwar period that the institution would alter its name from the Carson College for Orphan Girls to the Carson Valley School, a change that reflected new admissions policies and ended years of confusion in the public mind over just what was meant by "college." Meanwhile, the postwar baby boom prompted Carson to reopen its nursery school, much to the delight of mothers and fathers in the area.

Healthier enrollments, in addition to increases in income from the Carson estate (as the national and local economies prospered), permitted Carson to recover to a remarkable extent from the darkest days of the depression. Yet in the seventeen years between the American declaration of war in late 1941 and the retirement of Elsa Ueland as president of Carson in 1958, the institution did not regain the levels of income, enrollment, and national fame that it had known before the depression. Renewed attempts to raise additional funds or to contribute to community planning by building rental housing on the Carson property also met with failure, this time at the hands of the township zoning board. Elements of progressive living and learning remained in place, though these were more survivals from a receding past than the result of innovations in institutional programs.

Like the rest of the nation, Carson College felt some effects of the American entry into World War II and the full-scale mobilization that followed. Among the first of Carson's experiences with the war was the arrival of eight children and their mothers from England, part of a much larger exodus of women and children from the British Isles in anticipation of a German invasion. They resided for two weeks at Carson—according to an item in the Philadelphia *Evening Bulletin,* though the account did not reveal the name of the cottage where they stayed—before relocating in more permanent accommodations.[1] In addition, Carson took in eight Jewish refugees who had managed to escape from Germany. There were three boys, three girls, and a married couple. In addition to room and board, the adults were given jobs on campus.[2]

By May 1942 there were concerns about sugar rationing at Carson, especially since the canning-and-preserving season would soon be upon them.[3] A year later, during the summer of 1943, Carson expanded its vegetable gardens and purchased more pigs and chickens in order to supplement food supplies, and allowed homeowners in the adjoining College Park development to plant "victory gardens" on Carson land.[4] Gasoline shortages also hit Carson, especially during the winter months, sometimes leaving their equipment without enough fuel to plow snow from the roads.[5] Early in 1944 the Springfield Township Public Schools asked if it could use Thistle Cottage (which had been closed by Carson for now unknown reasons) as a child-care center for mothers employed in war industries. Carson agreed, but the local demand was not great enough to justify such a facility, and thus Thistle Cottage did not become a day-care center.[6] There were also "blackouts" and air-raid drills, both in the cottages and in school.[7] Beyond these relatively minor accommodations, Carson was not much disturbed by the nearly four years of war.

Yet the war set powerful forces in motion that would transform many aspects of American society for years to come. Among these were postwar prosperity, a sustained increase in the birth rate (which came to be known as the baby boom), a vast movement from cities into suburbs, and a postwar emphasis upon conformity, followed in the 1960s by a youthful rebellion known as the counterculture.

As if to register such changes in an official way, the Carson board began to consider altering the institution's name in March 1945. Later that year the administration started to receive numerous inquiries from returning servicemen, who were eligible for free tuition through the G.I. Bill of Rights. Because of the name Carson College, some veterans had assumed that Carson was an institution of higher learning. In addition to this sort of confusion, Carson was no longer an orphanage in the strictest sense of the word, and thus the name Carson College for Orphan Girls was doubly misleading. The board discussed a number of possible name changes, including Carson Farms, Carson Fields, Carson Green Acres, and Whitemarsh Valley School for Girls, before deciding on the Carson Valley School in July 1946. The board made the change "informally," on the advice of Shippen Lewis, again avoiding any legal challenge to the will itself.[8]

While the debate over changing Carson's name was in progress, Springfield Township and adjoining Whitemarsh Township were experiencing a tremendous housing boom, with parallel increases in population. Sleepy Flourtown was changing almost overnight into a busy suburban community very different from the place that Elsa Ueland had first seen in 1916, or that she knew in 1939, when she had lamented the absence of community planning in the local area. Although there are no reliable population figures for Flourtown itself, Springfield Township, to which Flourtown belonged, had grown from 5,500 in 1930 to 6,400 in 1940, and to an estimated 8,000 in 1948.[9] During 1947 alone the township issued building permits for new construction worth $3,237,000.[10]

A half dozen years later, in August 1953, a local weekly newspaper known as the *Herald* reported that a record number of building permits had been issued in Springfield Township the month before, amounting to nearly $450,000 in projected real estate. School enrollments rose apace, spurred by both the baby and housing booms: in the fall of 1953, 280 more pupils enrolled in the township's school district than had the year before, for a total of 2,596. In order to cope with the rising tide, the township had awarded contracts for a new high school the preceding February, to be built on Paper Mill Road, a little more than two miles east of the Carson campus. Even two-centuries-old St. Thomas Episcopal Church out on Bethlehem Pike, which a number of Carson children had attended over the years, had to expand its physical plant and parking facilities in 1953.[11]

In order to take advantage of growing markets in the new suburbs, investors raced to build shopping centers. In September 1952 the *Herald* announced that a shopping center had opened in the Springfield Township community of Oreland (just east of Flourtown). Three years later the same newspaper reported the grand opening of the Flourtown Shopping Center at the southeast corner of Bethlehem Pike and East Mill Road, only a block or two north of the Carson grounds.[12]

Not to be left out of the process, Carson again decided to investigate the possibility of some kind of real estate development on its property almost as soon as the war was over. Thus, at the board meeting of January 22, 1946, just four and a half months after the formal Japanese surrender had ended World War II, Otto Mallery (who was now chairman of the Carson board) proposed that the institution again explore the possibility of building rental houses on its land. The board assented, and in July it engaged the services of Eugene Henry Klaber, of Columbia University's School of Architecture, to undertake a feasibility study.[13]

There were several reasons for returning to the idea of building rental housing at Carson. One of these was financial. At a time of postwar inflation, income from the Carson estate was not keeping up with expenses. During the fiscal year 1946–47, for example, the total operating expenses were $95,600, as opposed to an income of $87,000, resulting in a deficit, which had to be made up by taking funds from the accumulated-income (or reserve) fund.[14] At the time, most of the estate funds were invested in U.S. government bonds, which were yielding about 2½ percent annually. Rental income from houses built on the Carson property, it was thought, might produce a real income far greater than this—in the range of 4 to 5 percent.[15] Mallery, for one, also believed that putting up such housing might be a first step toward moving Carson to a new campus further out from the city, where the land was much cheaper and suburban encroachment less advanced. This move might occur, he proposed, in about twenty years. By that time the entire Carson property would have been given over to residential housing, having been accomplished in several stages.[16]

In addition to taking advantage of the current housing shortage and the surge of population into the suburbs, it is certain in this case that the board was thinking of Dr. Woodward's rental properties on the west side of Chestnut Hill as something of a model, since the subject of the Woodward houses came up at board meetings as well as in correspondence.[17] Elsa Ueland, on the other hand, continued to hearken back to progressive concepts of modest, practical housing and to the Resettlement Administration's experiments in West Virginia and the Greenbelt towns developed under the same agency. She even obtained photographs of the Greenbelt developments from the Federal Public Housing Authority in Washington.[18] Thus Ueland saw Carson's rental development as more than just a money-making scheme. In a memorandum dated May 25, 1946, she wrote, "We would not wish to build without securing the advantages of out-of-the-city living—[such] as sun, trees, grass, no traffic hazard for children, playgrounds, open spaces, outlook."[19] Always the reformer, Ueland doubtless hoped that any housing project at Carson would serve as a model to private developers.

Ueland's views, rather than Mallery's, received emphasis in the report issued by Henry Klaber in January 1947. Indeed, one suspects that Ueland herself made sure to insinuate her ideas, and especially those about connecting Carson girls with the surrounding neighborhood. According to Klaber himself, Ueland had related "something of her efforts to avoid a sense of isolation on the part of the girls and give them a feeling of belonging to the local community." Moving the institution from Flourtown, he continued, "would mean that all this would go by the board and have to be started again in an environment conceivably less favorable."[20]

Although the trustees of the Carson estate were cool at first toward the idea of putting up houses on the Carson grounds, they eventually came around to the idea of lending the necessary money from estate funds. Most of the legal details were worked out between Shippen Lewis and officers of the Land Title Bank and Trust Company (as it was now known), which continued to manage the Carson trust.[21] The fact that Lewis had long been a close personal friend of Percy C. Madeira Jr., who was now president of the trust company, no doubt helped to smooth the way in these negotiations.[22]

Because of unsettled conditions in the building trades, and also because of protracted negotiations between the Carson board and the Carson estate trustees, the way was not clear to build until 1950.[23] In the meantime, Carson ordered more studies and feasibility reports.[24] There was considerable debate over just how many housing units to put up and where to locate them. Numbers ranged from a high of 342 units, according to one plan, to a low of 28 in another. Several of the plans called for a row of retail shops along Bethlehem Pike, likewise to be rented by Carson, on the strip that it owned to the south of Orchard Cottage.[25] Then there were debates over the best location for the residential units, with Carson's frontage along Wissahickon Avenue or that along West Mill Road being the two main alternatives.[26] During these years just after the war there was also some thought of selling certain pieces of Carson land, then estimated to be worth about $2,000 per acre, but this idea was rejected in favor of real estate development, which would theoretically produce more income over the years than land sales alone.[27]

The board authorized the search for an architect in April 1948, but took no action until the trustees of the Carson estate agreed to lend the necessary funds in early 1950.[28] Then Otto Mallery, as he had back in 1939, approached Frank Lloyd Wright about taking on the project, and in April 1946 the Carson board toured one of the Suntop houses that Wright had designed for Mallery over in Ardmore.[29] But the fees and other conditions demanded by Wright, who was now one of the most famous architects in the world, was doubtless the main reason why Carson did not offer him the commission.[30] Mallery then sent a query to Pope Barney, who agreed to take on the project and who received board approval as architect for the proposed development. By this time the development scheme had been scaled down to a dozen multiunit structures, in large part because of rising costs. These would be built on a five-acre tract along Wissahickon Avenue just east of the Carson entrance and slightly south of Upper Beech Cottage.[31]

Urging Carson to move ahead on the plan to put up rental housing was a new board member, Lawrence M. C. Smith (1902–75), elected in early 1949.[32] Smith was married to Eleanor Houston Smith, a granddaughter of Henry Howard Houston, who had begun the planned community on the west side of Chestnut Hill that featured rental housing. Eleanor Smith was also a niece-in-law of Dr. George Woodward, who had extended Houston's rental development in the early twentieth century. In early 1950, the Henry Howard Houston estate, of which Eleanor was an heir, had just begun a massive housing development called Andorra in the Roxborough section of Philadelphia, with plans to build dwellings for sale, as well as for rent. By circulating an article on the Andorra development that appeared in the Philadelphia *Bulletin,* Smith pointedly brought this project to the attention of Elsa Ueland and the Carson board.[33] He might also have pointed to yet another rental development being planned by others in the extended Houston family—the descendants of Sallie Houston Henry—on the west side of Chestnut Hill. Built on the Henrys' fifty-acre Stonehurst estate, the development was called Cherokee and featured some fifteen structures that included both "townhouses" and small apartments. The Cherokee complex was designed by Oscar Stonorov, who had been mentioned back in 1946 by the Carson board as a possible architect for its own development.[34] In any case, Smith was well aware of the feasibility of constructing rental developments in the immediate area.

Smith, an attorney, had left his practice in Philadelphia to work for the Home Owner's Loan Corporation and had become an enthusiastic New Dealer. He later would become an active member of Philadelphia's chapter of Americans for Democratic Action (ADA). Smith is also remembered as the founder of Philadelphia's classical-music radio station, WFLN-FM. Doubtless this interest in classical music, combined with his liberal credentials and activities as a New Dealer, made Smith very sympathetic to Elsa Ueland's bent for reform and desire to create a special residential development at Carson. That both Ueland and Smith were members of the ADA was yet another connection between the two of them.[35]

With new enthusiasm kindled in part by Smith, all seemed ready for Carson to proceed with its housing project in the summer of 1950. But the Korean War broke out in June of that year, and material shortages soon brought the housing project to a halt.[36] Once again external events forced Carson to alter its plans, this time until the Korean War ended in July 1953. Indeed, it was early 1954 before Carson resumed its development plans in earnest.

When serious discussion recommenced in January 1954, the scheme had to be scaled back, because of increased costs, to just four structures, each containing four units of varying sizes, with a total price for the four buildings not to exceed $200,000. Rents were projected to range from $80 to $100 per month. Although small compared to what had been envisioned originally, the board believed that this modest undertaking might be a first step toward a far larger development on the Carson grounds.[37]

With such projections in mind, the board decided to retain Pope Barney as the architect for this scaled-down version. In his correspondence with Barney, Otto Mallery insisted over and over again that the units must be designed in a "contemporary" style, a demand to which the architect agreed in principle, though it is unclear just what he understood by contemporary design, for detailed drawings were never made. The reason this time was Carson's failure to obtain the necessary zoning variances from Springfield Township, bringing the whole project again to a halt.[38]

In order to build the multiple units that Barney and the board envisioned, Carson had to apply for a zoning variance from the Residential-A designation that Springfield Township had applied to the area along Wissahickon Avenue, where Carson proposed to build. According to the township's zoning ordinance, passed in 1940, this meant that lots could not be less than 12,500 square feet, with no structure erected thereon to cover more than 20 percent of the property. Furthermore, the Residential-A classification prohibited multiple-unit dwellings.[39] On September 20, 1954, the Zoning Board of Adjustment of Springfield Township rejected Carson's request for a variance that would allow them to build multiple-unit housing on the Wissahickon Avenue plot.[40] Citing hardship, Carson appealed the decision to the Common Pleas Court of Montgomery County, but the court sustained the township in a decision handed down on April 28, 1955.[41] Nine years of planning and waiting had met with defeat.

It is likely that the small rental development, had it gone through, would have paid its own way, and even would have produced a modest income for Carson. Since the location was every bit as attractive and accessible as those of the highly successful rental developments built by various members of the Houston/Woodward families in nearby Chestnut Hill, there is no reason to suppose that Carson would have had trouble finding responsible, paying tenants. Yet any large-scale housing development at Carson would have destroyed the striking visual effect created by Albert Kelsey's landscape designs, and most certainly would have been lamented a generation later by historic preservationists. An ambitious housing development at Carson would also have marred one of the largest open spaces on the borders of a major city anywhere in the nation. For Carson's open spaces blend almost imperceptibly into the Philadelphia Cricket Club's golf course, the Widener/Dixon farm, and Fort Washington State Park (all on the Montgomery County side of the city limits), and also connect (on the city side) with the Morris Arboretum, Chestnut Hill College, and Fairmount Park. (Given Carson's own renaissance as a residential child-care facility just a decade later, it is fortunate that the institution did not develop large parcels of land in the 1950s.)

In any event, by the time the courts had ruled against the housing project in 1955, Carson had found other ways to raise income and balance its budgets. One of these was by enlarging its admissions policies still further. Accordingly, in early 1946 Ueland had renewed her long-standing desire to admit boys to Carson. Believing from the very beginning that an institution with both boys and girls would provide a more normal and more realistic atmosphere for the Carson children, she now emphasized that allowing boys to enter would enlarge the pool of applicants. Her idea was to admit the brothers of Carson girls as full-time residents, rather than as mere summer visitors, as had been done since the early 1940s. Her official justification was that by admitting brothers Carson would be able to keep siblings together, thus helping to maintain a vital family link, whereas by refusing to admit the brothers of girls it admitted, Carson in essence participated in the rupture of families. As with the decisions back in 1939 to admit half orphans, as well as girls who were younger than six or older than ten, Carson did not seek an official court order to break the Carson will, but simply submitted a brief to the Montgomery County Court that explained why the action seemed justified. The first brothers, five in all, entered Carson in the fall of 1947.[42]

Ueland proposed in early 1947 that Carson, besides admitting brothers, should open itself to children with parents (or other relatives) who were interested in continuing to have contact with the children but who, for any number of reasons, were not in any position to assume full responsibility for them. Since children in foster homes were prevented as a rule from seeing their original families, Carson could provide a necessary and much appreciated service.[43] Indeed, as early as 1925, Ueland had proposed in a professional address that the child who was without a single connection to any family member probably should not be placed in an institution, but was better off in a foster home, where he or she could experience some semblance of real family life. Institutions like Carson, on the other hand, were better for children who had some kinship ties, however tenuous, that could be nurtured through visits and thereby kept alive over the years.[44] Included in this category during the post–World War II period, Ueland believed, were the children of single parents whose work might keep them from caring for their children but who could afford to pay Carson some part of the children's expenses each month. During the late 1940s an unknown number of parents did in fact pay modest "tuitions" to Carson.[45]

Moreover, an increasing number of children—largely girls—were bound over to Carson from the juvenile courts. These "difficult teen age girls," as they were described in the board minutes of May 26, 1952, brought revenue to Carson in the form of board payments from the counties.

Troubled teens, in addition to half orphans, brothers, and children who were placed in Carson by parents themselves, allowed the institution to grow in the postwar years.

Another option for Carson, that of seeking some way to admit children of African American ancestry, was discussed and rejected in the fall of 1944. The impetus behind this discussion was a request from the Philadelphia Council of Social Agencies that Carson "consider the admission of Negro girls." However, it was the opinion of the management committee of the Carson board that Flourtown, with its overwhelmingly white population, would not offer a suitable atmosphere "for Negro girls [to have] a successful and happy life."[46]

Because of new admissions policies, even though these did not include African Americans, Carson rebounded with a peak enrollment during the postwar period of eighty-six children in the spring of 1947, a figure that was probably due in some degree to a high divorce rate and other disruptions in family life immediately after the war. In the early 1950s enrollments averaged in the high seventies and then fell to around sixty-five during the middle of the decade.[47] (As a reflection of Carson's improved health, Ueland's salary was raised in April 1951 to $6,500 a year.)[48] This gradual decline in numbers during the 1950s, despite Carson's relaxation of admissions policies, paralleled what was happening in similar institutions throughout the nation as aid to dependent children and increasing emphasis upon foster care eroded enrollments.[49]

In any case, the children being cared for at Carson by the middle 1950s were far different from those who had come to the institution thirty or thirty-five years before. As Ueland remarked at a board meeting on April 15, 1957, "[N]ot one of these children was sent to Carson under the age of 10, with father and mother both deceased," as had been directed by the Carson will. She noted further that not one of them had come from families in which both parents were living together: "They have all come from broken homes,—homes broken for many reasons."[50]

Carson had thus gone far beyond the initial guidelines set forth by Robert Carson a half century before. Changing social and demographic conditions had forced Carson to adapt in order to survive as an institution dedicated to the care of needy children. This successful adaptation, in addition to a growing national economy, had allowed Carson to regain some degree of financial health during the postwar period. Between 1948 and 1957 the corpus (or book value) of the Carson estate increased from $1,863,560 to $1,949,081. More important, the net annual income from the trust rose during the same time from $43,000 to $75,000. In 1957 board payments of an unknown amount from the various counties brought in additional revenue, allowing Carson to show a surplus of about $5,500, which went into the accumulated-income account.[51]

Yet another sign of well-being at Carson during the postwar period was the reopening of the nursery school in the fall of 1949, after a twelve-year hiatus.[52] Directing the revived nursery school was Miss Jean MacFarland, who had first come to Carson in 1933 as a student teacher in horticulture, as part of her training at the School of Horticulture for Women in nearby Ambler. She remained at Carson as a teacher until 1936 and became a student at the Bank Street School in 1937–38. She subsequently taught at several institutions, returning to work in the summer sessions at Carson, beginning in 1946.[53]

The nursery school program was much like the old one, with stress placed upon addressing the individual needs of children through meaningful play and learning by doing.[54] The children's exposure to nature and country life likewise remained an important part of the program. According to an article in one of the local newspapers, the youngsters explored the grounds twice each week to "visit the chickens and calves [and] see the cows milked." They walked past Sherwood Forest and wondered at the "wide expanse of corn shocks, standing in sentinel formation."[55] In these ways, the revived nursery school rekindled a link to Carson's progressive tradition.

The nursery school program was immediately popular with neighborhood parents, and by the spring of 1951 there were thirty-six children enrolled. These were divided into two groups: Nursery I (three to four years old) and Nursery II (four to five years old). Annual tuition was $145.[56] As before, the nursery school basically paid its own expenses and thus brought no additional income to Carson. Rather, the board saw it as a "contribution to the community" that Carson could afford to make during the daylight hours when its resident population was off campus in the public schools.[57] Yet another contribution to the local neighborhood was an agreement, made in 1947, to rent the basement playroom of Red Gables Cottage to the Springfield Township School District for use as a public kindergarten. The school district paid Carson $600 per year in rent for the facility.[58]

During the late 1940s and early 1950s, at least, Carson continued to open its summer activities to children in the neighborhood. In the summer of 1948, for example, sixteen boys and girls from the community were among the sixty-three residents in the program.[59] Carson also continued with certain offerings that might be of interest to adults in the area, such as ten classes in "rhythmic dance and exercise," given in the Mother Goose gym during 1950–51 and taught by Alice Kraft.[60]

Given Ueland's constant emphasis over the years upon the need for cooperation between Carson and the surrounding community, she must have been pleased by the reopening of the nursery school as well as by the use of Carson facilities for a public kindergarten. Continuing attendance of the Carson children in the Springfield Township public schools was, of course, another way of maintaining these connections. In this regard, Carson made a consistent effort to help its children fit in with the other students at school.[61] To save them from being seen as "charity cases" by their classmates, the board appropriated funds so that Carson girls and boys could participate in the same extracurricular activities and social events as the other students in the local schools. In the spring of 1956, for example, the board approved a $40 contribution toward the Springfield High School senior prom.[62] For its part, the high school assured Carson that its students, some forty-four of whom attended Springfield High in 1953, could participate in any program they wished, on the same basis as the others.[63]

At the same time, Ueland and the board recognized the tremendous contribution that the community made to Carson. In October 1950, the board drew up a list of the various persons and organizations that had helped Carson during the past year. These included the public school teachers who spent extra time assisting Carson children, various clergy and Sunday school teachers, Cub Scout den mothers who had Carson boys in their groups, the Flourtown Women's Club, which gave magazine subscriptions to the Carson cottages every year for Christmas, and the Flourtown League of Women Voters, who supplied each cottage with the Sunday *New York Times*.[64] In January 1953 the board recognized the contributions of area clubs that assisted with Christmas activities at Carson, among them the Flourtown Women's Club, the Oreland Women's Club, and the Beaver College Alumni Association.[65]

Yet changing times resulted in the breaking of certain ties to the community. In the fall of 1953, for instance, the board decided to ask the local Visiting Nurse Association to relinquish its office at Carson. The reasons were inadequate parking and "jammed telephone lines." Under the circumstances, the board concluded that it was better to send truly sick children to Chestnut Hill Hospital—and to pay the $2.50 fee for a visiting-nurse call in less serious cases—than to rely on the "free" services of visiting nurses in exchange for office space.[66]

Likewise a casualty to changing times was the Carson swimming hole down on Wissahickon Creek. Since the institution opened in 1918, it had been a mainstay of the summer program and the scene of many wonderful memories for Carson girls. However, the development of land along its banks during the postwar period had resulted in much larger runoffs, with mounds of debris collecting in the swimming area during and after rain storms, in addition to longer periods of low water during dry spells. Private septic tanks and the sewage systems of several towns upstream raised the bacteria levels in the creek to dangerous levels.[67] Also threatening Carson's use of the creek for bathing was the creation of Fort Washington State Park on land that included the 6.48 acres that Carson owned between West Mill Road and the bathing site. The state of Pennsylvania, acting on behalf of the Fort Washington Park Commission, seized the property through eminent domain, in compensation for which Carson received $6,400, or approximately $1,000 per acre. Protests by the Carson board against the price, which it deemed too low, as well as against the uncompensated destruction of the Carson bathhouses, were to no avail. The demolition of the bathhouses without warning, and the removal of the wood, particularly irritated Ueland and the board, since they had planned to donate the materials for the erection of a Boy Scout cabin. However, Carson children continued to swim at the creek until the summer of 1954, when the Pennsylvania Department of Health declared it unsafe for bathing.[68]

Carson and other interested parties in the community petitioned the state to build a swimming pool at the new Fort Washington State Park, but funds were denied.[69] In 1955 the Carson board again looked into constructing its own swimming pool on campus, at an estimated cost of $10,000, but did not go ahead, because of concern over the expense of maintaining it and worries over superintending it during the summer season.[70] Instead, the Carson children traveled to various swimming facilities in the area, going back and forth in the old green bus that had been purchased in 1931.[71]

In addition to the end of bathing at the creek and the removal of the Visiting Nurse Association, the community playground on Carson property along Bethlehem Pike had declined over the years and may have ceased operation altogether by the 1950s. The dwindling of such connections to the local community marked a serious movement away from the idea of shared facilities and in this sense was yet another sign that Carson's progressive program was losing momentum.

It was in social activities and cottage life that the progressive program survived most noticeably. In these areas there was not much difference between the postwar period and the late 1930s. The children, for instance, continued to play an integral role in the cooking, cleaning, laundering, and other chores at the individual cottages. In this regard, as well as in others, the progressive emphasis upon learning through doing still pertained.

A glimpse into the realization of this progressive concept during the late 1940s can be gleaned from a record entitled "Our Fall Diary, Oct.–Nov. 1948," kept by girls then living at Mother Goose (which had been returned to partial use as a residential cottage). On Thursday, October 28, they went for a visit to Dr. George Woodward's garden on his estate, Krisheim, in Chestnut Hill. There the gardener showed them how to make a compost pile and gave them russet apples to eat. Almost three weeks later, on Tuesday, November 16, the children started their own compost pile, carting the various materials in a wheelbarrow that they had named Spunky. Another day, after school, they went out behind Mother Goose and "edged the flower garden, . . . raked the lawn, . . . put the leaves on the mulch pile, [and] made holes for the tulips."[72]

In the spring and summer months there was plenty to learn from planting and tending the vegetable gardens at each cottage, helping with the farmwork, and preserving the various fruits and vegetables that were still grown on the grounds. As early as 1948, however, the board again began to examine farm costs in order to determine if it would be cheaper to buy certain foods in local markets than to continue producing them on site.[73] They took no immediate action, but in 1952 decided to discontinue Carson's poultry operation because they could buy both eggs and chickens more cheaply from commercial suppliers.[74] The Carson dairy continued to operate, but an oversupply of milk in the region during 1949 forced Carson to obtain a license to sell milk to its Flourtown neighbors (rather than to commercial distributors alone, as in the past). This was done from the Orchard Cottage complex, which fronted on Bethlehem Pike. During the summer, the children also operated a vegetable stand from this property.[75]

Because Carson was admitting more older children than formerly, social activities began to change somewhat by the mid-1950s. In January 1955, for example, forty-eight of the Carson children were over thirteen,

Fig. 40.   Cleaning up flower beds, autumn 1941. CVS.

and only thirteen under that age. Thus the question of "dating" came up
more and more frequently. Girls under sixteen could invite boyfriends to
Mother Goose on Saturday evenings, where they danced to records in the
gym, with Cokes and pretzels as refreshments. Sixteen-year-olds had permission to go off campus on "double dates"—to the movies and for a
snack afterward. Those seventeen and over could go out alone for similar
entertainments, but had to be back at Carson by 11:30, a rule not unlike

those adopted in local households for teenage daughters and sons.[76] In addition to dates off campus, Carson invited boys from Philadelphia's Girard College, as well as Valley Forge Military Academy, to dances and other activities during the 1950s.[77]

Although Carson allowed dating according to the standards of the day, there is no evidence of any kind of sex education. Caroline Vankouwenberg, who lived at Carson throughout the 1940s, remembered that no one warned her about menstruation, and that when her first "period" came, she assumed she had somehow injured herself during a long hike. The only words of advice from her housemother were, "Be careful now; this is how bad girls get babies."[78] Nor had the situation apparently been any different in earlier years at Carson. Helen Traiche Heath, who lived at Carson

Fig. 41.   Dance in the Carson gym with boys from Valley Forge Military Academy, 1950s. CVS.

College during the 1930s, reported that she was similarly ignorant about sexual matters. She had no idea about the sexual side of marriage or of what to expect from her first pregnancy.[79]

In any case, the increasing numbers of teenagers on campus led to new worries over relations with the surrounding community. In 1947, for instance, as the institution was just beginning to accept more "troubled children" from the courts, Ueland asked the board to contemplate the impact on Flourtown, and on Springfield Township in general, of admitting "children who [have] so little of any ordinary decent 'bringing up.'"[80] A half dozen years later, in the winter of 1953, she asked the board to consider just how many "disturbed and difficult" children the local churches and schools could handle, and what Carson could do to help them fit into community life.[81]

Such children understandably made greater demands on Carson's staff. In the fall of 1954, for example, Ueland shared her worries about finding and keeping good housemothers who could cope with troubled teenage residents. One of the biggest problems facing Carson, she told the board, was "how to find capable, strong, warm-hearted, sensitive housemothers who *want* to live with adolescents, many of whom seem full of rebellion, turmoil, evasion, and ... bitterness." Continuing in this vein, she asked, "Can we find adequate staff at any price?"[82]

Ueland probably associated this problem of staffing with the retirements or deaths of many individuals who had served Carson loyally for many years. Late in 1955 housemother Salome Jackson, of Orchard Cottage, became seriously ill and had to leave. She had been a housemother since the institution formally opened in 1918.[83] Three years later, in March 1958, Miss Gratia Balsh left for Norristown State Hospital, a mental health facility, and died the following year.[84] As Carson's music teacher and director of activities, Miss Balsh had been part of the campus scene since the early 1920s, though she had often been unhappy and was increasingly disliked by the children, who had taken to calling her "Miss Belch" behind her back.[85]

The postwar period saw the passing of Samuel Pinkerton in 1946, who had begun working for Carson as chief clerk in 1916 and who in 1919 became the business manager.[86] Death came in May 1952 to Shippen Lewis, one of Carson's (and Ueland's) most active supporters since joining the board in 1928.[87] That same spring Carson's first full-time social worker, Frances Jones, decided to retire.[88] Also stepping down that spring was Phoebe Allnutt (divorced and now using her maiden name of Crosby), who had been hired in 1918 as the principal of Carson's elementary school and who in recent years had been described as a "special teacher."[89] In late 1956 Carson lost the last of its original board members when Otto Mallery, who, while walking with a letter to the mail box near his home in Chestnut Hill, was struck and killed by a car.[90] In addition to such losses through retirement and death, Hurricane Hazel, which hit the Philadelphia area very hard in October of 1954, left its mark on the Carson grounds: About seventy large trees were lost, including half the white pines and spruces in Sherwood Forest. Many other trees, especially the willows, were twisted and broken.[91]

If some doubted that an era was passing, Elsa Ueland's own resignation as head of Carson in June 1958 presented them with unmistakable proof. The absence of any personal diaries from this period makes it impossible to know just what thoughts and feelings led to the decision. She had turned seventy in March of that year and may have concluded that age alone dictated retirement. The difficult challenges presented by the girls now being admitted to Carson, many of them with serious behavioral problems, may have contributed to the decision. Also influential must have been the death a year earlier (in June 1957) of Katherine Tucker, who had shared a house with Ueland for most of her years at Carson. This loss may have prompted something of an emotional crisis for Ueland.[92]

Whatever the reasons for her "retirement," Ueland must have spent some time reflecting on the forty-two years that had passed since, as a young woman of twenty-eight, she accepted the presidency of Carson College. In response to a board request that she provide some history of her years at Carson, Ueland composed a brief, fifteen-page typewritten account that was mimeographed and circulated among board members and staff.[93] Although her name was not attached to the document per se, it is similar in format to the reports that Ueland had written over the years. Filled with numbers and charts, it was reminiscent of the investigative projects that she had carried out as a young progressive during her settlement-house days in New York.

Ueland's brief account of Carson's preceding forty-two years gave no hint of the emotional and personal drama that had unfolded in her diaries and personal letters and that was so central to her commitment to the institution. In this sense, she had drawn a sharp line between her personal and professional lives. (Even close friends and family members were generally unaware of her personal trials. As her nephew Mark Ueland put it, "Aunt Elsa was a very private person.")[94] Nor was there any suggestion in the document that it was she who had molded Carson into a model

Fig. 42.   Portrait of Elsa Ueland, oil on canvas, by Alden M.
Wicks, 1961. CVS.

progressive institution, who had seen it through its darkest days during
the Great Depression of the 1930s, and who had found "a way through" to
health and a renewed sense of purpose in the postwar era.

Ueland's resignation from the leadership of Carson came just three
years after the final collapse of the Progressive Education Association in
1955 and one year after the disappearance of the association's journal, *Progressive Education.* The progressive-education movement, as a cohesive
and organized effort, had long been in difficulty. The domination of the
Progressive Education Association during the 1930s by advanced social
reformers, some of them with Marxist leanings, had taken it too far to the

Left for most American educators. Against the backdrop of the Cold War of the late 1940s and 1950s the association appeared subversive to various segments of the population. At the same time, a more widespread conservatism in the United States led many parents and voters to demand a return to "the basics" in education, which often meant a concentration on the learning of certain facts and skills in academic subjects.[95]

Ueland's old friend Alice Barrows was one of these so-called radicals of the latter-day progressive-education movement. Barrows had become an enthusiastic New Dealer and in 1934 had broken off all relations with her old mentor William Wirt, who had become increasingly conservative over the years. In the 1930s she vigorously opposed Congressman Martin Dies and his House Un-American Activities Committee and was a member of the executive committee of the Washington, D. C., chapter of the radical American League for Peace and Democracy. A decade later she become involved with a number of organizations with alleged ties to the Communist Party and was herself called before the Internal Security Subcommittee of the U.S. Senate in 1953, just a year before her death, where she took the Fifth Amendment upon being asked if she were a Communist.[96]

As time would show, many of the ideas and practices of progressive education survived such association with radicalism, along with charges that it lacked intellectual substance and academic discipline. Indeed, certain progressive ideas had become so much a part of the American school curriculum that they were taken for granted and were not even linked with progressive education by wide sectors of the public, including many professional educators.

Elsa Ueland's years as head of the Carson College for Orphan Girls and of the Carson Valley School had coincided in many ways with the rise and decline of the progressive-education movement. She had also lived through two great reform periods in the nation's history, the progressive era of the early twentieth century and the New Deal of the 1930s. In just a few years both she and the Carson Valley School would live through yet a third major reform movement of the century, which corresponded with what many Americans would simply call "the sixties." In the process, the legacy of progressivism would survive here and there at Carson and find some new channels of expression.

CHAPTER SEVEN

A
PROGRESSIVE
LEGACY

By the time Elsa Ueland stepped down as president of the Carson Valley School, it had ceased to be a traditional orphanage and was very much on its way to becoming an institution for what were being called "dependent and neglected children."[1] Yet certain elements of the old progressive philosophy and practice had remained a real part of residential life. Ueland herself continued to serve on the board of trustees until 1967, and thereafter remained a distinct presence in the Flourtown neighborhood until her death in 1980. By then she had become something of a legend at Carson, a status that would persist after her death as staff members continued to pass on stories about her and to speculate whether she would have approved the new directions in which Carson was moving as the twentieth century was nearing a close.

There were other continuities as well. Carson persisted in seeking ways to interact with its Flourtown neighbors and in pursuing plans for developing its land, though these plans were largely unsuccessful. After some confusion and hesitation during the years after Ueland's retirement, the institution resumed its adjustment to changing times. In the process, however, Carson made a major departure by altering its policies to admit children regardless of their racial or ethnic backgrounds, including African Americans. During this same period the Carson Valley School began admitting boys and girls on an equal basis, rather than enrolling only boys who were brothers of Carson girls, as had been the practice since the late 1940s.

During the 1980s Carson began to move into neighborhood-based child-care programs. These were partly in response to an intensified opposition to institutions within child-welfare and mental health circles, and partly in response to the need of public agencies to cut costs in a more conservative era of American life. This same cost-cutting program, combined with an ongoing anti-institutional movement, meant that those children who resided at Carson were staying for less and less time.

Unlike the genuine orphans of the past, who were generally judged to be "normal" and who entered at a young age and spent years at Carson, most residents at the end of the twentieth century suffered from a variety of emotional problems and learning disabilities. Such difficulties, combined with shorter and shorter stays at the institution (during which diagnosis and treatment were administered), forced Carson to reopen its own school on campus, after a hiatus of nearly fifty years.

The curriculum in Carson's new school, as well as the organization of cottage life, was no longer expressly rooted in the progressivism of a John Dewey or a William Wirt, but in behavioral and cognitive psychology, which held out the possibility of altering behavior patterns over a brief time span and of helping youngsters to take conscious responsibility for their own well-being. Yet to the extent that Carson tried to prepare its boys and girls to cope with practical challenges in the real world, its progressive traditions lived on in new ways.

Taking charge of Carson upon the retirement of Elsa Ueland was Dorothy "Dot" Moore (Fenstermacher). Born in 1912 in the nearby village of Broad Axe, Moore grew up at several locations in Montgomery County. She graduated from Ambler High School and Landsdale Business School, and first came to work at Carson as a bookkeeper in 1930.[2] By 1947 she had advanced to the position of business manager and assistant to the president.[3] In addition to her work in the business office, Moore took a personal interest in the Carson children almost from the beginning of her employment, and for many years ran a Sunday afternoon recreation program for the girls. She also superintended the older girls who lived and worked in households off campus.[4]

Moore's many years at Carson had given her much insight into the workings of the institution, and over that time she had taken several courses in social work at Temple University. She and Ueland were also well acquainted, Moore having been a regular visitor at Oak Run and a longtime member of the "Carson family."[5] In these circumstances Ueland asked Moore to succeed her as head of the institution when she stepped

Fig. 43.   Dorothy "Dot" Moore Fenstermacher, Carson's second executive director. Photo by Harold G. Fenstermacher, 1950. Courtesy of Dorothy and Harold Fenstermacher.

down in 1958, and the board affirmed her appointment. However, Moore would be known as executive director rather than as president, which had been Ueland's official designation since 1916 but which had become less appropriate after the name Carson College was discontinued just after World War II.[6] The designation of Ueland's successor thus must have seemed a good occasion on which to drop the title of president in exchange for that of executive director.

Despite the change in title, Moore does not seem to have been given any mandate to move Carson in new directions. According to Ueland herself, Moore "continued" with policies that were already in place. But as the years went by, it was clear to Ueland, other members of the board, and Moore herself that the Carson Valley School would have to undergo a major reorientation in order to meet the changing needs of children. In Ueland's words, "Carson was being asked to accept . . . more and more difficult children where intensive social case work—and possibly psychiatric treatment also—was needed for both child and parent."[7] There was also the matter of declining enrollments, with the numbers ranging between forty and fifty during the early 1960s.[8] After serious discussion with a delegation from the board, Moore herself concluded that she was not the person to institute new directions at Carson, and she submitted her resignation in February 1964.[9]

The situation that Carson faced in the mid-1960s should be understood within the context of larger cultural forces at work in the nation—and in the region as a whole. After a decade and a half of relative conservatism following World War II, the United States now entered another age of reform that is associated most of all with the Great Society programs of U.S. president Lyndon B. Johnson. Among Johnson's most dramatic initiatives was his War on Poverty and his sponsorship of broad civil rights legislation, which banned racial discrimination and ensured voting rights for all Americans.[10] At the same time—and somewhat ironically—many young people became disillusioned with their country and joined what has come to be known as the counterculture, a rebellion against middle-class values and traditional forms of authority.[11] The civil rights revolution would have a profound impact on Carson, and even the counterculture would make its presence known in certain ways at the school.

Among the changes closer to home were significant demographic shifts in the Philadelphia region, including Flourtown itself. The city of Philadelphia, after reaching a peak population of just over 2 million in 1950, consistently lost inhabitants during the next four decades and in 1990 stood at just under 1.6 million, for a net loss of 20 percent. In the process, Philadelphia fell from third largest city in the nation to fifth. While the city itself was shrinking, the entire region (defined as Philadelphia and the nine surrounding counties in Pennsylvania and New Jersey) continued to grow—from approximately 3.8 million in 1950 to about 5.2 million in 1990, for an increase of 37 percent.[12] Though Philadelphia lost both population and jobs during this period to the surrounding suburbs, it also suffered from competition with the southern and western regions of the United States—the so-called Sun Belt states—which provided better job opportunities and often a milder climate than southeastern Pennsylvania. Thus Philadelphians could no longer boast that their city was the "workshop to the world," as they had when Carson College opened in 1918, when jobs of almost every description for the skilled and unskilled alike were plentiful. Thus what had once been the industrial heart of the city was increasingly a desolate landscape, with hundreds of empty factories and mills, their windows smashed and walls covered with layers of ugly graffiti.

As Philadelphia lost population overall, it received substantial numbers of newcomers, many of them African Americans from the South who came in search of jobs and a better way of life. From just 11 percent of the population in 1930, African Americans made up 40 percent of the city's inhabitants in 1990.[13] Besides having to suffer the stings of racial prejudice, African Americans, arriving in Philadelphia at a time when the city's employment opportunities were declining, especially for those without advanced education and skills, faced economic uncertainty. Because of such conditions, African American families were badly stressed, with the result that growing numbers of their children needed help from the child-welfare system.

In contrast, Carson's own community of Flourtown continued to share in the region's postwar suburban expansion. At the time of this writing, census figures on Flourtown were not available for 1960, since the actual manuscript census, due to privacy considerations, would not be released for several more decades. However, census tracts, which were introduced in 1970, do provide something of a demographic profile for Flourtown in that year. Tract 2103, which includes all of Flourtown, along with a relatively small portion of surrounding Springfield Township, reveals that Carson's neighboring community contained 4,466 people in 1970. This is more than ten times the number who were counted in the somewhat smaller area designated as Flourtown in the 1920 manuscript census.

Although the 1970 tract does not include any information on occupations, it does report that median family income was $14,321 (as compared to $9,867 in the United States as a whole), thereby demonstrating that Flourtown was much more of a middle-middle- and upper-middle-class community in 1970 than it had been fifty years before.[14] Yet in other respects Flourtown had changed very little between 1920 and 1970: Its population remained overwhelmingly white, with just 65 persons (or 1.5 percent) classified as Negro (compared to 2 percent in 1920). The vast majority of local residents were still listed as native-born Americans, only 236, or 5.3 percent, being of foreign birth (as opposed to 11 percent of 1920's Flourtowners who had been born outside the United States).[15]

Twenty years later, in 1990, the picture had not changed substantially: The total population of the Flourtown census tract had declined somewhat to 3,846 people, largely (it would appear) because of an end to the postwar baby boom. Supporting this conclusion was the fact that the average number of persons per household had declined from 3.39 in 1970 to 2.50 in 1990, at the same time that the median age of Flourtowners increased by nearly a decade. Yet Flourtown remained an overwhelmingly white middle-class community. Median family income was now $49,718 (in contrast to $35,353 nationwide and to $27,000 in Philadelphia). African Americans were slightly fewer in absolute terms—62 in 1990 as opposed to 65 in 1970—but because the total population of the tract had declined, they now represented 1.6 percent of the total, a minuscule difference by any standard. The number of foreign-born was slightly higher, at 263, or 6.8 percent (though lower than in 1920).[16]

Back in the 1920s Elsa Ueland had asserted more than once that the families of Flourtown, then of very modest means, could provide Carson girls with a realistic view of the kinds of lives they themselves might know as adults. Those who led Carson after 1960, however, would have to face the prospect that children now entering the institution might find few similarities between Flourtown and the neighborhoods they had left behind—or between the lives of Flourtown's suburban families and the kinds of lives they could expect in the future.

Facing such realities was a new executive director, F. Herbert Barnes, engaged by the board in the spring of 1964 to replace Dorothy Moore. Born in 1926 in nearby Cheltenham Township, Barnes had earned a bachelor's degree in English from the University of Pennsylvania, with the intention of going on to law school. However, a job on the farm at Carson during the summer of 1948 resulted in a change of plans. At the end of the season, farm manager Bill Goss recommended Barnes to Elsa Ueland as a part-time recreation assistant for several afternoons a week during his senior year at Penn. Barnes became deeply interested in the work, and eventually asked Ueland how he could prepare himself for a career in child welfare. He followed her initial advice to obtain further education from the Bank Street School and then went on to earn a master's degree in social work (M.S.W.) from the University of Pennsylvania.[17]

Barnes's first position after graduate school was as a teacher at the Poughkeepsie Day School, which was affiliated with the highly acclaimed Child Study Department of Vassar College. He then became a caseworker at the Pennsylvania Training School at Canonsburg, run by the Pennsylvania Department of Welfare. In 1958 he left Canonsburg for the Children's Aid Society of Pennsylvania, with offices on South Juniper Street in

Fig. 44.   F. Herbert Barnes (far left), Carson's third executive director, posing with members of the Wyndmoor Women's Club (and unidentified man on right), Christmas 1965. CVS.

Philadelphia. There he worked in the society's foster-care section, where he developed a special program to train foster parents to care for emotionally disturbed children. He left Children's Aid in 1960 to become clinical director of the Wallingford Home in Wallingford, Pennsylvania. According to Barnes, the Carson board had asked him to consider becoming codirector of Carson several years before he actually took the position in 1964, but he had turned down the offer at the time, concluding that he lacked the necessary experience.[18]

In Herbert Barnes, Carson thus found a person with the academic background and experience that were necessary for the challenges that lay ahead. At the same time, they secured someone who had a history with Carson and had been inspired by Elsa Ueland herself to pursue a career in social work and child care. With Barnes, Carson would have a genuine link between past and present.

Among Barnes's early challenges at Carson as executive director was the whole question of racial integration. Collaborating with him on the matter was Carson board member Anderson Page, who was also closely associated with the institution's past. A son-in-law of Shippen Lewis, as well as a resident of Chestnut Hill, Page (1915–94) had taken his place on the board in 1952 just after Lewis's death.[19] Like Shippen Lewis, Page was an accomplished Philadelphia attorney. Of further interest, given Carson's progressive heritage, was the fact that Page was a grandson of Walter Hines Page (1855–1918). Though best known as Woodrow Wilson's controversial ambassador to Great Britain during World War I, Walter Hines Page had made a distinguished career as a progressive journalist and publisher before joining the Wilson administration and had taken a special interest in educational reform.[20] Just what this heritage may have meant to Anderson Page is unknown, but he might well have taken pride in realizing that reform activity was very much in the family tradition.

Reinforcing this family commitment to reform was Page's wife, Louise Lewis Page (1921–76), a daughter of Shippen Lewis and herself a community activist and reformer, who joined her husband as a member of the Carson board in 1963.[21] Louise, along with several other members of her family, had been much involved with settlement-house work in Philadelphia. Louise's aunt, Ellen Bradford, had founded the city's Lighthouse Settlement, and Louise herself had established a federation of settlements there. She was also instrumental in founding Women's Way, an organization for assisting women. (Louise's grandmother Dora Kelly Lewis had been a leading suffragist and a high officer of the American National Women's Suffrage Association.)[22]

In his capacity as a lawyer, Anderson Page directed the legal work on integration at Carson, with research assistance from Herbert Riband, then a young attorney in Page's firm who would go on to become an active Carson board member (as well as a future chairman of the board) several years later. Strong support for integration also came from Carson board president Robert L. Bast. Rather than attempt to break the Carson will through legal action, Page merely informed the Orphans Court of Montgomery County of what action the Carson board intended to take. When no objections were forthcoming from the court, the board proceeded with its plans.[23]

Carson's decision to integrate was made within the context of several national and local events. Of utmost importance was the Civil Rights Act, passed by the U.S. Congress in 1964, which forbade racial discrimination in all public accommodations. Agencies and institutions that did not integrate stood to lose their public funding. Although the Carson Valley School was a private agency, it received public funds from the federal, state, and municipal governments, and it undoubtedly served a public system of child welfare. Herbert Barnes and the Carson board were therefore concerned that a failure to integrate would lead to a loss of certain public funds and ultimately, perhaps, to a refusal by the counties to send any children at all to the school, with disastrous consequences for an already worrisome enrollment picture at the institution.[24] Furthermore, Carson was urged to reconsider its policy of not accepting "Negro children" at a meeting with representatives from public child-welfare administrations, held on the grounds in September 1964.[25]

Also pertinent was the case of Philadelphia's Girard College, which was then refusing to admit African American children, citing the Stephen Girard will, which had restricted the institution to white boys. After much protest, including demonstrations at the Girard campus and protracted legal battles, both the Pennsylvania and U.S. Supreme Courts ordered Girard to desegregate.[26] It is to Carson's credit that it avoided such a struggle and sought to integrate voluntarily.

More important than any of these considerations, as Herbert Barnes reflected three decades later, the Carson board believed that integration was the right thing to do.[27] Accordingly, the board's resolution, adopted on June 7, 1965, read in part:

> Whereas, it is the conviction of the Board . . . that the accident of
> birth or national origin, being an Act of Divine Creation, must not
> be made the basis for discrimination between human beings, and
> against a background of advancing and changing social, educa-
> tional and cultural philosophy. . . as reflected and evidenced by
> policy statements, Federal and local legislation and in the deci-
> sions of Federal and state courts . . . , be it hereby resolved that it
> is and shall be the policy of the Board of Directors . . . that [the
> Carson Valley School] be managed, maintained, and administered,
> with specific reference to the admission or enrollment qualifica-
> tions of any child who can be served thereby, without regard to
> race, color or creed.[28]

The first African American housemother was hired in 1966, and the
first black children (four little girls) were admitted to Carson in April
1967.[29] Yet integration proceeded slowly. One reason was a board decision to admit only young black children initially, those six or eight years
of age, in the belief that members of the local community would not per-
ceive them as being as much of a threat as black teenagers.[30] Another
reason was director Barnes's belief that Carson had to prepare itself carefully to meet the needs of African American children.[31]

Barnes's explanation was reiterated by Natline Thornton, a longtime
staff member at Carson and herself an African American. According to her,
there was no rapid increase in the number of black children at the school
because the institution was not prepared to handle the everyday needs of
this new population—to provide, for example, familiar kinds of food.
Knowing of these difficulties, some child-welfare authorities in Philadelphia, according to Thornton, were themselves reluctant to send African
American children to Carson, where they might feel out of place.[32] Carson overcame these concerns by the mid-1970s, at which time the pace
of integration quickened considerably. By the late 1980s the majority of
children at Carson were black, and in 1988 they made up 66 percent of
the residential population.[33]

In addition to facing the realities of the civil rights movement and the
growing need of African American children for Carson's services, director
Barnes, the board, and their successors had to confront a mounting opposition to institutional care within the child-welfare community. This attitude had existed since early in the century, as evidenced by statements

Fig. 45.   Car wash, Thistle Cottage, 1991. CVS.

from the White House Conference on the Care of Dependent Children back in 1909. But in the atmosphere of the 1960s, with its emphasis on civil rights and individual freedom, custodial institutions of all kinds—and especially mental health facilities—came under blistering attack. Leading the charge against such institutions was a book by Erving Goffman entitled *Asylums,* first published in 1959.[34] Works of fiction, like Ken Kesey's *One Flew over the Cuckoo's Nest* (1962), later made into a movie of the same name, reinforced the anti-institutional movement. These criticisms, combined with more effective drug therapies for a variety of mental illnesses, led to an emptying of traditional facilities for the mentally ill throughout the United States. In the same spirit, there was renewed criticism of institutional child care, which culminated in federal legislation known as the 1980 Adoption Assistance and Child Welfare Act. In one of its provisions, the law stipulated that children should be placed in "the least restrictive (most family-like) setting available."[35]

It would take the Carson Valley School a number of years to adapt to such new and constantly shifting circumstances. More immediately, director Herbert Barnes had to face a genuine crisis in enrollment upon assuming his duties in April of 1964, when there were only about thirty-five residents at Carson.[36] At the time of his hiring, the board told Barnes that they wanted him to try to turn the institution around without adopting a wholly psychiatric approach to child care, an approach then being adopted by many other institutions like Carson. While not rejecting psychological insights and treatment, the board wanted to continue with its emphasis upon a total living experience where all aspects of the child's life would be considered important to his or her well-being.[37]

Barnes launched into this project soon after he arrived, setting forth the challenges to Carson and proposing solutions in a number of meetings, reports, and planning documents. Indeed, Barnes's first step after taking up his duties was to initiate a self-study, resulting in what he called the two Community Survey Meetings, held on July 20 and September 21, 1964. These gatherings included representatives from public child-welfare agencies in Philadelphia and surrounding counties.[38]

Barnes combined the suggestions that emerged from the two meetings with his own extensive readings on child welfare to produce a planning document in January 1965.[39] In his opening paragraph he quoted from a recent report of the Child Welfare League of America on the broad social changes affecting child care in the United States:

> Major changes have occurred in the country's social and economic life and major progress has been made in understanding human development. . . . Advances in medical knowledge have almost eliminated the conditions which resulted in orphanhood for many children. . . . Basic shifts in concepts of governmental responsibility[,] represented primarily by the Social Security Act[,] have reduced financial need as a reason for child care outside their own homes. . . . Most children who must be cared for outside their own homes . . . come from families characterized by divorce, separation, marital discord, and the physical and mental breakdown of parents. . . . In addition to physical care [such children] often require extensive treatment of their emotional ills and [their] parents require help to restore the family to normal functioning.[40]

Later in his report Barnes observed that such conditions had been evolving for quite some time, and cited the observations that Elsa Ueland had made back in 1937 in her analysis of Carson that she had entitled "The Dilemma." It was Carson's task, Barnes concluded, to respond to the changing needs of children in the contemporary world, and he suggested several new programs that might meet these needs. Included in his list were "[r]esidential diagnosis, group care for 'normal' children, half-way houses for children returning from hospitals and training schools, adolescent group homes, [an] intensive treatment unit, [a] vocational training program, [and] special education services."[41] While none was put into effect immediately, some of these programs would be implemented at Carson, though often otherwise than originally envisioned, over the next quarter century. In spelling out how Carson might meet the emerging needs of children in a practical, pragmatic manner, Barnes wrote and spoke much in the spirit of John Dewey and other progressive educators and reformers from earlier in the century—or of Elsa Ueland herself, who remained an active member of the Carson board at the time. (Though Ueland was much appreciated, Barnes sometimes found her presence at board meetings unnerving, since all eyes would move in her direction whenever a question came up, as if to acknowledge that no discussion could really end until she had offered her opinion. Dorothy Moore Fenstermacher, who preceded Barnes as director, had sometimes found Ueland's continued membership on the board to be similarly intimidating.)[42] In Barnes's case, at least, Ueland realized that her presence at meetings posed difficulties for the director and explained to him that she would remain on the board only until he had established himself firmly as director. This having been accomplished, she stepped down from the board in 1967.[43]

Before putting any of the new programs into place, Barnes had to deal with considerable disarray in the Carson cottages. Although a few of the traditional housemothers remained, it was increasingly difficult to find the sorts of widowed or divorced women who had been the mainstay of such positions in the past. Social security benefits for their children and expanding job opportunities for women combined to make the role of housemother less appealing, as did the larger number of troubled children and youth that Carson now served. Of the six cottages operating in March 1966, three were headed by married couples (with the husbands attending graduate school), one by a woman who taught off campus during the day, and the two remaining cottages by single women (at least one of whom was a widow).[44] Two years earlier, in June of 1964, the couple in charge of Red Gables had proved so unsatisfactory that Barnes had had to dismiss them and close the cottage temporarily.[45]

At the same time, Barnes realized that even the most sincere and well-motivated houseparents were likely to encounter difficulties because the Carson residential program had not changed with the times. As Barnes himself put the matter, Carson's specialty had been—and remained—"an essentially undifferentiated program of tender, loving care which is highly successful with the eagerly responsive child but hardly meets the needs of the hostile or aloof youngster."[46] Barnes's most immediate response to the problem was the designation of two cottages for the older and more troubled teenage girls on campus, an arrangement that was abandoned a year or so later because the girls themselves complained of being isolated from the rest of the institution.[47] Another change was the admission for the first time, in 1968, of boys who were not related to Carson girls.[48]

Meanwhile, Barnes continued to cite the need for a "child-care model" at Carson in which those responsible for children in the cottages would have some formal training as child-care workers. Thus in October 1967, the institution adopted a plan of "in-service training." Cottage staff held weekly meetings with a psychologist from the Montgomery County Mental Health clinic, in addition to weekly sessions with a faculty member from Temple University. This initiative, combined with the others, led child-welfare agencies to conclude that Carson was addressing its most serious problems, and so they began to increase their referrals to the institution. Thus, from forty-three children in the summer of 1964, enrollment rose to sixty-one in the winter of 1972.[49]

Despite such steps Barnes was disappointed by "the gap between theory and practice," as he put it in March 1970.[50] That summer he attended the International Conference on Child Care Training in Switzerland and came back very excited about what was being done in Europe to train and make use of professional child-care workers.[51] The following year, in October 1971, Barnes brought two French professionals to Carson under a grant that he secured from a local donor. Calling themselves *educateurs,* as opposed to mere educators or teachers, the Frenchmen explained that the *educateur* was a highly trained professional who was capable of responding to any of the needs presented by the twelve to fifteen "maladjusted" children under his or her care.[52] As adapted by Barnes this program was labeled "educare." According to the board this meant "that at the center of the child's living experience there should be a specially trained professional child care worker who has prime responsibility for the care of the child."[53] Although the Carson board accepted this philosophy in principle, funds were never available to put it into practice.

Barnes himself, who was anxious to implement the educare concept, resigned in the spring of 1972 in order to establish his own child-care facility at Manchester, New Hampshire.[54] After conducting a brief search, Carson selected Peter Sutton-Smith as its new executive director in July 1972.[55] A Canadian by birth and education, Sutton-Smith had been director of administrative services of the Boy's Farm and Training School at Strawbridge, Quebec, immediately before coming to Carson.[56] Probably because of his short and controversial tenure as executive director of Carson, which lasted less than a year, nothing more was known about his background some two decades later. The board voted to terminate Sutton-Smith in May 1973, after he had been at Carson for only ten months. The reason given for the action was "differences between the Board and Mr. Sutton-Smith regarding the philosophy of the agency."[57]

Following an extensive search, the board selected John Taaffe as executive director, beginning in June of 1974.[58] His administration of Carson would become second in length only to Elsa Ueland's, and he remained director of the institution at the time of this writing. Born in 1939 in New York City, of Irish immigrant parents, Taaffe had received his bachelor's degree from Iona College at New Rochelle, New York. He then earned a master's in social work from New York University (located just a few blocks from the Richmond Hill Settlement where Elsa Ueland had lived and worked a half century before).[59] He became seriously interested in child welfare during his junior year at college, following a friend's suggestion that he apply for a job as a youth counselor at the Joseph P. Kennedy Home in the Bronx, which was an easy commute from Iona. Administered by the Sisters of St. Joseph Oblate, it had been named in honor of Joseph P. Kennedy Jr. (a brother of future U.S. president John F. Kennedy), who had been killed in World War II. Taaffe remained at Kennedy until 1962, the year after his graduation from Iona. While there he met his future wife, Shirley (Salak) Taaffe, who was also working as a counselor at Kennedy.

Following graduate school, Taaffe took a job in 1965 with the Catholic Guardian Society, which operated a number of group homes under the auspices of the Catholic Charities of New York City. These homes cared for children who had been long-term residents of area institutions and who needed to learn how to cope with the demands of everyday life. By this

Fig. 46.   John Taaffe, Carson's fifth executive director, 1995. CVS.

time Taaffe had married and, joined by his wife, Shirley, directed a group
home with nineteen adolescent boys. In 1969 Taaffe left this position for
the St. Agatha Home for Children in Nanuet, New York. Run by the Sisters
of Charity, St. Agatha's had begun as an orphanage and, like Carson, had
made the transition to residential child care. Taaffe was director of child
care and later director of all residential programs. He remained at St.
Agatha's until 1974.

Only thirty-four years old when he came to Carson, Taaffe nevertheless
had a wealth of experience behind him and was, in fact, some six years
older than Elsa Ueland had been when she was hired to lead the institution. In addition to having a background with group homes and residential child-care facilities, Taaffe came to Carson with much experience in
working with a diverse urban population. Although he was now taking
charge of an institution in suburban Flourtown, Pennsylvania, his rich
understanding of city life would greatly assist the Carson Valley School in
serving the evolving needs of urban children.

Taaffe was attracted to Carson in part because of its commitment to a child-care delivery model. He was also encouraged by the board's willingness to make changes in both the program and the personnel. Carson's beautiful campus was yet another reason for Taaffe's decision to take the job.

But this physical beauty masked a deeply troubled institution, as Taaffe was soon to discover during his first few days as director. Although there were a number of good staff members still at Carson, many of the younger employees were refusing to take directions from anyone and had allowed several of the cottages to fall into complete disorder, both physically and operationally, to the extent that Taaffe judged the children in them to be unsafe. Knowing of these conditions, child-welfare authorities in the region had once again become reluctant to make referrals to Carson.

One of Taaffe's early decisions was to close "intake" (as the admissions process was now being called) for approximately one month, until the institution could be put in order.[60] He also dismissed a number of insubordinate staff members and began looking for suitable replacements. Alarmed over the filth and general disarray at Lower Beech, he closed the cottage altogether until it could be cleaned up and repaired. His wife, Shirley, supported him wholeheartedly during this difficult period and herself volunteered to oversee the redecoration and refurnishing of several cottages. After about three months of reorganization and study, Taaffe's commitment to addressing the most serious problems became known to child-welfare agencies, and with renewed confidence they began referring cases to Carson again. Taaffe had also held several discussions with child-welfare authorities in the region in order to arrive at a common understanding of how Carson could best serve current needs.

Even while he was putting the institution in order, Taaffe moved quickly to start new programs. The first of these was called a "vocationally oriented halfway house," authorized by the board in May of 1974 (just before Taaffe arrived). It was designed for approximately eight girls, between the ages of sixteen and eighteen, who needed "to prepare themselves for independent living in the larger community."[61] The facility was located in South Fields, the residence that had been built back in 1928 for Elsa Ueland. Because it sat just across Wissahickon Avenue from the main campus, its semi-isolation from the rest of the cottages helped to emphasize its residents' partial independence from the institution at large. Under supervision, the girls at South Fields prepared themselves for full independence by working at part-time jobs, in addition to shopping, household planning, and various chores. During this time, they continued to attend Springfield High School.

Taaffe proposed another important initiative in the spring of 1975, the creation of a Diagnostic Reception Center, a program about which he had some knowledge from his work in New York. County child-welfare agencies needed such a place, where they could send children for a complete evaluation, followed at the end of sixty to ninety days by a recommendation for placement. Although a few of these children might be recommended for Carson, the program was not designed as a "feeder" for the institution, and it was never used as such. Answering this need, Carson reopened Lower Beech in the summer of 1975 as a diagnostic center for boys, and in 1977 Thistle Cottage became a second diagnostic facility, this one for girls.[62] Thus, within three years of coming to Carson, Taaffe had opened three new facilities, the two diagnostic centers and the halfway house at South Fields, that met the emerging needs of area children and their families. In the process, Carson became a leader in this field and renewed its reputation for flexibility and dependable service to the child-welfare community.

In its continuing response to local needs, Carson opened a coeducational diagnostic center in Lower Beech Cottage during the mid-1980s, with boys and girls occupying separate sleeping quarters, but interacting freely in the downstairs portion of the cottage.[63] This coeducational arrangement has produced beneficial results: It has allowed boys and girls to interact appropriately with one another, and it has helped them to experience members of the opposite gender as more than sexual objects, a living arrangement defended at the time by supporters of coeducational dormitories on college campuses.[64] In addition, accepting both boys and girls at Lower Beech allowed Carson the flexibility to meet the shifting requirements of child-welfare agencies, regardless of gender.[65]

In 1993 Carson opened an intensive treatment program for fourteen adolescent girls, also at Lower Beech. Because of the lack of such facilities locally, these girls otherwise would have been placed in facilities out of state—and at great expense. This initiative was named the Elsa Ueland Program in honor of Carson's first president.

Typical of those admitted to the Elsa Ueland Program was a nine-year-old girl whose single mother was a substance abuser. The child herself had been abused both physically and sexually, and came to Carson with little trust in anyone.[66] Although the other children at Lower Beech—as well as in the other cottages—may not have had such traumatic backgrounds as that of this particular girl, many, if not most, of them had suffered from drug-using parents and had known both physical and sexual abuse.[67] According to Donald Sobeck, program director of Lower Beech, Carson could assist such children "by providing predictable, appropriate responses to both positive and negative behaviors," and in the process "help make them feel better about themselves and learn how to deal successfully with their environment[s]."[68] Although this was a behavioral approach to residential life, it was still somewhat in the spirit of progressive education in that it sought to help boys and girls to cope successfully with their actual environments. Of course, it was without the wide freedom to explore on one's own, a luxury that children in need of a highly structured treatment setting could ill afford.

Early on in his tenure as executive director, Taaffe had decided to end the practice of having staff reside in the various cottages. Instead, child-care staff would work scheduled hours under the direction of a cottage supervisor. This policy signaled a clear break with the old housemother (or houseparent) style of cottage management and reflected Taaffe's commitment to the child-care model at Carson.

Meanwhile, the changes occurring in child-welfare practices, and the ever-present need to reduce expenditures, resulted in less time spent by children in the more restricted settings such as Carson. These changes also required adjustments in the educational experiences for residents. Since 1937, when Carson had closed its own school on campus, its residents had attended the Springfield Township public schools. But as the focus of Carson programs became short-term placement and assessment, it was increasingly evident that its residents' needs were best met in an on-campus educational program that combined behavioral management and remedial work.[69] Thus, in 1984 Carson secured a license from the state to operate its own "private school" on campus, with tuition to come from the students' districts of origin. Two years later, in 1986, Carson also qualified as a Private Residential Rehabilitative Institute (PRRI), which, among other things, allowed it to receive direct payments from the state for its educational services.[70] In addition to educating its own residents, Carson began to accept special-education students, who commuted to campus each day.[71] By 1995 there were approximately ninety resident students attending the school on grounds, along with some thirty day students. Classes were held in Mother Goose cottage, now given over almost completely to educational purposes.[72] (In order to open up additional space in Mother Goose, Carson's main administrative offices, including that of the executive director, moved to Orchard Cottage over on Bethlehem Pike during the late 1980s.)

According to Dr. Marie O'Donnell, who has directed the educational program at Carson since 1984, the goals of the school were to stabilize children educationally, to inculcate a more positive attitude toward school in general, to diagnose learning disabilities and provide appropriate treatment for them, and to make students understand that they must obey the rules. As in the cottages, the school used a "behavioral-levels system." Students who performed adequately and did not misbehave at school received a certain number of points each day, while students who failed to live up to these expectations lost points and privileges such as watching television, playing pool in the evenings, or going off campus to the nearby Plymouth Meeting Mall.[73] In so coordinating the school and cottage programs, Carson was returning to a practice that had prevailed during the time of its first school (1918–37). Such efforts to connect the school to a child's broader environment—in this case to cottage life—were also in the spirit of progressive education.

In addition to the greater emotional needs and more severe learning disabilities of Carson children, political and economic factors were driving the changes taking place in the educational and cottage-life programs. First, passage of the Adoption Assistance and Child Welfare Act in 1980 gave the decades-long movement against institutional care the force of federal law. Second, the election that same year of Ronald Reagan to the presidency of the United States signaled a return of conservatism to the mainstream of American politics, a mood that would continue to dominate government up to the moment of this writing. Campaigns against taxes, big government, the welfare state, and public spending were all characteristics of this conservative movement. (Ironically, this new conservatism had the effect of reinforcing an already long-standing liberal opposition to institutional care, though for different reasons.)

Carson responded to these wider challenges with flexibility and imagination. For one thing, the institution had to shorten the length of time that children resided on campus, both because of cutbacks in public funds and because of the goal of placing dependent children in the least restrictive environments. Thus, while residents were staying at Carson for an average of three or four years in the mid-1970s, most remained for less than a year two decades later.[74]

Carson showed additional imagination and flexibility in new programs to help children and families in Philadelphia. Thus, in 1987 Carson initiated a series of programs that were administered from an office at 6700 Germantown Avenue in the Mt. Airy section of Philadelphia (located about five miles southeast of the Flourtown campus). Eventually known as Carson Community Programs, these initiatives were under the direction of Cynthia Robinson and her assistant Natline Thornton.[75] The first of these was called Family Care, a foster-care treatment program for children with special needs—social, physical, and psychological. Foster parents participating in this program took training from the Carson staff, and these parents, along with the children in their charge, received support and supervision during regular visits from professional staff. Every attempt was made to maintain connections with the natural parents, who were also eligible for a range of treatment services, with the goal of reuniting them with their children. In cases where that proved impossible, Carson pursued adoption or permanent foster care. Commencing with just fourteen children in 1987, Family Care was assisting over seventy youngsters in 1993.[76]

In 1993 a second major initiative, Family Focus, was established to support and preserve family units and to prevent the removal of children

Fig. 47.   Natline Thornton of Carson Community Programs, 1987. CVS.

from their homes. Once a family entered the program, it participated in an intensive ten-week treatment intervention. Staff working in this program were assigned to only two families, making them available to provide daily support for each family.[77]

As one might expect, the changes in population and programs provided on campus at the Carson Valley School resulted in the disappearance of many traditional activities, though this process occurred gradually. During the 1970s, for example, there were still activities reminiscent of an earlier period. According to the *Communicator,* a student newspaper published at the time, the school held a Halloween party in October 1973, with residents in costumes, a bonfire behind Mother Goose Cottage, and the movie *Night of the Living Dead* shown in the Mother Goose gym.[78] In February 1974 some forty "Carson kids" and thirty-five guests attended a Valentine's Day dance in the gym.[79] In April of the same year, the residents held a talent show in the gym, and in July a group went hiking in the Finger Lakes district of New York. Indeed, ambitious excursions and camping trips were common throughout the 1960s and early 1970s, including a visit to the New York World's Fair in 1964. The fair became a theme for the entire summer program at Carson that year, with each cottage becoming a pavilion that represented a different country. In 1969 there were trips to Washington, D.C., Niagara Falls, and the Maine coast, and in 1974 to New York and Boston.[80] But by the late 1970s such activities appeared to cease as more and more children entered Carson with needs best met in a more structured environment.

The cottage vegetable gardens, long a part of the residential program, also disappeared by the late seventies, except for sporadic plantings undertaken by an enthusiastic staff member and several interested children.[81] In 1964 the board voted to discontinue milk production, which the local dairies would no longer buy unless Carson made it available in bulk tanks. The dairy herd was sold and replaced with beef cattle for use within the institution.[82] The cultivation of crops continued, however, and as late as 1971 Carson kids were helping with the planting, weeding, and harvesting of their own sweet corn. In a memorandum entitled "The Great Corn Planting," they were urged to keep their "eyes on the growth of the seeds we have planted... [and] find how long it takes the corn to sprout, to get six inches, then two feet and taller."[83] Yet in the spring of 1976 the board decided to discontinue what was left of Carson's unprofitable farming operation and to lease the cultivated land to a local farmer (an arrangement that remains in place two decades later).[84]

As the farm operation was winding down, most of the original furniture in the cottages, some of it especially crafted for the institution during the 1920s, was sold at an auction on the grounds in 1972 as part of a plan to refurnish the cottages along more contemporary lines. Among the items sold were solid oak trestle tables, gateleg tables, and desks, along with tea carts, bookcases, and ladder-back chairs. According to one employee who remembers the auction, antique dealers purchased much of the furniture at ridiculously low prices. Equally maddening, according to her, was the fact that the new furniture was far less durable than the old and only lasted several years before it had to be replaced. Fortunately, a few pieces of the original furniture did survive in several offices and are now greatly prized by the institution.[85]

One thing that did not change in the 1970s was the desire to provide vocational experiences for the residents, as the opening of Carson's halfway house at South Fields attested. For most of the residents, however, it was summer jobs that were most desirable. During the summer of 1972, for instance, fifteen of the older residents had jobs: at the Chestnut Hill Hospital, the Springfield School District, the day camp at St. Thomas Episcopal Church, and on Carson's own grounds.[86] Beginning about 1976, several dozen Carson kids participated in what was called the Youth Job Corps, a publicly funded program that provided paying jobs for teens mainly in nonprofit institutions. The elimination of such summer programs in 1981, a result of funding cutbacks by the federal government in particular, made it much less likely that Carson residents would find jobs thereafter, as did the changing nature of the residential population.[87] Still, at the time of this writing, some Carson residents earned money shoveling snow for neighbors, assisting the local Rotary Club with various activities, and working after-school jobs at Carson or in Flourtown.[88]

Carson's other contacts with the surrounding community also underwent a significant evolution during the thirty years or so after 1960. During the 1960s, for example, volunteers from Flourtown and vicinity gave considerable assistance to Carson. From the late 1950s to the early 1970s the police chiefs from surrounding communities treated the Carson children to an annual Christmas dinner—in 1960 complete with a tree, movies, and gifts.[89] During this same period the Montgomery County chapter of the American Institute of Banking provided Christmas stockings for each Carson child.[90] In 1966 some thirty students from neighboring Chestnut Hill College (an all-women's institution) volunteered to assist with a sports program and to help Carson kids with their homework.[91] In 1967 the Erdenheim Women's Club elected to take up Carson Valley as a special project and over the next several years provided funds for various social events and recreational activities.[92] About this same time, Carson established a somewhat formal organization of volunteers, who might tutor children, drive them to medical appointments, or take them on a shopping trip or some other off-campus outing.[93] Such volunteer activities appeared to dwindle during the upheavals between 1972 and 1974.

After settling in, director John Taaffe held a number of open houses for Carson's immediate neighbors.[94] Especially after the mid-1980s, when fewer and fewer Carson residents were attending the public schools, such occasions for the public to visit the grounds were one of the few ways that neighbors could make contact with the institution. Beginning in 1986 Carson held an annual May Festival that in the early years had a pronounced medieval theme, not unlike Carson's original May Festivals back

Fig. 48.   Area police chiefs at the annual Christmas party they sponsored at Carson, c. 1960. CVS.

Fig. 49.   Carson's May Festival, late 1980s. CVS.

in the 1920s, though it is not clear if the latter-day organizers were aware of this precedent. The modern May Festival featured a variety of foods, games, hay-wagon rides, jugglers, magicians, hot-air-balloon races, tours of Mother Goose and Red Gables Cottages, and a fireworks display after dark—the roads and walkways festooned with colorful banners. The festivals were open to the public and drew crowds of several thousands. Although they raised some money for the institution, their public relations value was just as important as any profits that might have been realized.[95] Another fund-raiser and public relations event was Carson's annual golf tournament, which began in 1988 and has commonly been held in August.[96]

Perhaps the most important ongoing connection with the outside community was the Carson Valley Nursery School, which continued to flourish over the decades. Jean MacFarland, who had presided over the nursery school since its revival in 1949, resigned as director in 1963 and was replaced by Becky Duryea, who remained in that position until 1974. Her successor was Dorothy Emhardt, who stepped down three years later. Since 1977 the director has been Judy Berger.[97] Throughout the 1960s and 1970s the enrollment averaged about seventy boys and girls each year.[98] In 1983 the nursery school added a day-care program for families who required child care before the nursery school program started, at nine in the morning (or after it ended, at noon), a feature that boosted total enrollments to about ninety.[99] In 1992 the nursery school established a kindergarten (a program that had existed before 1937, when the original nursery school closed).[100]

The nursery school's May Day celebration, to which parents and grandparents were invited, brought community residents to the campus at the same time that it recalled an earlier era at Carson. The children picked wildflowers and wrapped streamers around a Maypole.[101] Beginning in 1991, the nursery school reached out to elderly neighbors by visiting a local adult day-care facility operated by the Sisters of St. Joseph. These visits featured crafts, stories, songs, and refreshments, with the old and the young assisting each other.[102] As to the nursery school parents themselves, many became interested in the larger program at Carson and volunteered to assist in such events as the May Festival and golf tournament. Some nursery school parents have also been recruited as members of the Carson board.[103]

By the 1980s Carson no longer kept livestock for the nursery school youngsters to see, though they did go on walks around the grounds, as

Fig. 50.   Carson Valley Nursery School, 1996. Director Judy Berger, in center, and
Assistant Director Melissa "Miss Missy" Horrow, to the right, with children. Photo by
the author.

before, and took a hayride each fall. There was no return to the elaborate
indoor and outdoor projects of the 1920s, yet the progressive emphasis
upon acquiring social skills through play was still a foremost goal of the
program. So was the improvement of small motor skills through various
craft activities such as cutting, pasting, sewing, and drawing.[104]

As in the past, the main purpose of the nursery school was not so much
to raise revenue as it was to serve local families and to forge connections
with the surrounding community. The nursery school also continued to
provide part-time jobs for the resident population, and particularly in the
late afternoon day-care program.[105]

After experiencing difficulties with budgets during the 1960s and
1970s, Carson's new programs produced a healthy financial picture by
the mid-1980s. Both enrollments and incomes demonstrated this change.

From about sixty children annually during the early 1970s, average enroll-ment climbed to about seventy by the end of the decade, advancing to around eighty in the early 1980s and to ninety or so a decade later.[106]

Carson's budgets reflected these enrollment figures in many ways. Because the Carson estate provided only a fraction of the institution's yearly income (as had been the case for many years), with the bulk of its revenues coming from the counties as payment for child care, there was a direct relationship between enrollment and Carson's financial health. (The Carson estate was now handled by PNC Bank, which was a corpo-rate successor to the old Real Estate Land Title and Trust Company.) In 1970, for instance, only $92,000 out of a total expenditure of $453,000 (or 20.3 percent of the whole) was provided by the Carson estate, whose principal was just over $2 million at the time.[107]

Because there were especially low enrollments during the first half of the 1960s, deficits were the rule throughout the period, reaching a high of $50,000 in 1965 out of a total budget of $250,000. The deficits declined somewhat in the late 1960s as enrollment rebounded, but still ranged between $30,000 and $45,000 each year, only to rise to the $50,000 level again in 1970. Carson covered these regular shortfalls by drawing upon the accumulated-income fund.[108]

Although enrollments rose after the middle 1970s, serious nationwide inflation, brought on by the aftermath of the Vietnam War and by oil boy-cotts in the Middle East, forced Carson into continued deficit spending—$70,000 in 1974, $55,000 in 1975, $35,000 in 1976, and $41,000 in 1977.[109] An end to high inflation in the 1980s, combined with Carson's new programs and more stringent budgeting methods introduced by con-troller Jack Cavenaugh, led to balanced budgets by the middle of the decade and to modest surpluses by the end.[110] In 1991, when there was a total budget of $5.5 million, the finances were so healthy that Carson did not have to spend any of the $388,000 generated by the Carson trust for operating expenses and was able to dedicate it entirely to capital improvements. In 1995 the value of the Carson trust (including both principal and accumulated income) was approximately $6,500,000. Although this represented a considerable increase during the past two decades, it was not much more *in absolute terms* than the $5 million evaluation placed on the Carson estate at the time of Robert Carson's death in 1907.[111] Adjusted for inflation over the intervening nine decades, the amount was minuscule in comparison to the 1907 figure.

While the Carson Valley School's financial record can be traced with a large degree of accuracy, it is more difficult to measure the institution's success in treating the children under its care. For at no time in its history has Carson enjoyed the resources to follow up cases after individuals have left the institution. However, there are subjective indications that many former residents have maintained very warm feelings about Carson over the years, as attested by the letters they have written and the visits and telephone calls they have made to staff members.[112] The willingness of child-welfare agencies to send children to Carson, except for a few difficult years, was another measure of the perceived success of its programs.

Many other institutions that had begun as orphanages were not so successful as Carson and had to close as a result. One of these was the Ellis School, which had come into existence at virtually the same time as Carson and had been closely associated with Carson in the press and the social work community. In 1974 the Ellis trustees successfully petitioned the court to close the school and to use the income from the Ellis trust to provide scholarships to needy students.[113] Philadelphia's Girard College, which had helped to inspire Robert Carson, managed to survive, but by the early 1990s was facing a real financial crisis and was forced to rethink its status as a boarding school for children "from low-income, single-parent families."[114] The decline in the numbers of children in Pennsylvania institutions told essentially the same story—from 17,778 in 1932, to 7,434 in 1960, and to 3,248 in 1976. In the United States as a whole the numbers in institutional care had fallen from 144,000 in 1933, to 95,000 in 1951, to 77,000 in 1963, and to 43,000 in 1977.[115]

In its search for extra sources of revenue through maximum use of its resources, the Carson board once more looked into the plausibility of developing some of its land. This idea, first proposed in the late 1930s by Elsa Ueland herself, came before the board twice during the period under discussion—in 1972–73 and again ten years later. In 1972 the board commissioned the Philadelphia firm of Wallace, McHarg, Roberts, and Todd to conduct an extensive land-use study, which was completed in January 1973. Their report recommended the erection of both single- and multiple-family dwellings on the property as well as commercial structures on the Bethlehem Pike side of the campus. For its own use, the Carson Valley School would reserve a "core area" of open land around the residential cottages nearer to the center of the grounds. In addition to the commercial development on the Bethlehem Pike site (around Orchard Cottage), residential construction would take place along Wissahickon Avenue and Mill Road.[116] The land-use report suggested that Carson could either sell or lease the land in question to developers, who would take practical charge of the project.

In addition to the prospect of much needed additional revenue at a time of continuing deficits in the Carson budget, some of the board members saw the proposed development, once again, as a way of connecting Carson more closely with the Flourtown community, much as Ueland had proposed back in 1939 and again after World War II, by actually making it part of the residential area. As board chairwoman Louise Page observed in 1972, "Flourtown . . . does not have the total sense of community that a town might have or [that] . . . Chestnut Hill [does]."[117] According to her, building houses and shops on the Carson property—along with a swimming pool, tennis courts, and walking trails—might go a long way toward making up this deficit. There were also indications that Page and other board members planned to make this a racially integrated development from the very beginning, thereby quieting fears from child-welfare authorities, especially in Philadelphia, that the Carson Valley School could not provide a comfortable atmosphere for African American children.[118] (Though such integration may have been applauded in child-welfare circles, it probably would have been resented, or even resisted, by the overwhelmingly white population of Flourtown.)

As in the past, these plans would require zoning variances from a township that had not been sympathetic to Carson's development ideas before. However, the plan does not appear to have been submitted for consideration by the township. No explanation for this survives, but it is probable that the turmoil that gripped Carson during 1972 and 1973, resulting in the dismissal of Peter Sutton-Smith as executive director, was the principal reason why the plan was not carried through.

By May 1982 the Carson board was again discussing the possibility of selling, leasing, or otherwise developing some of its land, though it is not clear if members were aware of all four earlier and unsuccessful attempts to do so (that is, in 1939, 1946, 1954, and 1973).[119] In the spring of 1983 the board commissioned the firm of Cope/Linder to undertake yet another study that would look into the possibilities of developing Carson's "excess acreage."[120] In its report Cope/Linder recommended commercial properties for the strip along Bethlehem Pike owned by Carson (in an area that was already zoned commercial). For the parcel of land that ran back from the pike, then referred to as "the panhandle," the report suggested cluster housing, a use that would require a zoning variance from the township. After considering these possibilities the board decided not to go forward with either suggestion, concluding that the shape of these parcels, as well as problems with access, would not make their development all that profitable.[121]

Though these latest investigations into possible new land uses did not bear fruit, Carson did carry out two modest projects that fell into the category of physical development. One was the construction of a new residence for the executive director in 1965-66. This was a Tech-Built Home, a one-story prefabricated residence erected on institutional grounds just west of the entrance on Wissahickon Avenue, at a cost of about $35,000. Because of the evergreen trees in this area, it was named the Pines and has served as the director's residence ever since.[122] The second development was the sale in 1989 of South Fields, once the residence of Elsa Ueland. Carson obtained $276,000 for the house and a strip of land that ran west from South Fields along Wissahickon Avenue. A developer subsequently erected four small single-family residences there.[123] This sale made sense in light of the fact that the location of South Fields, across the road from the main campus, was out of sync with Carson's highly structured residential life, which at the time was best conducted within a concentrated area. (By the time the property was sold, the vocational halfway house at South Fields had been disbanded.)

A final change that bears notice was the further widening of board membership. To be sure, board members continued to be highly regarded members of the community, as well as successful professionals, but dominance by the upper class had lessened considerably over the past half century: Of the twenty board members listed for 1989, only two, or 10 percent, were included in the *Social Register,* compared to the 45 percent of board members who had appeared in the *Social Register* back in 1941— or the 57 percent in 1914.[124] The board had also contained African American members since the late 1960s or early 1970s, though there were no figures on just how many.

Ueland did not live to see all these changes, having died late in 1980. But she did express her approval of Carson's new programs in the 1970s and was always happy to give her views on "that fool Kelsey" to anyone who might inquire about Carson's original architect.[125] Yvonne Patterson, who had returned to live with "Aunt Elsa" in the late 1960s (after a very successful career in the ballet), recalled that Ueland remained a liberal Democrat until the end. According to Patterson, as well as members of the Ueland family, Elsa strongly approved of the civil rights movement, in addition to the many reforms passed under Lyndon Johnson's Great Society. She was also adamantly opposed to the Vietnam War.[126]

Ueland kept in touch with Carson through old friends and former students at the school. Every year at Christmas the Carson children rode over to Oak Run in a hay wagon, pulled by a tractor, and sang carols to "Miss Ueland," after which they went inside for hot chocolate.[127] Ueland enjoyed gardening in those years, taking particular care of her roses. She also savored long walks through the dramatic Wissahickon gorge, sometimes stopping for lunch or dinner at the Valley Green Inn along the creek banks just west of Chestnut Hill.[128] Her rosy complexion and bright blue eyes remained, now beneath a full head of curly white hair that her nephew Mark Ueland affectionately described as a "white Afro."[129] In March of 1979 Ueland fell and broke her hip in the bathroom at home. Following surgery she went to live at Priestley House, a nursing home in the Germantown section of Philadelphia run by the Unitarian Church. She died there of a stroke on December 1, 1980, just three months short of her ninety-third birthday. Among the last books that she had read were some novels by Charles Dickens, the author who had fired her with visions of social reform as a schoolgirl eight decades before.[130] In her will she left the Carson Valley School a bequest of $30,000, which the board decided to add to an endowment trust fund for helping Carson children to pursue their educations after leaving the institution.[131]

Although Ueland herself had proposed housing developments on the Carson property (always with provisions for plenty of open space), she would not have been unhappy over the board's decision to drop the idea of an intense development of Carson land, for in the last decades of her life she had become an even stronger advocate of conservation and environmentalism.[132] Within a half dozen years of her death, the Carson board itself would take up the cause of land conservation and architectural preservation.

If the board needed a local example for such preservation, they could refer to the decision in 1972 by the owners of the Widener property to place it into a perpetual land trust.[133] This property, which directly adjoined the Carson Valley School to the west, had once belonged to Robert Carson. In fact, the Widener estate and the Carson Valley property had once been joined as the Robert Carson farm. Historic preservation and land conservation were much in vogue around the United States at the time, including neighboring Chestnut Hill, where the local historical society was leading the preservation/conservation movement.[134] At least one member of the Carson board in the late 1980s also served on the board of the Chestnut Hill Historical Society, and another board member was heavily involved in the restoration of an eighteenth-century country house called the Highlands, located several miles from the Carson campus.[135]

To prepare for its preservation and conservation efforts, Carson commissioned John Milner and Associates in 1984 to conduct a "historic structures report."[136] Included in the Milner report, completed in April 1985, was the suggestion that Carson should have its buildings and grounds placed on the National Register of Historic Places.[137] The board agreed, and Carson received national register status in 1991. Meanwhile, Carson undertook to repair and restore its historic buildings, completing such work on Stork Hill in 1989 at a cost of over a half million dollars.[138] In 1991 and 1992 the school asked students from the horticulture program at the Temple University campus in nearby Ambler to study its landscape and plantings and make recommendations.[139] (This cooperative effort with the direct successor to the former School of Horticulture for Women represented the resumption of an old relationship for Carson, though it may not have been recognized by either institution at the time.)

In the last analysis, Carson stood to win far more good will in the local community for preserving its land and architecture (despite certain impractical features of the older buildings) than for any sort of real estate venture on its property—good will that probably outweighed whatever additional income might have been derived from developing its open land. Furthermore, many Carson staff believed that the charming buildings and tranquil rolling landscape exerted a subtle but beneficial influence on the boys and girls who came to Carson—too often from scenes of ugliness and turmoil. Thus, in Carson's first formal mission statement, adopted by the board in April 1989, the institution committed itself to "retaining the unique character of the historic buildings and their setting, which insure physical and emotional security."[140] Three years earlier, in November 1986, the board had asserted that any land-use decisions by Carson would have to be compatible with the Flourtown community and with the needs of the Carson Valley School, which would continue to require a *"generous acreage for the fulfillment of [its] unique mission"*[141] (emphasis is in the original).

The anticipation of Carson's seventy-fifth anniversary was doubtless another reason why attention became focused on historic preservation. The anniversary, in turn, provided a vehicle for raising funds to undertake the costly work of restoration. In observing this anniversary the board chose 1917 as the founding date (as opposed to the official opening date of July 1, 1918), since the first construction took place in that year.

The central event of the seventy-fifth-anniversary celebration was the May Festival held on May 9. In addition to the usual activities there was a historical exhibit of photographs and other objects assembled by Natline Thornton.[142] If Elsa Ueland had reappeared that day, she, more than anyone else, could have attested to how much Carson had changed over the seven and a half decades since she took charge of the institution. For nearly every requirement or suggestion of the original Carson will had been breached at one time or another. Instead of an orphanage for white girls, both of whose parents were deceased, Carson now served boys and girls regardless of race and whether or not one or both parents were alive. Yet the goal of helping children in need had been maintained over the years in the face of greatly changed conditions.

Although each facility is unique, the experiences of the Carson College and the Carson Valley School would appear to offer some guidance to those in both public and private spheres who will formulate child-care policy in the future: Carson's flexibility in meeting the needs of a changing national and local society have allowed it to survive and then to thrive as an institution. As an extension of this overall flexibility, there has been a continuing focus on each individual child—not merely on children as an age group with certain social or psychological characteristics in common. Also central to Carson's success has been an ongoing policy of trying to provide a homelike setting on the campus and, especially in recent decades, trying to maintain contacts between children and their families whenever possible. Carson's lush grounds and beautiful buildings, in a variety of subtle ways, have helped to make its children feel wanted and valued. Finally, consistent efforts to forge and maintain contacts between Carson and the surrounding community have engendered good will among its neighbors and have helped boys and girls at Carson to feel connected to a real world of work, school, families, and cultural expression.

Thus, with its practical, often experimental, and nondoctrinaire approach to child care, Carson has remained true to much of the spirit of progressive education. In its realistic focus on the needs of urban youth, it has continued to share one of the major preoccupations of the wider progressive movement of the early twentieth century: that of trying to repair the ills of modern urban society. Perhaps the most telling evidence of commitment to these goals appeared in Carson's 1989 mission statement. In part it read, "The school pays particular care to meeting educational needs and developing the life skills of those it serves.... [T]here is maximum opportunity for [them] to learn and to reach their individual potential." Although Carson Valley was no longer a progressive school in the same sense that it once had been, its buildings, grounds, and successful programs were genuine progressive legacies.

ABBREVIATIONS

These abbreviations are used in the captions for the illustrations and in the Notes and the Bibliographic Essay.

AQ	*American Quarterly*
AR	*Architectural Record*
CVS	Carson Valley School
CVV	*Carson Valley Views*
EUP	Elsa Ueland Papers
PH	*Pennsylvania History*
PMHB	*Pennsylvania Magazine of History and Biography*
SSR	*Social Science Review*
UA	Urban Archives, Samuel Paley Library, Temple University, Philadelphia

NOTES

Chapter 1

1. *Evening Bulletin* (Philadelphia), March 11, 1911.
2. *Philadelphia Record,* October 16, 1907.
3. *Public Ledger* (Philadelphia), October 16, 1907.
4. Ibid.; *Philadelphia Record,* October 16, 1907.
5. *Public Ledger,* October 16, 1907.
6. *Germantown Guide,* April 19, 1890, November 16, 1895, January 11 and May 2, 1896.
7. *Public Ledger,* October 16, 1907.
8. *Philadelphia Inquirer,* October 16, 1907.
9. *Evening Bulletin,* March 10, 1911.
10. The most recent biography of Girard is George Wilson, *Stephen Girard: The Life and Times of America's First Tycoon* (Conshohocken, Pa., 1995). An older but still helpful biography by a famous historian is John Bach McMaster, *The Life and Times of Stephen Girard,* 2 vols. (Philadelphia, 1918). A good brief account of Girard's life and the legal odyssey of Girard's will may be found in John Keats, "Consider the Curious Legacy of Stephen Girard," *American Heritage,* June-July 1976, 39-47.
11. Despite its many aspects, there is no recent history of Girard College. The most complete, though much outdated, work is Cheesman A. Herrick, *History of Girard College* (Philadelphia, 1927).
12. *Evening Bulletin,* October 23 and 24, 1907.
13. Will of Robert N. Carson, Carson Valley School collection (CVS), p. 9.
14. Ibid., 11.
15. Ibid., 10.
16. Ibid., 11.
17. Ibid., 12.
18. Ibid., 13.
19. Ibid.
20. See David J. Rothman, *The Discovery of the Asylum* (Boston, 1971), 206-36, and Susan Whitelaw Downs, "The Orphan Asylum in the Nineteenth Century," *SSR,* June 1983, 272-90.
21. Herrick, *Girard College,* 115-17.
22. Neva R. Deardorff, "The New Pied Pipers," *Survey,* April 1, 1924, 32, 33.
23. Ibid., 38.
24. *Evening Bulletin,* October 24, 1907.

25. Ibid., December 9, 1907. On Richmond, see James L. Leiby, *A History of Social Welfare and Social Work in the United States* (New York, 1978), 121–22.

26. *Proceedings of the Conference on the Care of Dependent Children* (1909; reprint, New York, 1917), 6.

27. Keats, "Legacy of Stephen Girard," 44–45.

28. Will of Robert N. Carson, pp. 6–7; *Evening Bulletin*, March 26, 1909.

29. *Evening Bulletin*, August 6 and November 17, 1910.

30. Martin J. Wade to J. Prentice Murphy, November 1, 1925. Wade appears to have been an attorney representing the Carson heirs who were then living in Iowa. In his letter Wade wrote in part, "Had Mr. Carson been free to act as he wished, there is no question but that these heirs would have received the bulk of his estate. The domination of his wife, who hated his kindred, arose out of unfortunate events which it is not necessary here to recite." (I am grateful to David N. Carson, a collateral descendant of Robert N. Carson, for supplying me with a copy of this letter and other materials relating to Robert Carson.)

31. *Evening Bulletin*, March 10, 1911.

32. Ibid., February 2, 1912.

33. Ibid., July 5, 1912, July 16, 1912, February 4, 1913, May 19, 1913, May 24, 1913; *Public Ledger*, May 20, 1913.

34. *Evening Bulletin*, September 24, November 29 and 30, 1913; *Public Ledger*, September 25 and 26, 1913, February 3 and March 9, 1914.

35. *Public Ledger*, May 24, 1916; *Philadelphia Inquirer*, May 10, 1916; *Evening Bulletin*, May 23, 1916.

36. Charter of the Carson College for Orphan Girls, in the Court of Common Pleas of Montgomery County, December Term, 1914, No. 19, CVS; Bylaws, Trustees, Carson College for Orphan Girls, CVS.

37. Will of Robert N. Carson, p. 7.

38. E. Digby Baltzell, *The Protestant Establishment* (New York, 1964). This work should be considered in conjunction with Baltzell's *Philadelphia Gentlemen: The Making of a National Upper Class* (1958; reprint, Philadelphia, 1979), which, as the title suggests, focuses on Philadelphia's socioeconomic elite.

39. *Social Register, Philadelphia*, 1922, 1929; *Who's Who in America*, 8 (1914–15): 2412, 15 (1928–29): 913, 29 (1956–57): 1630.

40. *Evening Bulletin*, February 27, 1919.

41. Ibid., October 17, 1945; James P. Carson to Walter W. Perkins, April 1, 1919.

42. It is not known for certain if the Thomas M. Thompson who served in Philadelphia's city government was the same man appointed to the Carson board. However, the only man of this name to receive an obituary in the Philadelphia newspapers who might plausibly have been on the Carson board was Thompson the city officeholder. See *Evening Bulletin*, February 1, 1922. The obituary did not state that this Thompson had served on the Carson board, but this fact may have been excluded because of Thompson's bitterness over the whole experience.

43. *Evening Bulletin*, November 5, 1929; *New York Times*, November 6, 1929; *Public Ledger*, March 24, 1930.

44. *Who's Who in America*, 15 (1928–29): 913; *Evening Bulletin*, August 26, 1936; *Philadelphia Inquirer*, August 25, 1936.

45. *Who's Who in America*, 8 (1914–15): 2412; *Evening Bulletin*, April 9, 1925, October 24 and 29, 1927. Mary W. James Vaux was the daughter of William and Henry James's brother Robertson. See *Evening Bulletin*, April 2, 1907.

46. *Who's Who in America,* 29 (1956-57): 1630; *Evening Bulletin,* January 29, 1915; Board Minutes, January 14, 1957, UA.

47. Board Minutes, October 13, 1927, UA. This quotation from Vaux appeared in a memorial resolution passed by the board following Vaux's death.

48. Memorandum on Budget, May 18, 1934, CVS.

49. This emulation of the Quaker worldview has been studied by E. Digby Baltzell in his *Puritan Boston and Quaker Philadelphia: Two Protestant Ethics and the Spirit of Class Authority and Leadership* (New York, 1979), 1-15, 79-91, 207-45, and more recently by David Hackett Fischer in his *Albion's Seed: Four British Folkways in America* (New York, 1989), 419-603. Also revealing are Baltzell's *Philadelphia Gentlemen* and *Protestant Establishment,* both cited above.

50. Memorandum on Budget, May 18, 1934, CVS. This sentiment on the part of the board was also reported in 1924 by Deardorff, "New Pied Pipers," 37.

51. Memorandum on Budget, May 18, 1934. One could argue, of course, that these statements made in 1934 were merely attempts to say that what Carson had actually done during the intervening years had been anticipated originally by the board. The fact, however, that there were no apparent objections to this interpretation by the board in 1934, which then contained a number of long-time board members, would lend some credence to these assertions.

52. Board Minutes, October 21, 1914, October 20, 1916, UA.

53. S. L. Pinkerton to Theron I. Crane, October 3, 1924, Correspondence, 1919-24, CVS.

54. *Evening Bulletin,* April 20, 1909.

55. *Philadelphia Press,* October 14, 1914; *North American* (Philadelphia), October 14, 1914.

56. In addition to Carson College and the Ellis School, neither of which was yet in operation, these other institutions and their endowments were Widener Memorial School for Crippled Children ($2,100,000), Thompson School for Girls ($1,829,000), Methodist Episcopal Orphanage ($900,000), Burd School ($685,000), Church Home for Children ($750,000), Gonzaga Memorial Asylum ($360,000), Foulke and Long Institute ($360,000), Elkins Masonic Orphanage for Girls ($350,000), Catholic Home for Girls ($315,000), Presbyterian Orphanage ($300,000), and some sixteen smaller institutions ($2,878,000). See *North American,* September 30, 1915.

57. Ibid., October 14, 1915.

58. Report of the Committee on Conclusions, Conference of the Prospective Work of Carson College and Ellis College, Philadelphia, October 13-14, 1915 (Philadelphia, 1915), pp. 5, 10, CVS.

59. Ibid., 6-9.

60. Hastings H. Hart to Leonard W. Coleman, February 6, 1917; Coleman to Hart, January 12, 1917, CVS; Hart, *Cottage and Congregate Institutions for Children* (New York, 1910).

61. Board Minutes, December 30, 1915, UA.

62. "Program of Competition for the Selection of an Architect for the Carson College for Orphan Girls," approved July 8, 1915, CVS; Board Minutes, June 4 and July 8, 1915, UA. One of the competitors, Warren and Wetmore, was a New York City firm. The others were all from Philadelphia: Bissell, Sinkler, and Tilden; Hewitt and Granger; Albert Kelsey; Watson and Huckel; and Zanzinger, Borie, and Medary.

63. "Program of Competition," 4-6.

64. Board Minutes, October 8, 1915, UA.

65. Sandra L. Tatman and Roger W. Moss, *Biographical Dictionary of Philadelphia*

Architects, 1700-1930 (Boston, 1985), 437-38; *Evening Bulletin,* October 7, 1915; *Philadelphia Inquirer,* October 9 and 16, 1915. On Cret, see Theodore B. White, *Paul Philippe Cret: Architect and Teacher* (Philadelphia, 1973), and Elizabeth Greenwald, "Paul Philippe Cret: Regionalism and Imagery in American Architecture" (Ph.D. diss., Brown University, 1980).

66. Ruskin's associationist ideas of art and architecture are discussed in Kristen Ottenson Garrigan, *Ruskin on Architecture: His Thoughts and Influence* (Madison, Wis., 1973). Ruskin developed these ideas most forcefully in his *Seven Lamps of Architecture* (1849) and *The Stones of Venice* (1851).

67. For an illuminating discussion of Anglophilia in Philadelphia and elsewhere, see Baltzell, *Protestant Establishment,* 4, 66-68, 113, 197-224. Anglophilia in neighboring Chestnut Hill is considered in David R. Contosta, *Suburb in the City: Chestnut Hill, Philadelphia, 1850-1990* (Columbus, Ohio, 1992), 80, 87-88, 106, 108, 152-54, 155-56.

68. See David R. Contosta, *Villanova University, 1842-1992: American—Catholic—Augustinian* (University Park, Pa., 1995), 61-67.

69. On the Gothic revival, see Calder Loth and Julius Trousdale Sadler Jr., *The Only Proper Style: Gothic Architecture in America* (Boston, 1975); for Collegiate Gothic in particular, see 90-91, 117, 150, 154-55, 161-62, 166. Also of interest is Kathleen Mahoney, *Gothic Style: Architecture and Interiors from the Eighteenth Century to the Present* (New York, 1995). An excellent study of revivalistic architecture in general during this period is Walter C. Kidney, *The Architecture of Choice* (New York, 1974). See also Jonathan Lane, "The Period House in the Nineteen Twenties," *Journal of the Society of Architectural Historians,* December 1961, 169-78.

70. On the Arts and Crafts movement in the United States, see Eileen Boris, *Art and Labor: Ruskin, Morris, and the Craftsman Ideal in America* (Philadelphia, 1986), and R. J. Clark, ed., *The Arts and Crafts Movement in America, 1876-1916* (Princeton, 1972). Also revealing is Paul Thompson, *The Works of William Morris* (New York, 1993).

71. Board Minutes, December 30, 1915, February 18, 1916, UA.

72. Ibid., July 23, 1917. The purchase price for this plot was $500.

73. Ibid., May 15, 1925.

74. Arthur Willis Colton, "The Carson College for Orphan Girls," *AR,* July 1921, 5.

75. *Public Ledger,* May 17, 1917.

76. Contosta, *Suburb in the City,* 10, 112.

77. John Ruskin, "Of Queens' Gardens," in *The Works of John Ruskin* (London, 1903), 18:131.

78. *Springfield Sun,* October 14, 1948; J. H. Dulles Allen to S. Gordon Smyth, March 19, 1914. Accompanying this letter is a five-page account of the founding and early years of Enfield Tile, probably written by Allen himself. I am indebted to Marie Kitto for providing me with photocopies of this material. Alan Selsor, telephone interview with the author, December 27, 1995; Selsor, "Enfield Chronology" (fall 1995; photocopy of unpublished typescript sent by Selsor to the author). See also Paul Evans, *Art Pottery in the United States* (New York, 1974).

79. Selsor, "Enfield Chronology."

80. Allen to Smyth, March 19, 1914.

81. Management Committee Minutes, October 25, 1919, UA; Furniture List, July 3, 1919, CVS. This last document directed that drawings for the tables from the Chapman Decorative Company be submitted for approval to "Mr. J. H. Dulles Allen."

82. Mantle Fielding, *Dictionary of American Painters, Sculptors, and Engravers* (New York, 1983), 835.

83. *Public Ledger,* May 18, 1917.

84. Ibid.

85. Colton, "Carson College," 12.

86. *North American,* March 7, 1917.

87. *Evening Bulletin,* October 13, 1916; Board Minutes, July 21 and October 11, 1916, UA. In a fifteen-page mimeographed work that was simply entitled "History," probably written by Elsa Ueland in 1958, she states that "the building program was started in 1916" (p. 1), CVS. It would appear from evidence in the board minutes, however, that the contracts were only awarded in 1916 and that actual building did not start until 1917.

88. *Evening Bulletin,* March 11, 1917.

89. Albert Kelsey to Theron I. Crane, November 8, 1917, and Kelsey to Walter W. Perkins, March 2, 1918, Committee Correspondence, 1915-18, CVS; C. E. Howland, Treasurer, Akron Roofing Tile Company, to Kelsey, March 25, 1918, Correspondence file of Elsa Ueland, CVS.

90. T. C. Powell, Member Priorities Committee, War Industries Board, to Walter W. Perkins, March 9, 1918, Committee Correspondence, 1915-18, CVS; Board Minutes, March 15, 1915, UA.

91. Elsa Ueland to Board of Trustees, May 6, 1918, CVS. Superintendent Coleman and his family made ready to move into their newly completed residence (soon to be called Stork Hill), only to find it appropriated by Ueland and the board as a residence for girls. Although the arrangement was supposed to be temporary, Stork Hill never reverted to its intended use as a superintendent's residence, a factor that may have led to Coleman's increasing bitterness and resignation as superintendent a year later. See Leonard W. Coleman to Theron I. Crane, April 29, 1918, CVS.

Chapter 2

1. For an interesting group profile of the kinds of men and women who became progressives, see Robert M. Crunden, *Ministers of Reform: The Progressives' Achievement in American Civilization, 1889-1920* (New York, 1982).

2. John E. Hayes, "Reformers, Radicals, and Conservatives," in *Minnesota in a Century of Change: The State and Its People Since 1900,* ed. Clifford E. Clark Jr. (St. Paul, Minn., 1989), 261-62.

3. For works on the Ueland family, see the Bibliographic Essay.

4. Brenda Ueland, "Clara Ueland of Minnesota" (typescript dated 1967), 1-22, and *Me* (New York, 1939), 13-15; Andreas Ueland, *Recollections of an Immigrant* (New York, 1929), 59-60.

5. Andreas Ueland, *Recollections,* 60-62; a photograph of the Ueland residence on Lake Calhoun appears opposite page 64. On the demolition of the house in 1953, see the *Minneapolis Morning Tribune,* July 22, 1953.

6. Brenda Ueland, "Clara Ueland," 419.

7. Ibid., 57, 419.

8. Ibid., 57-58.

9. Ibid., 58.

10. Ibid., 17-18, 31-32, 47-48.

11. Ibid., 60.

12. Laurence Cremin, *The Transformation of the School: Progressivism in American Education, 1876-1957* (New York, 1961), 5.

13. Ibid., 64.

14. Brenda Ueland, *Me*, 23, 55.

15. Brenda Ueland, "Clara Ueland," 68.

16. Brenda Ueland, *Me*, 48.

17. Brenda Ueland, "Clara Ueland," 77.

18. Brenda Ueland, *Me*, 36.

19. Ibid.

20. Ibid., 20.

21. Ibid., 36.

22. Ibid., 76–77. Brenda Ueland wrote a portrait of Simmons, which appears in *Sword Arm*, 182–86.

23. Brenda Ueland, *Me*, 77.

24. Ibid., 28.

25. Barbara Stuhler, *Gentle Warriors: Clara Ueland and the Minnesota Struggle for Woman Suffrage* (St Paul, Minn., 1995).

26. Margaret (Mrs. Rolf) Ueland to the author, July 23, 1996.

27. Memorials to Clara Ueland appeared in the *Minnesota Woman Voter* for March 1927. The best account of Clara's role as a feminist is Stuhler, *Gentle Warriors*.

28. Brenda Ueland, "Clara Ueland," 106–7, 164, 178, 198, 233, 246, 247, 256, 290, 292, 496.

29. Sigurd Ueland, "Sense and Senility," 20.

30. Undated and unidentified newspaper clipping found among the personal papers of Elsa Ueland. The papers of Elsa Ueland were located by the author at Ueland's former home, Oak Run. Ueland's heir, Yvonne Patterson, who occupied Oak Run at the time of this writing, has generously allowed the author to make use of these papers.

31. Brenda Ueland, *Me*, 83.

32. *Who's Who in America*, 15 (1928–29): 2097; *Evening Bulletin*, November 24, 1916; *Public Ledger*, November 24, 1916; Stuhler, *Gentle Warriors*, 71.

33. Margaret Ueland to the author, July 23, 1996.

34. Ada Comstock, Dean of Women, University of Minnesota, to the Committee of Selection for the English Scholarship Offered by the General Federation of Women's Clubs, EUP. This letter is undated, but it would appear to have been written about 1909, around the time that Elsa graduated from the University of Minnesota.

35. Brenda Ueland, "Clara Ueland," 179.

36. Elsa Ueland to her parents, quoted in ibid., 191. Brenda Ueland does not include a date for this letter, but it appears to have been written from New York during the summer of 1909.

37. In particular, see Erik H. Erikson, *Identity, Youth, and Crisis* (New York, 1968).

38. An excellent profile of settlement workers may be found in Allen F. Davis, *Spearheads for Reform: The Social Settlements and the Progressive Movement, 1890–1914* (New York, 1967), 33–39. See also Jill Conway, "Women Reformers and American Culture, 1870–1930," in *Our American Sisters: Women in American Life and Thought*, ed. Jean E. Friedman and William G. Slade (Boston, 1976); Allen F. Davis, *An American Heroine: The Life and Legend of Jane Addams* (New York, 1973); John P. Rousmaniere, "Cultural Hybrid in the Slums: The College Woman and the Settlement House, 1889–1894," *AQ*, spring 1970, 45–66.

39. Davis, *Spearheads for Reform*, 3–14.

40. Crunden, *Ministers of Reform*, ix–xii. On progressivism and the progressive movement, see John D. Buenker, *Urban Liberalism and Progressive Reform* (New York, 1967); Michael Ebner and Eugene M. Tobin, eds., *The Age of Urban Reform: New Perspectives on the Progressive Era* (Port Washington, N.Y., 1977); Eldon J. Eisenbach, *The Lost Promise of*

Progressivism (Lawrence, Kans., 1994); Arthur A. Ekirch Jr., *Progressivism in America* (New York, 1974); Peter G. Filene, "An Obituary for the 'Progressive Movement,'" *AQ*, January 1970, 20-34; David W. Noble, *The Progressive Mind, 1890-1917* (Minneapolis, 1981); William L. O'Neill, *The Progressive Years: America Comes of Age* (New York, 1975); Alan Ryan, *John Dewey and the High Tide of American Liberalism* (New York, 1995); Bruce M. Stave, ed., *Urban Bosses, Machines, and Progressive Reformers* (Lexington, Mass., 1971); Robert H. Wiebe, *The Search for Order, 1877-1920* (New York, 1967).

41. Davis, *Spearheads for Reform*, 29-33.

42. Elsa Ueland to her mother, November 4, 1916. See also ibid., November 2, 1916, EUP.

43. *New York Times*, May 10, 1961.

44. Brenda Ueland, *Me*, 100.

45. Elsa Ueland to her parents, August 8, 1909, quoted in Brenda Ueland, "Clara Ueland," 179-80.

46. Elsa Ueland to her parents, December 1909, quoted in ibid.

47. Brenda Ueland, *Me*, 100, 105.

48. Ibid., 100, 133.

49. Elsa Ueland, Diary, October 21, 1909-May 3, 1910. See also the entries for October 24, 25, 26, and 29, EUP.

50. Ibid., January 11, 1910.

51. Ibid., April 18, 1910.

52. Ibid., January 29, March 5, March 8, and March 15, 1910; Brenda Ueland, "Clara Ueland," 250. On February 11, 1911, Elsa wrote to her father that she had attended a performance of Richard Wagner's *Götterdämmerung*, EUP.

53. Elsa Ueland to her father, February 22, 1911, EUP.

54. Roy Lubove, *The Professional Altruist: The Emergence of Social Work as a Career, 1880-1930* (New York, 1969), 19, 144-45; David M. Austin, *A History of Social Work Education* (Austin, Tex., 1986), 4, 51. See also Stanley Wenocur and Michael Reisch, *From Charity to Enterprise: The Development of American Social Work in a Market Economy* (Urbana, Ill., 1989). Elsa Ueland's entry in *Who's Who in America* for 1928-29 (15:2097) states that she received a Master of Arts degree from Columbia University. Since there is no evidence that she took separate classes at Columbia, one is left to conclude that her Columbia degree was granted on the basis of the extensive research work that she did while at the New York School of Philanthropy.

55. Pearl Goodman and Elsa Ueland, "The Shirtwaist Trade," *Journal of Political Economy*, December 1910, 816-28.

56. On this phenomenon, see Lubove, *Professional Altruist*, 13-32.

57. Quoted in Brenda Ueland, "Clara Ueland," 244.

58. Quoted in ibid., 372.

59. Quoted in ibid., 376. To her mother she wrote on March 22, 1917, "As the war looks nearer I find myself getting to be more and more unilaterally peaceful" (EUP).

60. Elsa Ueland to her parents, August 8, 1918, EUP. Ueland's refusal to accommodate herself to the war, as did many other progressives, was very similar to the position taken by the writer and essayist Randolph Bourne, whom she had met while in New York. See Bourne, "The War and the Intellectuals," *Seven Arts*, June 1917, 133-46, and Edward Abrahams, *Randolph Bourne, Alfred Steiglitz, and the Origins of Cultural Radicalism in America* (Charlottesville, Va., 1986).

61. Lubove, *Professional Altruist*, 36-37. See also Cremin, *Transformation of the School*, 60-64; Earl Russell Yaillen, "Progressive Education and Social Group Work" (Ph.D. diss., University of Pittsburgh, 1977); *Evening Bulletin*, November 24, 1916.

62. Davis, *Spearheads for Reform*, 53–54; *Who's Who in America*, 15 (1928–29): 2097. See also Martin Lazerson and W. Norton Grubb, eds., *American Education and Vocationalism: A Documentary History* (New York, 1974).

63. *Who's Who in America*, 15 (1928–29): 2097. Elsa's pay for a year's work at Vocational Guidance, according to an undated letter to her mother, was about $1,200. EUP.

64. *Who's Who in America*, 15 (1928–29): 239; *New York Times*, October 3, 1954; Elsa Ueland to her mother, October 4, 1922, EUP. Barrows married a poet named W. G. Tinckon Fernandez in 1914, but divorced him in 1922. Following her father's death, Barrows had grown up in the Portland, Maine, household of the famous Speaker of the U.S. House of Representatives Thomas B. "Czar" Reed. For an excellent and concise biography of Barrows, see Ronald D. Cohen and Raymond A. Mohl, *The Paradox of Progressivism: The Gary Plan and Urban Schooling* (Port Washington, N.Y., 1979), 22–34.

65. A typewritten copy of the report was found among Elsa Ueland's personal papers, EUP.

66. "A Study of Eighty-Seven Working Paper Boys Who Left One School in District 9, Manhattan, in the Year 1911–1912," 1, 2, 4. In an article entitled "Juvenile Employment Agencies," which appeared in the June 1915 issue of the *American Labor Legislation Review*, Ueland continued to express her concerns about the employment of adolescents.

67. The best and most comprehensive work on progressive education remains Cremin, *Transformation of the School*, cited above. Also enlightening are Walter Feinberg, "Progressive Education and Social Planning," *Teachers College Record* (1971–72), 486–505, and Arthur Zilversmit, *Changing Schools: Progressive Education Theory and Practice, 1930–1960* (Chicago, 1993). For a good biography of John Dewey, see George Dykhuizen, *The Life and Mind of John Dewey* (Carbondale, Ill., 1973). Some recent reflections on Dewey as a pragmatist appear in James T. Kloppenberg, "Pragmatism: An Old Name for Some New Ways of Thinking?" *Journal of American History*, June 1996, 100–138.

68. For example, Richard Weissbourd, *The Vulnerable Child: What Really Hurts America's Children and What We Can Do About It* (New York, 1996); L. Katz, "Do You Foster Children's Self-Esteem or Promote Selfishness?" *Instructor*, March 1996, 62–66; T. Glaser, "Do Schools Overrate Self-Esteem?" *American Teacher* (May–June 1994), 4; A. Kohn, "The Truth About Self-Esteem," *Phi Delta Kappan*, December 1994, 277–83.

69. Raymond A. Mohl to Elsa Ueland, October 11, 1973, EUP; *Who's Who in America*, 15 (1928–29): 239.

70. Cohen and Mohl, *Progressivism*, 24.

71. *New York Times*, May 10, 1961; Elsa Ueland to her mother, September 6, 1915, November 4, 1917; Ueland to her father, January 5, 1916, EUP. Ueland and Roemer invited Alice Barrows to visit them at Gary in the fall of 1914. It was an exhilarating experience for Barrows, who became even more avid in her support for the Gary Plan back in New York. See Cohen and Mohl, *Progressivism*, 24–25.

72. On the failed campaign to have New York City adopt the Gary Plan, see Cohen and Mohl, *Progressivism*, 35–66, and Mohl, "Schools, Politics, and Riots: The Gary Plan in New York City, 1914–1916," *Paedagogica Historica*, 1975, 39–72.

73. *Who's Who in America*, 15 (1928–29): 2097; Adeline Levine and Murray Levine, introduction to Randolph S. Bourne, *The Gary Schools* (1916; reprint, Cambridge, Mass., 1970), xiv, xxxiii, xxxv, xxxix.

74. Dewey had moved on to Columbia University and was a professor there during Elsa Ueland's time in New York. There is no evidence that she took any courses from him, but she did single him out in a letter as a top professor at Columbia. See Ueland to her mother, September 28, 1912, EUP.

75. John Dewey and Evelyn Dewey, *Schools of Tomorrow* (New York, 1915), 181-94.

76. Bourne, *The Gary Schools* (Boston, 1916); Cohen and Mohl, *Progressivism*, 25.

77. See Abraham Flexner and Frank P. Bachman, *The Gary Schools: A General Account* (New York, 1918).

78. Levine and Levine, introduction to *Gary Schools*, xii-xxxix; Raymond A. Mohl and Neil Betten, "The Failure of Industrial City Planning: Gary, Indiana, 1906-1910," *AIP Journal*, July 1972, 203-14; Richard Elwell, "The Gary Plan Revisited," *American Education*, July 1976, 16-22. Further insights into the evolution of the Gary Plan may be found in a periodical called the *Platoon School*, issued between 1927 and 1936.

79. Cohen and Mohl, *Progressivism*, 17.

80. Elsa's enthusiasm comes through in a feature newspaper article about her that appeared in the *Minneapolis Journal* on June 20, 1915.

81. Elsa lived at 328 West 6th Avenue. Elsa Ueland to her mother, September 6 and 20, 1915, August 4, 1916, EUP.

82. Elsa Ueland to her mother, August 10, 1916, EUP.

83. Elsa Ueland to her father, January 5, 1916, EUP. On Chairman Gary's gift to Wirt, see Cohen and Mohl, *Progressivism*, 19.

84. Cohen and Mohl, *Progressivism*, 19.

85. Ibid. Also revealing is Elsa Ueland to her mother, April 7, 1916, EUP.

86. Elsa Ueland to her father, March 8, 1916, EUP.

87. Elsa Ueland, "The Teacher and the Gary Plan," *New Republic*, July 1, 1916, 219-21.

88. Elsa Ueland, "The Gary System," reprinted in W. J. McNally, ed., *The Gary School System* (Minneapolis, 1915), 42-43.

89. Elsa Ueland, Diary, February 14, 1910.

90. Quoted in Brenda Ueland, "Clara Ueland," 215-16.

91. Ibid., 216.

92. On her fifty-fifth college reunion in 1964, Elsa accompanied Harold Taylor to the event at the University of Minnesota. Margaret Ueland to the author, July 23, 1996.

93. Brenda Ueland, *Me*, 91.

Chapter 3

1. Board Minutes, November 17, 1916, UA.

2. Carson College for Orphan Girls to William Wirt and to Alice Barrows Fernandez, October 1, 1915. On the same day, Carson also sent the same materials to John Dewey at Columbia University, CVS.

3. Virginia Robinson, *Jessie Taft, Therapist and Social Work Educator: A Professional Biography* (Philadelphia, 1962), 44-45.

4. Board Minutes, January 19, 1917, UA.

5. *Evening Bulletin*, December 1, 1916; William A. McGarry, "A College for Wives," *Green Book*, March 1921, 18.

6. The precise date of her first visit to the site of Carson College, according to Elsa Ueland herself, was May 26, 1916. See Ueland, "History," 1.

7. Quoted in Brenda Ueland, "Clara Ueland," 330-31.

8. Ibid., 330; Elsa Ueland to her mother, April 7, 1916, EUP.

9. Elsa Ueland to her parents, March 20, 1916, EUP.

10. Quoted in Brenda Ueland, "Clara Ueland," 331.

11. Elsa Ueland to her parents, May 28, 1916, EUP. The official vote came at the board

meeting of May 26, 1916. See the board minutes of that date and also of September 15, 1916, UA.

12. Andreas Ueland to Elsa Ueland, June 11, 1916, EUP.

13. Elsa Ueland to her mother, November 10, 1916, June 17, 1917, October 11, 1918, EUP.

14. Elsa Ueland to her parents, May 28, 1916, EUP.

15. Ibid., July 11, 1916.

16. Elsa Ueland to her mother, October 13, 1916, January 19, 1917, EUP; Ueland, "History," 1.

17. Elsa Ueland to her mother, October 6, 1916, EUP.

18. *Evening Bulletin,* November 24, 1916.

19. *Public Ledger,* November 14, 1916.

20. *Evening Bulletin,* November 24, 1916.

21. Ibid., December 1, 1916.

22. Ibid.

23. Horace Mather Lippincott, *A Narrative of Chestnut Hill, Springfield, Whitemarsh, Cheltenham* (Jenkintown, Pa., 1948), 100-114; John T. Faris, *Old Roads out of Philadelphia* (Philadelphia, 1917), 234-56; *Survey Atlas,* Springfield Township, 1916.

24. Fourteenth Decennial Census of the United States (1920), Montgomery County, Springfield Township, Pennsylvania. T 625, Reel 1605, Supervisor's District 3; Enumeration District 17.

25. The census taker used Wissahickon Avenue as the unofficial southern boundary and Mill Road as the unofficial northern boundary of Flourtown, as opposed to the somewhat enlarged boundaries of the post-World War II period, which have placed Flourtown between Haws Lane and Valley Green Road.

26. Edward Pessen, *The Log Cabin Myth* (New Haven, Conn., 1984), 63. Instead of the terms "skilled workers" and "unskilled workers," Pessen uses the labels "lower-lower" and "upper-lower class" respectively.

27. For a socioeconomic profile of Chestnut Hill during this period, see Contosta, *Suburb in the City,* 118-37.

28. Nathaniel Burt and Wallace E. Davies, "The Iron Age, 1876-1905," in *Philadelphia: A 300-Year History,* ed. Russell F. Weigley (New York, 1982), 495-96.

29. On the subject of political corruption in Philadelphia during the early twentieth century, see Lloyd Abernethy, "Progressivism, 1905-1919," in *Philadelphia: A 300-Year History,* ed. Weigley, 524-65; Arthur P. Dudden, "Lincoln Steffens' Philadelphia," *PH,* October 1964, 449-58; Peter McCaffery, *When Bosses Ruled Philadelphia: The Emergence of the Republican Machine, 1867-1933* (University Park, Pa., 1993); and Michael P. McCarthy, "The Unprogressive City: Philadelphia at the Turn of the Century," *PH,* October 1987, 263-81. Also informative are Allen F. Davis and Mark H. Haller, *The Peoples of Philadelphia: A History of Ethnic Groups and Lower-Class Life, 1700-1940* (Philadelphia, 1973), and Sam Bass Warner, *The Private City: Philadelphia in Three Periods of Its Growth* (Philadelphia, 1968).

30. Board Minutes, April 20, 1917; Elsa Ueland to her mother, April 22, 1917, EUP.

31. Management Committee Minutes, April 20, 1917, UA.

32. *Evening Bulletin,* June 7, 1957; *New York Times,* June 7, 1957.

33. Yvonne Patterson, interview with the author, November 11, 1994.

34. Elsa Ueland to her mother, June 24, 1919, EUP.

35. Ibid., March 20, 1918.

36. Ibid., May 22, 1924; Management Committee Minutes, April 25, 1924, UA.

37. Management Committee Minutes, May 7, 1921, UA.

38. *Philadelphia Record,* January 4, 1930; *Evening Bulletin,* June 8, 1960; *New York Times,* June 8, 1960.

39. *Evening Bulletin,* June 30, 1977; *New York Times,* June 30, 1977.

40. Undated salary list from 1917; Salary Lists and Other Regular Charges, 1918, CVS; Management Committee Minutes, March 14, 1922, February 9, 1923, UA.

41. Management Committee Minutes, December 24, 1917, UA. See also Elsa Ueland to her parents, December 13, 1918, September 26, 1921, January 4, 1922, January 20, 1927, EUP.

42. Robinson, *Jessie Taft,* 72–73; Management Committee Minutes, March 16, 1923, UA; *Philadelphia Record,* January 4, 1930.

43. Elsa Ueland to her mother, October 29, 1918, EUP.

44. Ibid., February 16, 1919, September 3, 1924.

45. Ibid., February 20, 1919; *Evening Bulletin,* February 20 and 27, 1919; *Public Ledger,* February 20, 1919; *North American,* February 19 and 27, 1919.

46. Elsa Ueland to her mother, February 20, 1919, EUP.

47. Leonard W. Coleman to Theron I. Crane, April 29, 1918, CVS.

48. Elsa Ueland to her mother, September 23, 1918, EUP.

49. Ibid., January 17, 1919.

50. Ibid., February 20, 1919.

51. Ibid. See also ibid., February 6, 1919.

52. *Evening Bulletin,* February 20, 27, and 28, 1919.

53. Elsa Ueland to her mother, February 20, 1919, EUP.

54. Ibid., January 19, 1917. See also ibid., January 20, 1917.

55. McGarry, "College for Wives," 19.

56. Management Committee Minutes, October 11 and November 14, 1919, April 17, 1920, UA; Furniture List, July 3, 1919, CVS.

57. That Ueland was fascinated by the theory of evolution is evident from a letter to her father on March 3, 1921, in which she is full of enthusiasm over a book about evolution that she has just finished reading and that she plans to send to her father, EUP.

58. Yvonne Patterson, interview with the author, November 14, 1994; Management Committee Minutes, November 15, 1922, March 16, October 12, and December 14, 1923, UA; Elsa Ueland to Board of Trustees, May 6, 1918, CVS. According to the minutes of the Management Committee for October 12, 1923, Ninth House was obtained in the fall of that year.

59. Elsa Ueland to her mother, December 24, 1917, EUP; Ueland to the Finance Committee of Carson College for Orphan Girls, February 23, 1918, CVS.

60. Elsa Ueland to her mother, February 13 and March 20, 1918, EUP; Ueland, "History," 1.

61. For example, Leonard W. Coleman to Chief Probation Officer, West Chester, Pa., February 11, 1916, and to Associated Charities, Norristown, Pa., February 14, 1916, CVS.

62. Coleman to Crane, February 10, 1916, CVS.

63. Ueland, "History," 2.

64. Elsa Ueland, President's Annual Report, January 16, 1925, CVS; Management Committee Minutes, November 16, 1921, May 11 and September 26, 1923, UA; Annual Report of the Management Committee, February 17, 1922, January 19, 1923, CVS.

65. Social Worker's Report, October 1, 1926, April 15 and September 23, 1927, UA; President's Annual Report, January 1, 1931, CVS.

66. Ueland discussed such cases in some detail in a letter, dated January 17, 1918, to the Carson board of trustees (CVS). Forty years later, in her brief history of Carson, Ueland

wrote, "In the absence of a death certificate, a sworn statement was accepted" ("History," 3).

67. For a discussion of this phenomenon, see Marshall B. Jones, "Crisis of the American Orphanage, 1931-1940," *SSR,* December 1989, 612-23. On the subject of orphanages and child welfare in general, see Grace Abbott, ed., *The Child and the State,* 2 vols. (Chicago, 1938); Leroy Ashby, *Saving the Waifs: Reformers and Dependent Children, 1890-1917* (Philadelphia, 1984); Ellen Key, *The Century of the Child* (New York, 1909); Leroy H. Pelton, "Not for Poverty Alone: Foster Care Population Trends in the Twentieth Century," *Journal of Sociology and Social Welfare,* June 1987, 37-62; Susan Tiffin, *In Whose Best Interest? Child Welfare Reform in the Progressive Era* (Westport, Conn., 1982); and Martin Wollins and Irving Piliavin, *Institution or Foster Family: A Century of Debate* (New York, 1964).

68. Elsa Ueland to the Management Committee, Carson College for Orphan Girls, September 20, 1918, CVS.

69. Social Worker's Report, September 23, 1927, UA.

70. Ibid., April 15, 1927.

71. Ibid., January 20, 1928.

72. Ibid., May 10, 1929.

73. Elsa Ueland to Russell L. Pullinger, Secretary, Springfield Township School Board, May 20, 1918; D. Yeakel Miller, School District of Springfield, to Ueland, May 23, 1918; Pullinger to Ueland, July 15, 1918, CVS.

74. Pullinger to Ueland, July 25, 1918, CVS; Ueland to her mother, July 16, 1918, EUP.

75. Elsa Ueland to Dr. Bradley C. Algee, Chairman, Springfield Township School Board, August 26, 1918, CVS.

76. Pullinger to Ueland, October 2, 1918; Ueland to Pullinger, October 5, 1918, CVS; Management Committee Minutes, December 17, 1920, March 18, 1921, UA.

77. Elsa Ueland to her mother, July 16, 1918, EUP. In writing about the early days of the institution some forty years later, Ueland did not mention these conflicts with the local school board and instead spoke of a "close cooperation" with Springfield Township school authorities. See Ueland, "History," 3.

78. Elsa Ueland to her mother, September 10, 1918, EUP.

79. Board Minutes, September 20, 1918; Phoebe [Crosby] Allnutt, "Educational Adventures in an Institution," *Family,* June 1923, unpaginated reprint. At the time that she came to work at Carson, Allnutt's husband was living and working in Baltimore, Maryland. In the fall of 1920 he left his position there and joined Phoebe in Flourtown. They later divorced, and she reverted to her maiden name of Crosby. See Board Minutes, October 11, 1920, and April 15, 1921, UA.

80. Lucy Sprague Mitchell, *Two Lives: The Story of Wesley Clair Mitchell and Myself* (New York, 1953), 272-73; *New York Times,* October 17, 1967. See also Ueland's entry in *Leaders in Education* (New York, 1932), 945. An excellent biography of Mitchell is Joyce Antler, *Lucy Sprague Mitchell: The Making of a Modern Woman* (New Haven, Conn., 1987).

Chapter 4

1. Cremin, *Transformation of the School,* viii.

2. Memorandum on Salaries, June 1922; Management Committee Minutes, June 13, 1924, June 3, 1927, UA.

3. Dorothy Moore Fenstermacher, interview with the author, December 2, 1995.

4. *Philadelphia Press,* July 14, 1918.

5. Notes on School Program, School Programs, 1920–22, CVS.

6. Ibid.

7. "Flourtown: A Study by the Eighth Grade," Flourtown, Pa., 1928, CVS. In 1923, 1924, and 1925 (and possibly in other years) the ninth grade printed booklets containing an assortment of entries, ranging from accounts of field trips and the findings of their various researches to the programs of social events held throughout the year. In 1923 this publication was called "An Inkling," and in 1924 and 1935 it was simply entitled "A Class Book."

8. Elsa Ueland, President's Annual Report, January 19, 1932, CVS.

9. Elsa Ueland to her mother, July 1921, EUP.

10. *Jabberwock*, June 1927.

11. Ibid.

12. Allnutt, "Educational Adventures."

13. Harriet R. Smith to Elsa Ueland, April 10, 1941; Greta M. Murray to Ueland (undated but probably written in early 1941); Notes on Trips, CVS.

14. Smith to Ueland, April 10, 1941, CVS.

15. As cited in note 5 above.

16. Report on Assemblies: October–November–December, 1924, CVS.

17. "The Record of Our Mice," Little School, June 1926, CVS.

18. *Yesterday and Today*, School Program, 1927–31, CVS.

19. See, in particular, David Glassberg, *American Historical Pageantry* (Chapel Hill, N.C., 1990), 71–101.

20. Ibid., 43–67.

21. *Public Ledger*, May 22, 1920.

22. Business Manager to William L. Turner, Correspondence, 1919–24; School Programs, 1927–31, CVS.

23. *Jabberwock*, Christmas 1925; Treasurer to Elsa Ueland, December 22, 1919, CVS.

24. Yvonne Patterson, interview with the author, November 11, 1994; Fenstermacher, interview with the author, December 2, 1995; Elsa Ueland to her mother, December 16, 1924, December 29, 1925, January 20, 1927, EUP.

25. Festivals, School Programs, 1927–31, CVS.

26. Mary Bordogna, telephone interview with the author, March 15, 1996. Mary Bordogna's mother-in-law was Josephine Bordogna, the housemother at Tanglewood Cottage.

27. Elsa Ueland to Tony, Clara, and Margaret Bordogna, August 23, 1934, CVS. The occasion of this letter was the board's recent and sad decision to close Tanglewood Cottage, where the Bordogna family had lived.

28. Deardorff, "New Pied Pipers," 32–35.

29. Helen Traiche Heath, telephone interview with the author, June 3, 1996; Florence MacFarlane, telephone interview with the author, July 28, 1996.

30. Heath, telephone interview with the author, June 3, 1996; Bordogna, telephone interview with the author, March 15, 1996.

31. MacFarlane, telephone interview with the author, July 28, 1996; Caroline Conley Vankouwenberg, interview with the author, October 14, 1995.

32. Alice Wandel, telephone interview with the author, June 30, 1996.

33. Vankouwenberg, interview with the author, October 14, 1995.

34. Bordogna, telephone interview with the author, March 15, 1996.

35. Salary Adjustments Recommended June 1922, July 1, 1927; Treasurer's Report, 1926, CVS.

36. Deardorff, "New Pied Pipers," 31–50.

37. Heath, telephone interview with the author, June 3, 1996.

38. Wandel, telephone interview with the author, June 30, 1996.

39. MacFarlane, telephone interview with the author, July 28, 1996; Vankouwenberg, interview with the author, October 14, 1995.

40. Elsa Ueland to the Management Committee, Report: July 1 to September 20, 1918, Management Committee, CVS.

41. McGarry, "College for Wives," 18. See also Elsa Ueland to her mother, July 19, 1921, EUP.

42. Board Minutes, January 19, 1917; Resolution of Management Committee, January 18, 1917, UA.

43. Elsa Ueland to her mother, November 17, 1917, EUP.

44. Elsa Ueland to her mother, March 22, 1917, December 12, 1920, EUP.

45. Management Committee Minutes, February 13, 1922, December 12, 1924, UA.

46. Ibid., February 13, 1922, July 26, 1924, December 2, 1927; Board Minutes, April 22, 1930, UA; Salary Adjustments Recommended July 1, 1927, CVS; Elsa Ueland to Leo Nelson Sharpe, October 20, 1927, CVS; President's Annual Report, January 1, 1931, CVS; Ueland to Robert W. Meeker, Manager, U.S. Employment Service, April 27, 1943, CVS.

47. Elsa Ueland to Theron I. Crane, October 19, 1917; Crane to Ueland, November 15, 1917, Committee Correspondence, 1915-18, CVS; Ueland to her mother, November 17, 1917, EUP.

48. Ueland, Memorandum to Management Committee, November 10, 1917, CVS.

49. Alice Mary Steiner, "A Potato Party," *Jabberwock,* December 1930.

50. Management Committee Minutes, April 19, 1922, UA.

51. Heath, telephone interview with the author, June 3, 1996.

52. Cremin, *Transformation of the School,* 150.

53. Management Committee Minutes, April 19 and June 16, 1922, September 26, 1923, October 15, 1924, UA; Annual Report of the Management Committee, January 11, 1923, CVS; Salary Lists and Other Regular Charges, 1918, CVS.

54. McGarry, "College for Wives," 18, 19; Management Committee Minutes, March 19, 1924, UA.

55. McGarry, "College for Wives," 18.

56. Board Minutes, November 21, 1919, UA.

57. McGarry, "College for Wives," 18.

58. Annual Report of the Management Committee, January 19, 1923, and January 18, 1924, CVS.

59. Ibid., February 17, 1922. The first serious consideration of vocational training seems to have been taken up at the management committee meeting of March 18, 1921, UA.

60. Board Minutes, April 22, 1930, UA.

61. Vocational Report, November 16, 1926, CVS.

62. Management Committee Minutes, May 18, 1922, UA.

63. Ibid., September 26, 1923.

64. Ibid., November 14, 1924.

65. Ibid.

66. Ibid., February 17, 1922.

67. Allnutt, "Educational Adventures." Similar ideas were repeated by Allnutt in her annual school report dated January 17, 1924, CVS.

68. Allnutt, "Educational Adventures."

69. Management Committee Minutes, September 19, 1924, UA; Memorandum for Management Committee, March 18, 1927, UA; Social Worker's Report, September 23, 1927, UA.

70. C. Madeleine Dixon, "Nursery School Experience as Pre-vocational Training," *Jabber-wock*, May 1926, 6.

71. McGarry, "College for Wives," 19; Memorandum to Board, undated but probably sometime in 1928, UA.

72. Elsa Ueland to her mother, September 26, 1921, EUP.

73. Cremin, *Transformation of the School*, 204.

74. Ibid. See also Alice Burnett, "Pioneer Contributions to the Nursery School" (Ph.D. diss., Columbia University, 1964); Hamilton Craven, *Before Head Start* (Chapel Hill, N.C., 1993); Ilse Forest, *Preschool Education: A Historical and Critical Study* (New York, 1927); Florence L. Goodenough and John E. Anderson, *Experimental Child Study* (New York, 1931); and Caroline Pratt and Jessie Stanton, *Before Books* (New York, 1926).

75. Cremin, *Transformation of the School*, 202–3; Management Committee Minutes, November 16, 1921, UA.

76. Mitchell, *Two Lives*, 272–73, 406–9.

77. Board Minutes, September 10, 1930, UA; *Philadelphia Inquirer*, December 24, 1945.

78. C. Madeleine Dixon's 1930 book *Children Are Like That* was published in New York by John Day, which carried a substantial list of titles in progressive education. Dixon's second book on nursery schools, also published by Day, was *High Wide and Deep: Discovering the Preschool Child* (New York, 1938). Dixon later published several novels, including *The Devil and the Deep* (New York, 1944).

79. Elsa Ueland, Carson College Nursery School, 1926–27: Memorandum upon Tuition and Financial Support, CVS.

80. Carson College Nursery School, September 1926, Nursery School, CVS.

81. Ibid.; *Jabberwock*, February 1928.

82. Management Committee Minutes, May 11, 1923, October 1, 1926, UA.

83. Management Committee Minutes, May 13, 1926, UA.

84. Present School Groups and Their Work, Teachers' Meetings, 1924–'25, CVS.

85. Elsa Ueland to her father, July 6, 1929, EUP.

86. Board Minutes, October 17, 1924, May 18, 1928, UA; Phoebe [Crosby] Allnutt to Mrs. Gould, June 19, 1928, CVS.

87. Teachers Meeting, June 17, 1924, Teachers Meetings, 1923–24, CVS.

88. Board Minutes, May 20, 1921; Management Committee Minutes, February 17, 1922, UA.

89. Ueland to Pullinger, April 3, 1923, CVS; Management Committee Minutes, April 16, 1923, January 17, 1924, UA.

90. Ueland to Pullinger, April 3, 1923, CVS.

91. Russell L. Pullinger to Elsa Ueland, April 9, 1923, CVS.

92. Elsa Ueland to her mother, January 16, 1923, EUP; Management Committee Minutes, January 12, 1923, UA.

93. Patterson, interview with the author, November 11, 1994.

94. Board Minutes, September 20, 1918, UA.

95. Ibid.

96. Vankouwenberg, interview with the author, October 14, 1996.

97. Board Minutes, February 19, 1919, November 19, 1926, UA; Patterson, interview with the author, May 23, 1995.

98. Board Minutes, May 21, 1920, UA; Management Committee Minutes, April 30, 1921, December 14, 1923, October 15 and November 14, 1924, March 18, 1925, UA; Patterson, interview with the author, May 23, 1995; *Norristown Times-Herald*, July 5 and July 7, 1952.

An obituary of Willets appeared in the *Ambler Gazette* on January 20, 1966. A complete list of the dental equipment purchased (dated April 30, 1921), along with the prices paid, is among the materials generated by the management committee, CVS.

99. Elsa Ueland to her mother, November 17, 1917, EUP. On the playground movement during this period, see Dominick Cavallo, *Muscles and Morals: Organized Playgrounds and Urban Reform* (Philadelphia, 1981), and Lawrence A. Finfer, "Leisure as Social Work in the Urban Community: The Progressive Recreation Movement, 1890-1920" (Ph.D. diss., Michigan State University, 1974).

100. Management Committee Minutes, May 15, 1925, UA.

101. Patterson, interview with the author, May 23, 1995; Management Committee Minutes, May 11, 1923, January 17 and June 13, 1924, May 15, 1925, May 13, 1926, UA. An undated list of all the equipment purchased for the playground was found among the management committee records. It was probably drawn up during the winter or spring of 1919, CVS.

102. Elsa Ueland to her parents, August 8, 1918, EUP.

103. Elsa Ueland to her father, July 6, 1929, EUP.

104. Board Secretary to Elsa Ueland, April 12, 1920, Correspondence, 1919-24, CVS; Board Minutes, May 15, 1925; Management Committee Minutes, May 13, 1926, UA; Ueland to William Harper, March 7, 1919; Ueland to E. K. Krumbhaar, Commandant, December 1, 1919; Krumbhaar to Ueland, December 5, 1919, both letters in Community—General Transactions, CVS; Visitor's Bulletin, March 1926, Teachers Meetings, 1925-26, CVS.

105. *Ambler Gazette,* December 25, 1975.

106. Patterson, interview with the author, May 23, 1995; Board Minutes, May 20, 1930, UA.

107. Management Committee Minutes, April 17 and June 17, 1925, UA.

108. Board Minutes, June 20, 1924, May 21, 1926; Management Committee Minutes, June 13, 1924, UA; *Jabberwock,* August 1925 and midsummer 1928.

109. Elsa Ueland to her father, July 6, 1929, EUP.

110. Wandel, telephone interview with the author, June 30, 1996; Heath, telephone interview with the author, June 3, 1996.

111. Marie Kitto, interview with the author, February 1, 1995; Management Committee Minutes, April 25, 1924, May 15, 1925; Board Minutes, October 23 and December 18, 1925, UA; Business Manager to Theron I. Crane, May 2, 1922, CVS.

112. Elsa Ueland, "A Re-evaluation of Methods of Child Care: The Case of Children in Institutions," June 26, 1924.

113. Elsa Ueland, "Celery Child or Strawberry Child: Handicaps of Institutional Life for Children," *Survey,* February 15, 1924 (unpaginated reprint). Ueland had already presented much of what appeared in this article in her annual report of February 17, 1922, which she had entitled "Handicaps of Institutional Life" (CVS). It thus seems clear that the *Survey* article was based in part on this earlier presentation.

114. Ueland, "Celery Child or Strawberry Child."

115. Zilversmit, *Changing Schools,* 15-16.

116. Elsa Ueland, "Every Child—Where and How He Plays," *Annals of the American Academy of Political and Social Science,* September 1925, 1-6, and "The Rights of the Child," in *Proceedings of the Thirty-Third Session of the Minnesota State Conference, Second Session of the Institute for Social Work, September 19-25, 1925.*

117. Management Committee Minutes, June 13 and September 18, 1924, March 19 and April 16, 1926; Board Minutes, January 21 and April 15, 1927, UA; entry for Elsa Ueland in *Leaders in Education: A Biographical Directory* (New York, 1932), 945.

118. Management Committee Minutes, December 12, 1924, March 18, 1925, UA.

119. Deardorff, "New Pied Pipers," 36.

120. Ibid., 37.

121. Ellen C. Potter, M.D., Secretary of Welfare, to John Gribbel, January 10, 1926, CVS.

122. See, for example, Elsa Ueland to her mother, July 6, 1919, July 19, 1921, August 21, 1922, EUP.

123. Elsa Ueland to her father, July 6, 1929, EUP.

Chapter 5

1. Carson College for Orphan Girls, Annual Reports, 1920-37, CVS; Board Minutes, September 20, 1918, UA.

2. Treasurer's Report, June 30, 1919, December 31, 1928, UA; Board Minutes, March 21, 1945, UA.

3. Board Minutes, February 17, 1922, UA.

4. Ibid., March 19, April 16, and December 28, 1926, February 18, 1927, December 21, 1928, April 22, 1930.

5. See, for example, ibid., October 23, 1929.

6. Ibid., October 1, 1926, December 28, 1926; Management Committee Minutes, February 13, 1922, November 14, 1924, May 13, 1926, UA; Report of Building Committee, 1927, UA.

7. Memorandum from Elsa Ueland to Theron I. Crane, June 15, 1929, CVS.

8. Board Minutes, April 16, 1925, UA.

9. Ibid., December 28, 1926, June 13 and October 23, 1929. Hepburn and Norris charged Carson College a legal fee of $5,000 for these services.

10. Ibid., April 19, 1929, May 22 and June 18, 1930; Leo Nelson Sharpe to C. J. Hepburn, Esq., April 3, 1926; Charles Townley Larzelere to Hepburn, April 15, 1930, CVS; Petition of the Carson College for Orphan Girls for Order upon Trustees to pay cost of Erection of Certain Buildings from Income Account, CVS.

11. Elsa Ueland, President's Annual Report, January 16, 1925, CVS.

12. On the subject of progressive and feminist housing reform, see Clifford Edward Clark Jr., *The American Family Home, 1880-1960* (Chapel Hill, N.C., 1986), 131-92; Dolores Hayden, *The Grand Domestic Revolution: A History of Feminist Designs for American Homes, Neighborhoods, and Cities* (Cambridge, Mass., 1981), 151-53; and Gwendolyn Wright, *Moralism and the Modern Home* (Chicago, 1980), 231-53.

13. Elsa Ueland, President's Annual Report, January 16, 1925, CVS.

14. Ibid.

15. Elsa Ueland, "Our Next Cottage: What We Would Like to Have Included in Any Cottage Built by the College," *Jabberwock*, June 15, 1925, CVS.

16. Ibid., 1.

17. Ibid.

18. Ibid., 3.

19. Ibid.

20. Ibid., 4-5.

21. Albert Kelsey to Elsa Ueland, October 14, 1925, CVS.

22. Theron I. Crane to Albert Kelsey, October 16, 1925, CVS.

23. Ueland to Kelsey, October 27, 1925, CVS.

24. Ibid.

25. Management Committee Minutes, May 13, 1926, UA.

26. Ueland to Kelsey, May 18, 1926, CVS; Ueland, Diary, December 26, 1939, EUP.

27. Elsa Ueland to her mother, July 23, 1916, EUP.

28. Ibid., October 12 and October 13, 1916.

29. Ueland was not the only one at Carson who was displeased with Kelsey from an early period. In the summer of 1918 Superintendent Coleman was furious about a letter in which Kelsey had accused Coleman of neglecting the grounds. Kelsey to Coleman, June 17, 1918; Coleman to Ueland, June 21, 1918, CVS.

30. Ueland to Kelsey, February 16, 1927, CVS.

31. Leo Nelson Sharpe to Walter W. Perkins, February 12, 1927, CVS.

32. Board Minutes, January 21 and April 15, 1927, UA; Leo Nelson Sharpe to C. J. Hepburn, February 8, 1927, CVS.

33. Milner Associates, "An Architectural and Historical Survey, Carson Valley School," April 1985, 46; Kelsey to Crane, May 14, 1926; Sharpe to Perkins, February 12, 1927, CVS; Board Minutes, January 21 and April 15, 1927, UA. An article on the Loves' "English Village" in Wynnewood appeared in the *Evening Bulletin* on August 4, 1968. See also *Main Line Chronicle,* October 22, 1975.

34. Board Minutes, July 23, 1917, UA.

35. At that time Chestnut Hill College was known as Mount Saint Joseph Academy. The sisters had first come to this site in 1858, when they purchased the former Joseph Middleton Estate and began operating a series of schools; these activities culminated in the founding of a college in 1924. On the sisters and their various activities on the Chestnut Hill site, see Maria Kostka Logue, S.S.J., *Sisters of Saint Joseph: A Century of Growth and Development, 1847-1947* (Westminster, Md., 1950), and John Lukacs, *A Sketch of the History of Chestnut Hill College* (Philadelphia, 1975).

36. Yvonne Patterson, interview with the author, November 14, 1994.

37. See David R. Contosta, *A Philadelphia Family: The Houstons and Woodwards of Chestnut Hill* (Philadelphia, 1988), 68-70.

38. Board Minutes, September 19, 1930, UA.

39. Tatman and Moss, *Philadelphia Architects,* 47. See also William Pope Barney, *Some Domestic Architecture in Surrey and Sussex* (New York, 1930); "House Beautiful's 13th Annual Small House Competition," *House Beautiful,* February 1941, 18-19; "Juniata Housing Corp. Project in Philadelphia," *AR,* April 1958, 328-29.

40. Board Minutes, September 19, 1930, UA.

41. Ibid., December 18, 1930, November 20, 1931.

42. See Wendy Hitchmough, *C.F.A. Voysey* (New York, 1995).

43. Elsa Ueland, "The New Buildings," *Jabberwock,* December 1930, 1.

44. Board Minutes, April 13, 1932, UA.

45. Elsa Ueland to William Pope Barney, January 20, 1932; Barney to Ueland, January 25, 1932, CVS; Board Minutes, May 21, 1926, UA.

46. Report of the Finance Committee, Carson College for Orphan Girls, 1932, pp. 2, 15, CVS; Board Minutes, April 20 1934, March 21, 1945, UA.

47. Report of the Finance Committee, 1932, CVS; Board Minutes, February 19, 1932, May 19, 1933, April 20, 1934, UA.

48. Board Minutes, April 24, 1935, UA.

49. Ibid., October 18, 1935. These same findings were conveyed in a letter of November 6, 1935, from Sharpe, Lewis, and Lukens to the Real Estate Land Title and Trust Company, CVS.

50. Agreement Between Land Title Bank and Trust Company and the Carson College

for Orphan Girls, October 1, 1936, CVS. See also Board Minutes, June 19 and October 16, 1936, UA.

51. Leo Nelson Sharpe to Percy C. Madeira Jr., Vice-President, Land Title Bank and Trust Company, December 2, 1936, CVS.

52. Leo Nelson Sharpe to Lewis N. Lukens Jr., May 17, 1933, CVS.

53. Board Minutes, October 16, 1936, UA

54. Ibid., May 28, 1934.

55. Dorothy Moore Fenstermacher, interview with the author, December 2, 1995.

56. Board Minutes, June 15 and September 21, 1934, UA; Elsa Ueland to Tony, Clara, and Margaret Bordogna, August 23, 1934. In a letter to Josephine Bordogna on August 23, 1934, Ueland wrote that the remaining cottages were Red Gables, Stork Hill, Thistle, Orchard, and the two Beeches, CVS.

57. These salary cuts were partially reversed in 1936. See Board Minutes, October 16, 1936, UA.

58. Ibid., June 3, 1929, January 18, April 24, and October 16, 1935.

59. Ibid., June 5 and November 20, 1931, September 16 and October 21, 1932.

60. Ibid., September 22, 1937.

61. Elsa Ueland to Dorothy Hoyle, September 8, 1953, CVS.

62. Summer Jobs, 1939, CVS.

63. Board Minutes, December 22, 1931, UA.

64. Elsa Ueland, Memorandum on Budget, May 18, 1934, CVS.

65. Mitchell, *Two Lives,* 423-32.

66. Board Minutes, December 22, 1931, UA; Finance Committee Report to Board of Trustees, May 15, 1936, UA. Ueland wrote an account of this trip for a publication called *69 Bank Street.* It appeared in the issue for May 1935 (pp. 10-14). On the Resettlement Administration itself, see Bernard Sternsher, *Rexford Tugwell and the New Deal* (New Brunswick, N.J., 1964), 262-306, and James S. Olson, ed., *Historical Dictionary of the New Deal* (Westport, Conn., 1985).

67. Patterson, interview with the author, November 11, 1994; Margaret Ueland to the author, July 23, 1996. Elsa Ueland praised Eleanor Roosevelt strongly in a diary entry from November 3, 1940, EUP.

68. On the connections between progressives and the progressive movement and the later New Deal reforms, see Donald Feinman, *Twilight of Progressivism and the New Deal* (Baltimore, 1981), and Otis L. Graham Jr., *An Encore for Reform: The Old Progressives and the New Deal* (New York, 1973).

69. Hayes, "Reformers, Radicals, and Conservatives," 361-63. Ueland's continuing identification with Minnesota ways was confirmed by Margaret Ueland in her letter to this author on July 23, 1996.

70. Leo Nelson Sharpe to Horace C. Jones, August 7, 1935, CVS.

71. Board Minutes, October 18, 1935, April 22, 1938, UA.

72. *Evening Bulletin,* November 25, 1938.

73. Elsa Ueland to Otto T. Mallery, October 16, 1936, CVS.

74. Clara Ueland to the author, August 4, 1996; Julia E. Moore, interview with the author, June 10, 1996. Moore, who knew Ueland from the mid-1930s, remembered that Ueland had once become enraged and had "blown up" at a board meeting, but she was unsure of the date.

75. Ueland was given two months off with salary and three months without. See Board Minutes, June 3, 1938, UA.

76. Ibid., March 16 and 23, 1923, April 22 and November 25, 1938; Elsa Ueland, Diary,

July 1913, November–December 1938, EUP; Ueland to her father, August 21, 1923, March 18, 1929, EUP; Ueland, Plans for a trip, July 1, 1938, EUP; *Philadelphia Inquirer,* November 25, 1938.

77. Patterson, interview with the author, November 11, 1994; Board Minutes, October 20, 1939, UA. As early as April 9, 1917, Ueland wrote her father, Andreas, and asked him to invest $500 for her. On May 7, 1921, she wrote her mother about a plan to save $50 each month as part of a personal pension plan. See also Ueland to her mother, July 19, 1921, EUP.

78. Russell A. Allen to Elsa Ueland, December 10, 1938, EUP.

79. Ueland to Mallery, May 31, 1938, CVS; Ueland, Diary, May 9, 1939, EUP; Patterson, interviews with the author, November 11 and 14, 1994.

80. Patterson, interviews with the author, November 11 and 14, 1994.

81. Ueland willed the house to Yvonne Patterson, who returned to live with her in the late 1960s. At the time of this writing (fall 1996), the house looks much as it did when Elsa Ueland lived there with Kate Tucker, including the rugs, furniture, books, paintings, and other interior features.

82. Elsa Ueland, Diary, September 14 and September 29, 1939, EUP. Patterson, interview with the author, June 12, 1995.

83. Elsa Ueland, Diary, April 19, 1939. Similar sentiments appear in her entry from April 16, 1939, EUP.

84. As early as November 8, 1920, in a letter to her mother, Ueland expressed her disgust at conservative, Republican Pennsylvania, EUP.

85. Margaret Ueland to the author, June 23, 1996.

86. Ueland may also have been dropped from *Who's Who* because she had virtually ceased to publish articles or to give addresses at important national conferences, a turn of events that appeared to start at about the time of her mother's death in early 1927 and a serious bout of depression that accompanied it.

87. Moore, interview with the author, June 10, 1996. Elsa's sister-in-law, Margaret Ueland, also wrote to this author, in her letter of July 23, 1996, that she knew nothing of Elsa's depression during the late 1930s.

88. Elsa Ueland to Horace C. Jones, April 21, 1939, CVS; Ueland, Diary, April 22, 1939, EUP.

89. Elsa Ueland to her father, December 16, 1928, EUP.

90. In fact, in early 1927 Taft had written to Rank, who was then in Paris, asking him if he would see Elsa when he came to Philadelphia later in the year. This is made clear from the letter that Rank wrote to Ueland on April 25, 1927. Elsa's father, Andreas Ueland, also refers to her depression in a letter to her dated May 4, 1928. Ueland, Diary, May 5, 1939, EUP.

91. Elsa Ueland, Diary, February 26, 1940, EUP.

92. Rank's most important works on the role of will are *Truth and Reality:A Life History of the Human Will* and *Will Therapy:An Analysis of the Therapeutic Process in Terms of Relationship,* both published in English by Alfred A. Knopf (New York, 1936). The translator of both volumes was Ueland's close friend Jessie Taft. I found copies of both works in Oak Run, Elsa Ueland's home during the last four decades of her life, in the autumn of 1994.

93. Jessie Taft, *Otto Rank:A Biographical Study Based on Notebooks, Letters, Collected Writings, Therapeutic Achievements, and Personal Associations* (New York, 1958). I likewise found a copy of this book at Oak Run. It was autographed by Taft, with the inscription "To Elsa—with affection, Jessie."

94. Elsa Ueland, Diary, May 7, May 9, May 22, and May 28, 1939, January 7, 1940, EUP.

95. Ibid., October 26, 1939. Ueland to her mother, September 11, 1918, February 23, 1924, October 8, 1926, EUP; Patterson, interview with the author, November 11, 1994.

96. Margaret Ueland to the author, June 23, 1996; Clara Ueland to the author, August 4, 1996; Mark Ueland, interview with the author, May 20, 1996.

97. Elsa Ueland, Diary, December 18, 1939, EUP.

98. Ibid., April 29, 1939; Ueland to her mother, September 26, 1926; Almena Dawley to Ueland, January 3, 1947, EUP; Management Committee Minutes, October 12, 1923, UA; Cohen and Mohl, *Progressivism*, 26-27.

99. Elsa Ueland, Diary, April 17, 1939. The quartet also played on New Year's Day 1940 and on Elsa's birthday, March 10 of the same year, according to diary entries of January 3 and March 12, EUP.

100. Clara Ueland to the author, August 4, 1996.

101. Moore, interview with the author, June 10, 1996.

102. The name "Pocket," according to Yvonne Patterson, derived from the fact that Taft and Robinson had been forced to dig deeply into their pockets in order to purchase the house.

103. Elsa Ueland, Diary, June 8, September 26, and January 12, 1939, EUP.

104. Board Minutes, May 26, 1952, UA; *Evening Bulletin*, May 18, 1952. For more on Shippen Lewis, see Mary Wickham Bond, *Ninety Years at Home in Philadelphia* (Bryn Mawr, Pa., 1988). For the story of Philadelphia's James Bond and his connection to Agent 007, see David R. Contosta, *The Private Life of James Bond* (Lititz, Pa., 1993).

105. Mary Wickham Porcher Bond (the former Mrs. Shippen Lewis), interview with the author, May 27, 1995.

106. Elsa Ueland, Diary, June 4, 1930, EUP.

107. Ibid., June 26, 1940.

108. See Contosta, *Philadelphia Family*, 69-70, and *Suburb in the City*, 108-11. See also Cynthia Ann McLoed, "Arts and Crafts Architecture in Suburban Philadelphia Sponsored by Dr. George Woodward" (master's thesis, University of Virginia, 1979), and Mary Corbin Sies, "American Country House Architecture in the East and Midwest, 1877-1917" (Ph.D. diss., University of Michigan, 1987).

109. On the Greenbelt towns, see Joseph Arnold, *The New Deal in the Suburbs: A History of the Greenbelt Town Program, 1935-1954* (Columbus, Ohio, 1971). For a brief description of the Greenbelt towns, see Olson, *Historical Dictionary of the New Deal*, 221-22. A wider perspective on the Greenbelt projects may be found in Carol A. Christensen, *The American Garden City and the New Towns Movement* (Ann Arbor, Mich., 1986), and Robert Fishman, *Urban Utopias in the Twentieth Century* (New York, 1977).

110. Ueland was clearly wrong in stating that there was a lack of public recreation for the underprivileged children in Chestnut Hill. In the early 1920s the Woodward family had built the so-called Water Tower Recreation Center on the East Side of the Hill, where the less prosperous population of the community then resided. On this matter, see Contosta, *Philadelphia Family*, 88, 109.

111. Elsa Ueland to Shippen Lewis, April 11, 1939, CVS.

112. Otto T. Mallery to Leo Nelson Sharpe, May 10, 1938, CVS; Elsa Ueland, Diary, April 20 and May 14, 1939, EUP; Milner Associates, "Architectural and Historical Survey," 18. On Wright's more general interest in such residential planning, see Robert C. Twombly, "Undoing the City: Frank Lloyd Wright's Planned Communities," *AQ*, October 1973, 538-49.

113. Elsa Ueland, Diary, July 15, 1939, EUP.

114. Ibid.

115. Ueland, "History," 4.

116. Elsa Ueland, "Admission of New Children: Some Notes on Our Experience of the Past Twenty Years, for Discussion in Considering Our Direction During the Next Chapter," December 2, 1936, CVS; Ueland, "History," 4.

117. Elsa Ueland, "The Dilemma," 1, CVS.

118. Ibid., 3.

119. Ueland, "History," 7.

120. Leiby, *Social Welfare and Social Work,* 191-92, 197, 212-13, 232, 246-47; Jones, "American Orphanage, 1931-1940," 623-29. Aid to Dependent Children was repealed by Congress in August 1996.

121. Annual Report, 1930, CVS; Social Worker's Report, March 1, 1931, UA; Board Minutes, September 21, 1934, UA; Memorandum on the Admission of New Children, December 2, 1936, UA; Treasurer's Report, 1939, UA; Elsa Ueland to Arnold Look, President, Ellis College, September 12, 1946, CVS; Caroline Conley Vankouwenberg, interview with the author, October 14, 1995; Fenstermacher, interview with the author, December 2, 1995; Fenstermacher, telephone interview with the author, January 9, 1996.

122. Ueland, "The Dilemma," 3.

123. Ibid., 14.

124. Ibid., 15.

125. Board Minutes, April 6, 1937, UA. One board member who opposed the change, at least initially, was Leo Nelson Sharpe. See Sharpe to Ueland, June 8, 1938, CVS.

126. As part of this research, Ueland solicited the advice of numerous child-care agencies. Several of their responses were quite copious and more or less in agreement that Carson should loosen its admissions requirements. These letters include Helen Glenn Tyson, United States Children's Bureau, to Ueland, January 14, 1937; Irene Liggett, Children's Aid Society of Pennsylvania, to Ueland, April 26, 1937; Edith M. Everett, White-Williams Foundation, to Ueland, May 20, 1937; Ora Pendleton, Children's Bureau of Philadelphia, to Ueland, June 18, 1937; Betsy Libbey, Family Society of Philadelphia, to Ueland, June 21, 1937, CVS.

127. Leo Nelson Sharpe, Charles Townley Larzelere, and Shippen Lewis to the Trustees of the Carson College for Orphan Girls, April 11, 1939, CVS; Board Minutes, April 21 and May 19, 1939, UA. See also Lewis N. Lukens Jr. to Elsa Ueland, June 8, 1938, and Lewis to Ueland, June 9, 1938, CVS.

128. Elsa Ueland to Board of Trustees, January 17, 1918, CVS.

129. Social Worker's Report, December 20, 1929, UA. Another girl whose mother had been committed to a mental institution was admitted in September 1933.

130. Board Minutes, June 18, 1940, UA; Brothers and Sisters, 1942, CVS.

131. Social Worker's Report, December 16, 1927, UA; Ueland, "History," 5.

132. Judge Harold G. Knight to S. L. Pinkerton, September 28, 1935; Leo Nelson Sharpe to Judge Harold G. Knight, October 15, 1935, CVS; Board Minutes, November 19, 1937, November 18, 1940, UA; Ueland, "History," 4.

133. Board Minutes, September 16, 1939, May 8, 1941, UA.

134. Inquiries and Applications for the Admission of New Children, June 1939-May 1940, CVS.

135. Ibid.

136. Bylaws, adopted by the Board of Trustees, November 18, 1940, CVS.

137. Elsa Ueland, Diary, July 25 and 26, 1939, EUP.

138. Board Minutes, January 21, 1941, UA; Philadelphia *Social Register,* 1940.

139. *Springfield Sun,* April 22, 1948; Board Minutes, March 5, 1945, February 13, 1950, UA.

140. Student scrapbook, "Our New Cottages," CVS.

141. *Carson News,* November 4, 1932, June 16, 1933; Ueland, memorandum, July 3, 1934, CVS.

142. Board Minutes, April 27, 1937, UA; Ueland to Lukens, Mallery, and Sharpe, February 15, 1938; Sharpe to Lewis, May 15, 1937; Samuel Emlen to Shippen Lewis, April 14, 1938; Shippen Lewis to Thomas B. K. Ringe, May 19, 1937, CVS.

143. Itinerary for Sea-Shore Trip, July 20, 1938; itinerary for Southern Bus Trip, August 30–September 1, 1938, summer 1938, CVS; Margaret E. Roberts to Horace C. Jones, August 6, 1938, CVS.

144. Board Minutes, April 22 and July 22, 1941, UA.

145. Summer notices, 1933, CVS.

146. Summer notices, 1934, 1938, CVS; Ueland to Lewis, September 1, 1933; Ueland to Lukens, September 1, 1938, CVS.

147. Board Minutes, March 15, 1940, UA.

148. Elsa Ueland, "Graduation from Carson College: The New Plan, 1930," *Jabberwock,* spring 1930, 1–2.

149. Ueland to Lewis, May 26, 1933; Ueland, memorandum, "To the Staff and to the Big Girls," June 11, 1934; Program, Eighteenth-Birthday Dance, June 15, 1934; Program, Eighteenth-Birthday Party, June 18, 1936, CVS.

150. Week End Notice, January 17, 1941, CVS.

151. Otto T. Mallery to Margaret E. Roberts, December 5, 1938; Elsa Ueland to Glenn Clark, April 5, 1944, CVS.

152. The only brief biography of Kraft would appear to be her obituary. See *Evening Bulletin,* April 19, 1973. On Duncan, see Victor Seroff, *The Real Isadora* (New York, 1971).

153. Isadora Duncan, quoted in *The Vision of Modern Dance,* ed. Jean Morrison Brown (Princeton, 1979), 9.

154. Ibid., 11. Elsa Ueland was also apparently an admirer of Duncan and owned a "painted dress" that had once belonged to Duncan, though just how she acquired it is unclear. Elsa's niece, Clara Ueland, has donated the dress to the Metropolitan Museum in New York. Clara Ueland to the author, August 4, 1996; Mark Ueland, interview with the author, May 20, 1996.

155. *Evening Bulletin,* May 3, 1970.

156. Patterson, interview with the author, November 14, 1994.

157. Helen Traiche Heath, telephone interview with the author, June 3, 1996.

158. Christmas file, 1930–39, CVS.

159. Elsa Ueland, Diary, January 1, 1940, EUP. The tradition of caroling in Flourtown and then retiring for hot chocolate at Oak Run was remembered with much warmth and vividness by Fenstermacher, in an interview with the author, December 2, 1995.

160. Elsa Ueland to Housemothers and Senior Staff, June 29, 1940, CVS.

Chapter 6

1. *Evening Bulletin,* August 14, 1940.

2. Caroline Conley Vankouwenberg, interview with the author, October 14, 1995; Dorothy Moore Fenstermacher, interview with the author, December 2, 1995. It is unclear just when these Jewish refugees came to Carson, whether it was before or after the American entry into World War II.

3. Memorandum, "About Sugar Rationing," May 2, 1942, CVS.

4. Board Minutes, January 19 and July 27, 1943, UA.

5. Ibid., January 24, 1945.

6. A. L. Gehman, Superintendent, Springfield Township Public Schools, to Elsa Ueland, March 23 and May 4, 1944; Ueland to Gehman, May 24, 1944, CVS; Board Minutes, April 11, 1944, UA.

7. Vankouwenberg, interview with the author, October 14, 1995.

8. Board Minutes, March 21, 1945, January 22, July 1, and October 22, 1946, UA.

9. *Springfield Sun,* January 29, 1948.

10. Ibid., December 25, 1947.

11. *Herald,* February 26, August 27, September 24, and October 1 and 23, 1953, November 3, 1955, January 3, 1957.

12. Ibid., September 4, 1952, February 5 and October 29, 1953.

13. Board Minutes, January 22 and July 1, 1946, UA; Carl G. Horst Jr. to Otto T. Mallery, May 10, 1946, CVS.

14. Carson Valley School Housing Investment Studies: Concluding Remarks, 1946–47, CVS.

15. Otto T. Mallery to M. T. Cooke, August 13, 1947, CVS.

16. Otto T. Mallery to Shippen Lewis, May 13, 1946, CVS.

17. According to the board minutes of January 29, 1947 (UA), Shippen Lewis, who was himself living in a Woodward house in Chestnut Hill, specifically invoked the Woodward precedent. In a letter to architect Pope Barney on February 22, 1954 (CVS), Otto Mallery again compared the Carson project to the Woodward houses.

18. Elizabeth Coit, Technical Division, National Housing Agency, Federal Public Housing Authority, to Elsa Ueland, May 5, 1947, CVS.

19. Elsa Ueland, Memorandum: Houses for Rental (As I See It Now), May 25, 1946, CVS. Ueland reiterated and expanded these sentiments in a memorandum dated May 16, 1950 (CVS).

20. Eugene Henry Klaber, Report to the Land Use Committee, Carson College, January 20, 1947, p. 3, CVS.

21. Robert A. Bast, Vice-President, Land Title Bank and Trust Company, to Otto T. Mallery, July 2 and November 13, 1946; Mallery to Bast, December 3, 1946, December 31, 1949; Lewis to Mallery, July 3 and December 12, 1946, June 4, 1947; Mallery to Lewis, February 5, 1947; Percy C. Madeira Jr., President, Land Title Bank and Trust Company, to Mallery, February 17, 1950; Mallery to Madeira, February 24, 1950, CVS.

22. Mary W. P. Bond (the former Mrs. Shippen Lewis), interview with the author, December 23, 1994.

23. Concern over the unsettled state of both the real estate markets and the building trades was expressed in the Klaber report of January 1947 to Carson's Land Use Planning Committee (p. 10).

24. For example, see Edward L. Fortin, Housing Investment Studies, Carson Valley School, March 31, 1948; William W. Jeanes, Report to the Housing Investment Committee, Carson College, April 1, 1948; Edward L. Fortin to Otto T. Mallery, March 31, 1948; Otto T. Mallery to A. Kenneth Lindsley, May 23, 1950; Lindsley to Mallery, May 31, 1950, CVS.

25. Klaber, Report to the Land Use Committee, pp. 3, 6.

26. For example, Board Minutes, April 10, 1948, UA.

27. Housing Investment Studies, 1946–47; Bast to Mallery, July 2, 1946; Mallery to Bast, December 3, 1946; Lewis to Mallery, December 12, 1946, CVS.

28. Lindsley to Mallery, May 31, 1950, CVS.

29. Staff member Dorothy Moore Fenstermacher, who would later become director of the Carson Valley School, lived in one of Mallery's Suntop homes, and it was her house that the board visited. Indeed, they seem to have held their entire board meeting there on April 2, 1946, UA.

30. Otto T. Mallery to Frank Lloyd Wright, June 12, 1950; Wright to Mallery, June 22, 1950, CVS.

31. Barney to Mallery, April 20, 1950; Memorandum by Ueland to the Housing Investment Committee, April 26, 1950, CVS; Board Minutes, April 24 and June 5, 1950, UA.

32. Board Minutes, February 16, 1949, UA; Lawrence M. C. Smith to Housing Investment Committee of Carson Valley School, undated but probably written in March 1950, CVS.

33. *Evening Bulletin,* March 18, 1950. On the Andorra development, see Contosta, *Philadelphia Family,* 120, and *Suburb in the City,* 212.

34. Contosta, *Philadelphia Family,* 115-17, and *Suburb in the City,* 200-201. On Carson's interest in Stonorov, see Shippen Lewis to F. A. Pitkin, Pennsylvania State Planning Commission, January 11, 1946; Pitkin to Lewis, January 14, 1946, CVS.

35. For more on Smith, see Contosta, *Philadelphia Family,* 163-69. Ueland's membership in the ADA is cited in her obituary in the *Evening Bulletin,* December 4, 1980.

36. Board Minutes, October 30, 1950, UA.

37. Ibid., April 24, 1950.

38. William Pope Barney to Elsa Ueland, January 28, 1954; Bast to Mallery, February 25, 1954; Lindsley to Mallery, February 26, 1954; Mallery to Barney, February 17 and February 22, 1954; Barney to Mallery, March 12, 1954, CVS; Minutes, Land Use Planning Committee, March 9, 1954, CVS; Board Minutes, April 7, 1954, UA.

39. *Springfield Township Zoning Ordinance of 1940,* 4-9, CVS.

40. Request for Variance for Land on North Side of Wissahickon Ave., July 9, 1954, CVS; Robert A. Bast to Lawrence M. C. Smith, October 13, 1954, CVS; Board Minutes, October 25, 1954, UA.

41. Court of Common Pleas of Montgomery County, Pennsylvania, Appeal of the Carson College for Orphan Girls from the Board of Adjustment of Springfield Township, No. 18, September Term, 1954, CVS.

42. Lewis, memorandum, "Talk with Miss Ueland," February 1, 1946, CVS; Board Minutes, July 1, 1946, May 7 and October 29, 1947, UA. The decision to admit brothers was reinforced by a letter to Ueland from Madeleine S. Marris, casework supervisor of the Philadelphia Bureau of the Children's Aid Society, April 4, 1946 (CVS). In this communication Marris asked Carson to consider admitting brothers so that siblings would not have to be separated upon being placed in residential care.

43. Board Minutes, January 29, 1947, November 16, 1953, UA.

44. Elsa Ueland, "Given Good Foster Homes and Good Institutions[,]Which Children Should Go to Institutions?" in *Proceedings of the Thirty-Third Session of the Minnesota State Conference, Second Session of the Institute of Social Work, September 19-25, 1925,* 6-10.

45. Board Minutes, October 21, 1948, February 16, 1949, UA; Frances Jones to Elsa Ueland, May 25, 1948, CVS.

46. Board Minutes, November 15, 1944, UA.

47. Ibid., May 7, 1947, April 16, 1951, February 4, 1952, January 12, 1953, May 3, 1954, November 14, 1955, October 21, 1957.

48. Ibid., April 16, 1951.

49. Marshall B. Jones, "Decline of the American Orphanage, 1941–1980," *SSR,* September 1993, 459–80.

50. Board Minutes, April 15, 1957, UA.

51. Ibid., May 26, 1958.

52. Ibid., November 2, 1949. Some of the subsequent literature on the nursery school led readers to believe that it had been in continuous existence since 1924, but according to Fenstermacher, in her interview with the author on December 2, 1995, this claim was made in order to avoid from township officials any objections, based on zoning regulations, to reopening the school. In subsequent years the fact that the nursery school had been closed for a dozen years was largely forgotten, resulting in the widespread but incorrect belief at Carson that the nursery school had been in continuous existence since 1924.

53. Board Minutes, November 2, 1949, UA; Elsa Ueland to Dorothy Hoyle, Acting Director, Department of Early Childhood and Elementary Education, Temple University, September 8, 1953, CVS.

54. Jean MacFarland recorded some of her ideas about teaching young children in an article entitled "How Nursery Children Learn," *Parish School* (a publication for Lutheran Sunday school teachers), September 1954, 19–20.

55. *Herald,* November 29, 1951.

56. Carson Valley Nursery School (application form and letter), May 17, 1951, CVS.

57. Carson Valley Nursery School, Budget Study, September 1952, CVS.

58. Board Minutes, October 29, 1947, UA; Elsa Ueland to Richard Rosenberry, Chief, Private Academic School Registration, Pennsylvania Department of Public Instruction, April 27, 1953, CVS.

59. Enrollment Reports, Summer 1945, 1948, 1949, 1950, 1951, 1952, CVS. See also Board Minutes, May 7, 1947, UA.

60. Flyer, "Rhythmic Dance and Exercise," CVS.

61. Board Minutes, November 16, 1953, UA.

62. Ibid., April 23, 1956.

63. Ibid., May 11, 1953.

64. Ibid., October 30, 1950.

65. Ibid., January 17, 1953.

66. Ibid., November 16, 1953.

67. Shippen Lewis to John F. McCloskey, M.D., June 7, 1948; E. S. McCawley, Deputy Secretary, Pennsylvania Department of Forests and Waters, to Fort Washington Park Commission, January 20, 1950, CVS.

68. Howard D. King, Chief Division of Land Acquisition, Pennsylvania Department of Forests and Waters, to Otto T. Mallery, December 6, 1949; Mallery to King, December 29, 1949, April 26, 1950; Mallery to Ueland, September 27, 1950; Elsa Ueland to W. B. Jeffries, Director of Engineering and Construction, Pennsylvania Department of Property and Supplies, April 7, 1950; Ueland to Board, July 26 and November 11, 1950, CVS; Board Minutes, May 10, 1949, April 24 and June 5, 1950, October 25, 1954, UA; Board Resolution, April 24, 1950, UA. The state's posting of health warnings at the bathing site appeared to have been motivated in part by complaints of the owners of new homes in the area, who felt the swimming hole was a nuisance. See Board Minutes, October 25, 1954.

69. McCawley to Commissioners of Fairmount Park, February 3, 1950, CVS.

70. Board Minutes, January 17, 1955, UA.

71. Ibid., November 14, 1955.

72. "Our Fall Diary," November 8, 1948, CVS.

73. Board Minutes, October 21, 1948, UA.

74. Ibid., February 4, 1952.

75. Ibid., May 10, 1949.

76. Ibid., January 17 and March 28, 1955.

77. Ibid., November 25, 1957.

78. Vankouwenberg, interview with the author, October 14, 1995.

79. Helen Traiche Heath, telephone interview with the author, June 3, 1996.

80. Board Minutes, May 7, 1947, UA.

81. Ibid., January 12, 1953.

82. Ibid., October 25, 1954.

83. Ibid., November 14, 1955.

84. Ibid., March 31, 1958; Dorothy Moore Fenstermacher to Charles Plank, National Health and Welfare Retirement Association, September 3, 1959, CVS.

85. F. Herbert Barnes, interview with the author, January 9, 1995; Vankouwenberg, interview with the author, October 14, 1995; Fenstermacher, interview with the author, December 2, 1995.

86. Board Minutes, July 1, 1946, UA.

87. Ibid., May 26, 1952.

88. Jones had left Carson in 1932 to become superintendent of the Alderdyce School and had then returned to Carson on a part-time basis about 1944. See ibid., October 29, 1947, May 26 and June 30, 1952.

89. Ibid., February 4, May 26, and October 27, 1952; Elsa Ueland to Joint Vocational Service, November 7, 1919, CVS. Allnutt's return to her maiden name, occasioned by a divorce, is reflected on her personnel folder: Both "Mrs." and "Allnutt" were crossed out in pencil, and "Crosby" was written in above the crossed-out name "Allnutt." Fenstermacher, interview with the author, December 2, 1995.

90. Board Minutes, January 14, 1957, UA.

91. Ibid., October 25, 1954.

92. *New York Times,* June 7, 1957; *Herald,* June 13, 1957.

93. The author is indebted to Dorothy Moore Fenstermacher for a copy of this history by Ueland.

94. Mark Ueland, interview with the author, May 20, 1996.

95. Cremin, *Transformation of the School,* 258-70, 338-53; Zilversmit, *Changing Schools,* 104-17. See also Patricia A. Graham, *Progressive Education: From Arcady to Academe: A History of the Progressive Education Association, 1919-1955* (New York, 1967).

96. Cohen and Mohl, *Progressivism,* 30-31.

Chapter 7

1. This phrase was used to describe Carson in an evaluation by the Pennsylvania Department of Welfare in 1963. See C. Wilson Anderson, Commissioner, to Robert L. Bast, May 17, 1963, CVS.

2. Dorothy Moore Fenstermacher, interview with the author, December 2, 1995.

3. Elsa Ueland to F. Herbert Barnes, March 29, 1965, CVS; Board Minutes, October 29, 1947, June 23, 1958, UA.

4. Fenstermacher, interview with the author, December 2, 1995.

5. Ibid.

6. Board Minutes, June 23, 1958, UA.

7. Ueland to Barnes, March 29, 1965.

8. Board Minutes, September 1960, January 1961, July 13, 1964, UA.

9. Moore [Fenstermacher] to "All Carson Staff," February 24, 1964, CVS; Board Minutes, January 27 and July 17, 1964, UA; Fenstermacher, interview with the author, December 2, 1995.

10. These reforms were achieved in the Civil Rights Act of 1964 and the Voting Rights Act of 1965.

11. For a good overview of this period, see Edward P. Morgan, *The 60s Experience: Hard Lessons About Modern America* (Philadelphia, 1991).

12. Kenneth Finkel, ed., *Philadelphia Almanac* (Philadelphia, 1995), 182.

13. Stephanie G. Wolf, "The Bicentennial City," in *Philadelphia: A 300-Year History,* ed. Weigley, 707; *Municipal Reference Guide: Pennsylvania, 1994-1995* (Shrewsbury, N.J., 1994), C-40.

14. *Statistical Abstract of the United States, 1992* (Washington, D.C., 1992), 449.

15. 1970 Census of Population and Housing, Census Tracts, Philadelphia, Pa.-N.J. Standard Metropolitan Statistical Area, Montgomery County Tract 2103.

16. Ibid.; Bureau of the Census, 1990 Census of Housing: Population and Housing Characteristics for Census Tracts and Block Numbering Areas, Philadelphia-Wilmington-Trenton, Phila.-N.J. PMSA, Montgomery County, Tract 2103; *Statistical Abstract of the United States, 1992,* 449.

17. F. Herbert Barnes, interview with the author, January 9, 1995. A brief biography of Barnes appeared in the *Ambler Gazette,* June 4, 1964.

18. Barnes, interview with the author, January 9, 1995; telephone interview with the author, January 8, 1996.

19. Board Minutes, May 26, 1952, UA.

20. *Dictionary of American Biography,* 13-14:142-44; Cremin, *Transformation of the School,* 82, 86, 128, 142.

21. Board Minutes, February 11, 1963; *Ambler Gazette,* November 18, 1971.

22. Cary Page (daughter of Anderson and Louise Lewis Page), telephone interview with the author, January 9, 1996.

23. Barnes, telephone interview with the author, January 8, 1996.

24. These fears were expressed in the board minutes of September 27 and November 8, 1965, UA. Anderson Page's legal opinion on the matter of Carson's integration appeared in a long letter addressed to Robert L. Bast, chairman of the board of directors, June 23, 1965, CVS.

25. Minutes, Second Community Survey Meeting, September 21, 1964, CVS.

26. Joseph S. Clark Jr. and Dennis J. Clark, "Rally and Relapse," in *Philadelphia: A 300-Year History,* ed. Weigley, 680-81.

27. Barnes, telephone interview with the author, January 8, 1996.

28. Board Minutes, June 7, 1965, UA.

29. Barnes, telephone interview with the author, January 8, 1996.

30. Ibid., January 23, 1967. According to the board minutes of March 7, 1966, this first black cottage employee was Fannie Goins, who was assigned to Red Gables.

31. Barnes, telephone interview with the author, January 8, 1996.

32. Natline Thornton, interview with the author, March 8, 1995.

33. Residential Care Demand Analysis, Carson Valley School, June 1993, pp. 1–8, CVS. By 1991 the percentage of African American children at Carson had fallen to 58 percent but only because the institution, which had been experiencing difficulties in obtaining payment for its services from Philadelphia, purposely increased the numbers of children it took from suburban counties, where the white population was higher than in Philadelphia.

34. Erving Goffman, *Asylums: Essays on the Social Situation of Mental Patients and Other Inmates* (Chicago, 1959). See also Marshall B. Jones, "Decline of the American Orphanage, 1941–1980," *SSR,* September 1993, 470–72, and Jeffrey Koshel, *Deinstitutionalization—Dependent and Neglected Children* (Washington, D.C., 1973).

35. Quoted in Jones, "Decline of the American Orphanage," 476.

36. Barnes, telephone interview with the author, January 8, 1996.

37. Ibid.

38. Barnes to invitees to Second Community Survey Meeting, September 21, 1964; Minutes, Second Community Survey Meeting, September 21, 1964, CVS; Board Minutes, September 28 and November 9, 1964, UA.

39. Barnes, Some Considerations for Planning of Future Directions, Report Prepared for the Board of Directors, January 18, 1965, CVS.

40. Joseph N. Reid, foreword to *Principles and Policies on Administration of Voluntary and Public Child Welfare Agencies,* Child Welfare League of America, 1958, as quoted in Barnes, Some Considerations for Planning, CVS.

41. Barnes, Some Considerations for Planning, p. 9.

42. Barnes, interview with the author, January 9, 1994; Fenstermacher, interview with the author, December 2, 1995.

43. Barnes, telephone interview with the author, January 8, 1996.

44. Barnes, Report of the Executive Director, in Board Minutes, March 7, 1966, UA.

45. Ibid., June 15, 1964.

46. Barnes, Report of the Executive Director, in Board Minutes, January 18, 1965.

47. Ibid.; Barnes, telephone interview with the author, January 8, 1996.

48. Board Minutes, April 8, 1968; Barnes, telephone interview with the author, January 8, 1996.

49. Board Minutes, July 13, 1964, February 7, 1972.

50. Ibid., March 9, 1970.

51. Ibid., October 19, 1970.

52. *Springfield Sun,* October 1, 1971.

53. Board Minutes, June 6, 1972, UA.

54. Ibid., May 1 and June 6, 1972.

55. Ibid., July 27, 1972. The board had advertised the position in social-work and child-welfare journals, as well as through regional organizations and institutions. They received approximately thirty applications.

56. Ibid.

57. Ibid., May 23, 1973.

58. Board Minutes, February 20, March 4, and March 25, 1974, UA.

59. This biography of John Taaffe is based upon the interview that he gave to the author on January 18, 1995.

60. The period during which intake ceased was September 23 to October 28, 1974. See Board Minutes, October 28, 1974, UA.

61. Proposal: Vocationally Oriented Halfway House, in Board Minutes, May 13, 1974.

62. Taaffe, interview with the author, March 3, 1995; Board Minutes, April 28 and September 29, 1975, January 24, 1977, UA. Originally, the program at Lower Beech was called a Crisis Reception Center.

63. Donald Sobeck, interview with the author, August 3, 1995.

64. See Contosta, *Villanova*, 249–50.

65. Sobeck, interview with the author, July 25, 1995.

66. *CVV,* fall 1993; Board Minutes, February 22 and March 22, 1993. Board Minutes generated after 1980 are a part of the Carson Valley School collection and are not to be found at the Urban Archives at Temple, which houses the Board Minutes before 1980.

67. Sobeck, interview with the author, July 25, 1995.

68. *CVV,* fall 1993.

69. Marie O'Donnell, interview with the author, July 18, 1995.

70. Board Minutes, September 24, 1984, January 27, 1986, CVS.

71. Ibid., February 27, 1984.

72. O'Donnell, interview with the author, July 18, 1995.

73. Ibid.

74. Taaffe, interview with the author, January 18, 1995.

75. *CVV,* fall 1993.

76. Thornton, interview with the author, March 15, 1995; *CVV,* fall 1993, spring 1994.

77. Board Minutes, February 22, 1993, CVS; Thornton, interview with the author, March 15, 1995; *CVV,* spring 1994.

78. *Communicator,* October 26, 1973.

79. Board Minutes, February 25, 1974, UA.

80. Thornton, interview with the author, March 15, 1995; Board Minutes, June 15, 1964, September 15, 1969, UA; Jean MacFarland, Summary Report of Summer Program, 1964; World's Fair Bulletin, July 22, 1964, CVS; *Communicator,* August 21, 1974.

81. John Carver, interview with the author, October 5, 1994; Thornton, interviews with the author, March 8 and March 15, 1995. In July 1995 this author noticed that the Lower Beech Cottage had put out a small vegetable garden.

82. Board Minutes, June 15, 1964, UA.

83. Undated Memos, 1971, CVS.

84. Board Minutes, April 26, 1976, UA.

85. Thornton, interviews with the author, March 8 and 15, 1995.

86. Ibid., September 11, 1972.

87. Neighborhood Youth Corps Program, Summer 1976, included with the Board Minutes of February 28, 1977, UA. See also Board Minutes, May 23, 1977, UA; June 21 and September 18, 1981, CVS.

88. John Taaffe, interview with the author, September 20, 1996.

89. *Ambler Gazette,* December 22, 1960; Police Chiefs Christmas Party file; F. Herbert Barnes to Chief Robert Baxter, January 8, 1968, CVS; *Communicator,* December 15, 1972; Fenstermacher, interview with the author, December 2, 1995.

90. *Springfield Sun,* December 22, 1960.

91. *Evening Bulletin,* February 17, 1966.

92. Mrs. John W. Caldwell, President, Women's Club of Erdenheim, February 3, 1967; F. Herbert Barnes to Mrs. George Wormley, November 4, 1969, CVS; *Ambler Gazette,* June 11, 1970.

93. Anderson Page to Dear Volunteer, n.d., CVS.

94. Board Minutes, February 24, 1975, UA; September 27, 1982, February 27, 1984, April 24, 1989, CVS.

95. Ibid., January 27, 1986, May 22, 1989, May 20, 1991, CVS.

96. Ibid., October 24, 1988; *Intelligencer/Record,* October 4, 1988.

97. Board Minutes, April 22 and June 24, 1963, May 23, 1977, UA.

98. Ibid., September 15, 1960, April 9, 1973.

99. Ibid., May 23 and September 26, 1983, September 23, 1991, CVS.

100. *CVV,* fall 1993.

101. Board Minutes, April 26, 1982, CVS; *CVV,* spring 1994.

102. Board Minutes, October 28, 1991, CVS; Judy Berger, interview with the author, June 8, 1995.

103. Berger, interview with the author, June 8, 1995; Taaffe, interview with the author, March 3, 1995.

104. Berger, interview with the author, June 8, 1995.

105. Ibid.

106. Board Minutes, February 7, 1972, April 26, 1976, February 28, 1977, UA; June 21, 1981, April 22, 1985, February 27, 1989, April 22, 1991, CVS.

107. Ibid., April 7, 1969; Account of the Estate of Robert N. Carson, Deceased ... in the Court of Common Pleas of Montgomery County, Pennsylvania, February 19, 1969; Annual Report, 1970, CVS.

108. Board Minutes, September 15, 1960, October 16, 1961, UA; Page to the Honorable Walter Morley, [Pennsylvania] House Appropriations Committee, May 21, 1965; Page to the Honorable Paul D'Ortona, President, City Council, Philadelphia, December 4, 1967; Annual Report, Carson Valley School, 1970, CVS.

109. Board Minutes, September 23, 1974, May 31, 1975, January 26, 1976, UA; Budget Summary, Carson Valley School, FY 1977-78, CVS.

110. Annual Budget, Carson Valley School, FY 1986-87, CVS.

111. Ibid., FY 1991-92; Jack Cavenaugh, interview with the author, July 18, 1995; Cavenaugh to the author, August 5, 1995.

112. Taaffe, interview with the author, March 3, 1995; Sobeck, interview with the author, July 25, 1995.

113. Board Minutes, January 21 and September 23, 1974, UA; Anderson Page to Nochem S. Winnet, January 14, 1974, CVS.

114. *Philadelphia Inquirer,* September 29, 1994.

115. Jones, "Decline of the American Orphanage," 459.

116. Wallace, McHarg, Roberts, and Todd, "A Land Use Study for the Carson Valley School Site," January 1973, CVS.

117. Louise Page to George C. Toop of Wallace, McHarg, Roberts, and Todd, November 21, 1972, CVS.

118. On this last point, see the letter from Jerome Beker, editor, *Child Care Quarterly,* to F. Herbert Barnes, May 4, 1972, CVS.

119. Board Minutes, March 22, 1982, CVS.

120. Ibid., April 24, 1983.

121. Ibid., April 23, 1984.

122. Ibid., July 19, 1965, April 25, 1966, March 25, 1974, UA.

123. Ibid., June 23, 1986, November 24, 1988, February 27, 1989, CVS.

124. [List of] Board of Directors, Carson Valley School, 1989, CVS; *Social Register,* 1989.

(Around 1980 the social registers from individual metropolitan areas were combined into one, large, national register.)

125. Taaffe, interview with the author, March 3, 1995. Ueland used the phrase "that fool Kelsey" in conversation with John and Shirley Taaffe when they went to call on her at Oak Run shortly after they came to Carson.

126. Yvonne Patterson, interviews with the author, November 11 and 21, 1994; Mark Ueland, interview with the author, May 20, 1996; Margaret Ueland to the author, July 23, 1996.

127. Thornton, interview with the author, March 8 and 15, 1995.

128. Margaret Ueland to the author, July 23, 1996.

129. Mark Ueland, interview with the author, May 20, 1996.

130. Patterson, interview with the author, November 21, 1994; Clara Ueland to the author, August 4, 1996.

131. Board Minutes, January 26, 1981, CVS; *Evening Bulletin,* December 4, 1980; *Ambler Gazette,* December 4, 1980; Patterson, interviews with the author, November 11 and 21, 1994. Ueland left her home, Oak Run, and its contents to Yvonne Patterson.

132. Patterson, interview with the author, November 21, 1994; *Montgomery County Advertiser,* May 24, 1973; Tribute to Elsa Ueland for the Springfield Township League of Women Voters.

133. *Beacon,* May 1972 (a publication of Philadelphia Conservationists, Inc.).

134. Contosta, *Suburb in the City,* 245-47, 285-87, 290.

135. [List of] Board of Directors, Carson Valley School, 1989, CVS.

136. Board Minutes, April 23, 1984, CVS.

137. Ibid., May 20, 1985. The official name of the Milner study was "An Architectural and Historical Survey."

138. Board Minutes, April 24, 1989, CVS.

139. Ibid., January 28, 1991, April 27, 1992.

140. Ibid., April 24, 1989.

141. Criteria for Land Use/Land Development, adopted by the Board of Trustees, November 24, 1986, CVS.

142. *Philadelphia Inquirer,* April 30, 1992, Montgomery Neighbors section.

BIBLIOGRAPHIC ESSAY

Three collections of primary sources have proved essential to this study. Only one of these has been organized and catalogued at the time of this writing: the records that the Carson Valley School donated in 1982 to the Urban Archives in the Samuel Paley Library of Temple University in Philadelphia. Included in this repository are the board minutes of the Carson Valley School (and the Carson College for Orphan Girls) and the minutes, reports, and correspondence of the various board committees and officials through the late 1970s, as well as early case records for children who were wards of the institution.

The second group of items generated by the institution was assembled by the author and Carson Valley School staff from various informal storage spaces at the school. These are in the process of being organized, catalogued, and preserved. Among these materials are institutional correspondence, legal briefs, internal reports, inactive personnel files, memoranda, scattered committee minutes and correspondence, curricular materials, photographs, architectural and landscape plans, circulars, fliers, advertisements, newspaper clippings, newsletters, student newspapers and other publications generated by students, as well as a large body of ephemera. Many of these items were located over the years and stored by Carson staff member Natline Thornton.

The third repository of materials is what might be called the private papers of Elsa Ueland, who served as president of Carson from 1916 to 1958. These are in the possession of Ueland's principal heir, Yvonne Patterson. Of greatest interest in this collection are the personal letters of Elsa Ueland. The diaries that Ueland kept on a sporadic basis also offer important insights into her thinking about Carson, as well as into many other topics of interest to her. Besides the letters and diaries, Ueland's papers contain photographs, copies of her own publications and those of close friends or professional associates, and biographical materials relating to the Ueland family.

The author was fortunate in being able to interview a number of persons who knew Elsa Ueland, or who were in a position to offer insights into the workings of the institution at various periods. Their names, and the dates of the interviews with them, are listed in the notes.

Newspaper accounts of Carson, and of matters relating to it, were helpful in many ways. Several of these accounts have appeared in the Philadelphia daily newspapers (some of them no longer in existence): the *Evening Bulletin,* the *North American,* the *Philadelphia Inquirer,* the *Philadelphia Press,* the *Philadelphia Record,* and the *Public Ledger.* In addition, several local newspapers (all of them weeklies) have carried numerous stories about Carson and Carson people: the *Ambler Gazette,* the *Chestnut*

Hill Local, the *Germantown Guide,* the *Herald,* and the *Springfield Sun.* Beyond the Philadelphia region there have been items of interest on Carson, or on individuals connected to Carson, in the *Minneapolis Journal,* the *Minneapolis Morning Tribune,* the *New York Evening Post,* and the *New York Times.*

Historical studies of Philadelphia that place Carson into a wider regional context include several that appear in Russell F. Weigley, ed., *Philadelphia: A 300-Year History* (New York, 1982): Lloyd M. Abernethy, "Progressivism, 1905-1919," 524-65; Arthur P. Dudden, "The City Embraces Normalcy, 1919-1929," 566-600; Margaret B. Tinkcom, "Depression and War, 1929-1946," 601-48; Joseph S. Clark Jr. and Dennis J. Clark, "Rally and Relapse," 649-703; and Stephanie G. Wolf, "The Bicentennial City, 1968-1982," 704-34. Also helpful in understanding Philadelphia during Carson's existence as an institution are three works by E. Digby Baltzell: *Philadelphia Gentlemen: The Making of a National Upper Class* (1958; reprint, Philadelphia, 1979), *The Protestant Establishment* (New York, 1964), and *Puritan Boston and Quaker Philadelphia* (New York, 1979). Besides these, see Allen F. Davis and Mark H. Haller, *The Peoples of Philadelphia: A History of Ethnic Groups and Lower-Class Life, 1700-1940* (Philadelphia, 1973); Arthur P. Dudden, "Lincoln Steffens' Philadelphia," *PH,* October 1964, 449-58; John Lukacs, *Philadelphia: Patricians and Philistines, 1900-1950* (New York, 1981); Peter McCaffery, *When Bosses Ruled Philadelphia: The Emergence of the Republican Machine, 1867-1933* (University Park, Pa., 1993); Michael P. McCarthy, "The Unprogressive City: Philadelphia at the Turn of the Century," *PH,* October 1987, 263-81; Sam Bass Warner, *The Private City: Philadelphia in Three Periods of Its Growth* (Philadelphia, 1968).

On Flourtown and Springfield Township, where Carson is located, there are only a few works of interest, none of them by professional historians: Horace Mather Lippincott, *A Narrative of Chestnut Hill, Springfield, Whitemarsh, Cheltenham* (Jenkintown, Pa., 1948), and Velma Thorne Carter, *Penn's Manor of Springfield* (Springfield Township, Pa., 1976). The girls of Carson College wrote a charming study of their neighborhood, which they printed on their own hand press: "Flourtown: A Study by the Eighth Grade," Flourtown, Pa., 1928. In attempting to understand the socioeconomic contours of Flourtown and surrounding Springfield Township, the author made use of the manuscript, on microfilm, of the Fourteenth Decennial Census of the United States (1920), in addition to the U.S. Census Tracts of 1970, 1980, and 1990 for the Flourtown area. The *Survey Atlas* of 1916 for Springfield Township, which may be found at the Springfield Township Building, offered important insights into the layout and size of Flourtown at the time that Carson was established.

On the Chestnut Hill section of Philadelphia, where many members of the Carson board have resided and which has had multiple influences on the institution, see Mary Wickham Bond, *Ninety Years at Home in Philadelphia* (Bryn Mawr, Pa., 1988); David R. Contosta, *A Philadelphia Family: The Houstons and Woodwards of Chestnut Hill* (Philadelphia, 1988), *Suburb in the City: Chestnut Hill, Philadelphia, 1850-1990* (Columbus, Ohio, 1992), "George Woodward, Philadelphia Progressive," *PMHB,* July 1987, 341-70, and "Suburban Quasi Government in Chestnut Hill, Philadelphia," *PMHB,* July 1992, 259-93; John T. Faris, *Old Roads out of Philadelphia* (Philadelphia, 1917); Maria Kostka Logue, S.S.J., *Sisters of Saint Joseph: A Century of Growth and Develop-*

ment, 1847-1947 (Westminster, Md., 1950); and John Lukacs, *A Sketch of the History of Chestnut Hill College* (Philadelphia, 1975).

Intellectual and cultural context for the physical evolution of Carson may be found in Joseph Arnold, *The New Deal in the Suburbs: A History of the Greenbelt Town Program, 1935-1954* (Columbus, Ohio, 1971); Eileen Boris, *Art and Labor: Ruskin, Morris, and the Craftsman Ideal in America* (Philadelphia, 1986); Carol A. Christensen, *The American Garden City and the New Towns Movement* (Ann Arbor, Mich., 1986); Clifford Edward Clark Jr., *The American Family Home, 1880-1960* (Chapel Hill, N.C., 1986); R. J. Clark, ed., *The Arts and Crafts Movement in America, 1876-1916* (Princeton, 1972); Paul Evans, *Art Pottery in the United States* (New York, 1974); Robert Fishman, *Urban Utopias in the Twentieth Century* (New York, 1977); Kristen Ottenson Garrigan, *Ruskin on Architecture: His Thoughts and Influences* (Madison, Wis., 1973); David Glassberg, *American Historical Pageantry* (Chapel Hill, N.C., 1990); Dolores Hayden, *The Grand Domestic Revolution: A History of Feminist Designs for American Homes, Neighborhoods, and Cities* (Cambridge, Mass., 1981); Wendy Hitchmough, *C.F.A. Voysey* (New York, 1995); Walter C. Kidney, *The Architecture of Choice* (New York, 1974); Jonathan Lane, "The Period House in the Nineteen Twenties," *Journal of the Society of Architectural Historians,* December 1961, 169-78; Calder Loth and Julius Trousdale Sadler Jr., *The Only Proper Style: Gothic Architecture in America* (Boston, 1975); Roy Lubove, *The Urban Community: Housing and Planning in the Progressive Era* (Englewood Cliffs, N.J., 1967); Cynthia Ann McLoed, "Arts and Crafts Architecture in Suburban Philadelphia Sponsored by Dr. George Woodward" (master's thesis, University of Virginia, 1979); Kathleen Mahoney, *Gothic Style: Architecture and Interiors from the Eighteenth Century to the Present* (New York, 1995); Program of Competition for the Selection of an Architect for the Carson College for Orphan Girls, July 8, 1915 (CVS); Mary Corbin Sies, "American Country House Architecture in the East and Midwest, 1877-1917" (Ph.D. diss., University of Michigan, 1987); Bernard Sternsher, *Rexford Tugwell and the New Deal* (New Brunswick, N.J., 1964); Sandra L. Tatman and Roger W. Moss, *Biographical Dictionary of Philadelphia Architects, 1700-1930* (Boston, 1985); Paul Thompson, *The Works of William Morris* (New York, 1993); Robert C. Twombly, "Undoing the City: Frank Lloyd Wright's Planned Communities," *AQ,* October 1973, 538-49; and Gwendolyn Wright, *Moralism and the Modern Home* (Chicago, 1980).

Because little is known about benefactor Robert N. Carson, the author was forced to rely almost entirely on obituaries in the Philadelphia newspapers: *Evening Bulletin,* October 16, 1907; *Philadelphia Inquirer,* October 17, 1907; *Philadelphia Press,* October 16, 1907; *Philadelphia Record,* October 16, 1907; *Public Ledger,* October 16, 1907. Genealogical information on the Carson family, along with some insights into the legal disputes over the Carson will, were supplied to the author by David Carson, a collateral descendant of Robert Carson. Marie Kitto of the Springfield Township Historical Society conveyed material relating to Carson's house at the Erdenheim Stock Farm in her letter to the author of February 6, 1995.

The drawings and papers of Albert Kelsey, the earliest and most important architect of the Carson College for Orphan Girls (and the Carson Valley School), are located at the Library of Congress, the Archives of the American Institute of Architects in

Philadelphia, and in the University of Pennsylvania Architectural Archives. A biographical entry and a list of Kelsey's most important commissions appear in Tatman and Moss, *Biographical Dictionary* (cited above), 437-38. There is also an insightful, though much dated, article on Kelsey's work at Carson by Arthur Willis Colton, "Carson College for Orphan Girls at Flourtown near Philadelphia: Albert W. Kelsey, Architect," *AR*, July 1921, 1-25. On Pope Barney, Carson's other significant architect, see William Pope Barney, *Some Domestic Architecture in Surrey and Sussex* (New York, 1930). See also "House Beautiful's 13th Annual Small House Competition," *House Beautiful*, February 1941, 18-19; "Juniata Housing Corp. Project in Philadelphia," *AR*, April 1958, 328-29; and the entry in Tatman and Moss, *Biographical Dictionary*, 47-48. Barney's drawings and papers may be found at the Atheneum of Philadelphia, the University of Pennsylvania Architectural Archives, and the Georgia Institute of Technology. On Paul P. Cret, who greatly influenced both Kelsey and Barney, see Theodore B. White, *Paul Philippe Cret: Architect and Teacher* (Philadelphia, 1973), and Elizabeth Greenwald, "Paul Philippe Cret: Regionalism and Imagery in American Architecture" (Ph.D. diss., Brown University, 1980).

Elsa Ueland did not compose an autobiography or leave any organized account of her life. Her personal letters and diaries, cited above, were valuable sources in reconstructing that life. Ueland's father, Andreas Ueland, did publish an autobiography, *Recollections of an Immigrant* (New York, 1929), which was very helpful in providing background on the Ueland family as well as on Elsa's childhood. Even more revealing about Elsa's early years was her sister Brenda Ueland's autobiography, *Me* (New York, 1939). This may be supplemented by some selected writings by Brenda published under the title *Strength to Your Sword Arm* (Duluth, Minn., 1993). Then there is the unpublished autobiography by Elsa and Brenda's brother Sigurd Ueland, "Sense and Sensibility" (1971), a copy of which was provided to the author by Elsa and Brenda's nephew, Mark Ueland. There is also the unpublished biography that Brenda wrote of their mother, "Clara Ueland of Minnesota" (typescript dated 1967). This work gives much information not only about their mother but also about the Uelands' lives together as a family and contains long quotations from numerous family letters, including a number written by Elsa to her parents. Also helpful in understanding the Ueland family and especially the influence of Elsa's mother is Barbara Stuhler, *Gentle Warriors: Clara Ueland and the Minnesota Struggle for Woman Suffrage* (St. Paul, Minn., 1995). For a good history of Minnesota during Elsa Ueland's formative years, including the state's strong tradition of reform, see Clifford E. Clark Jr., ed., *Minnesota in a Century of Change: The State and Its People Since 1900* (St. Paul, Minn., 1989).

There are several works by or about Ueland's friends and professional associates. Virginia Robinson published a biography about their mutual friend Jessie Taft, *Jessie Taft, Therapist and Social Work Educator: A Professional Biography* (Philadelphia, 1962). Robinson also authored several books on social work: *Supervision in Social Case Work* (Chapel Hill, N.C., 1936), *A Changing Psychology in Social Case Work* (Chapel Hill, N.C., 1939), and *The Dynamics of Supervision Under Functional Controls* (Philadelphia, 1949). Ueland, Taft, and Robinson all profited from their friendship with and the professional insights of psychologist Otto Rank, two of whose most influential works were translated from the German by Taft: *Will Therapy: An Analysis of the Therapeutic Process in Terms of Relationship* (New York, 1936) and *Truth and*

Reality: A Life History of the Human Will (New York, 1936). In addition, Taft wrote an important book about Rank's life and work, *Otto Rank: A Biographical Study Based on Notebooks, Letters, Collected Writings, Therapeutic Achievements, and Personal Associations* (New York, 1958). Helpful too in understanding Ueland's circle of friends are Lucy Sprague Mitchell, *Two Lives: The Story of Wesley Clair Mitchell and Myself* (New York, 1953), and Joyce Antler, *Lucy Sprague Mitchell: The Making of a Modern Woman* (New Haven, Conn., 1987).

Ueland herself authored a good many articles and professional papers, especially during the period 1910-25. In chronological order these are "The Shirtwaist Trade" (with Pearl Goodman), *Journal of Political Economy,* December 1910, 816-28; "A Study of Eighty-Seven Working Paper Boys Who Left One School in District 9, Manhattan, in the Year 1911-1912" (typescript found among the private papers of Elsa Ueland); "Juvenile Employment Agencies," *American Labor Legislation Review,* June 1915, 203-37; "The Gary System," in W. J. McNally, ed., *The Gary School System* (Minneapolis, 1915), 42-43; "The Teacher and the Gary Plan," *New Republic,* July 1, 1916, 219-21; "A Re-evaluation of Methods of Child Care: The Case of Children in Institutions" (paper presented at the Children's Division of the National Conference on Social Work, June 26, 1924); "Celery Child or Strawberry Child: Handicaps of Institutional Life for Children," *Survey,* February 15, 1924 (unpaginated reprint); "Every Child—Where and How He Plays," *Annals of the American Academy of Political and Social Science,* September 1925, 1-6; "The Rights of the Child" and "Given Good Foster Homes and Good Institutions[,] Which Children Should Go to Institutions?" in *Proceedings of the Thirty-Third Session of the Minnesota State Conference, Second Session of the Institute for Social Work, September 19-25, 1925;* and "Milestones in the Progress of Children's Institutions," *Better Times,* June 3, 1935, 15-16. In addition to these professional articles and papers, Ueland wrote a number of internal reports and position papers for Carson. The most significant of these are "The Dilemma" (1937) and "History" (c. 1959). Both of these writings give a good deal of straightforward but largely dispassionate history of the institution. Ueland also published an account of the bus trip she took with the Bank Street School to observe the activities of the Resettlement Administration in West Virginia, "Eight Days," *69 Bank Street,* May 1935, 10-14.

Works on the progressive movement in general are as follows: John D. Buenker, *Urban Liberalism and Progressive Reform* (New York, 1967); John D. Buenker et al., *Progressivism* (Cambridge, Mass., 1977); Dominick Cavallo, *Muscles and Morals: Organized Playgrounds and Urban Reform* (Philadelphia, 1981); Robert M. Crunden, *Ministers of Reform: The Progressives' Achievement in American Civilization, 1889-1920* (New York, 1982); George Dykhuizen, *The Life and Mind of John Dewey* (Carbondale, Ill., 1973); Michael Ebner and Eugene M. Tobin, eds., *The Age of Urban Reform: New Perspectives on the Progressive Era* (Port Washington, N.Y., 1977); Eldon J. Eisenbach, *The Lost Promise of Progressivism* (Lawrence, Kans., 1994); Arthur A. Ekirch Jr., *Progressivism in America* (New York, 1974); Peter G. Filene, "An Obituary for the 'Progressive Movement,'" *AQ,* January 1970, 20-34; Lawrence A. Finfer, "Leisure as Social Work in the Urban Community: The Progressive Recreation Movement, 1890-1920" (Ph.D. diss., Michigan State University, 1974); James T. Kloppenberg, *Uncertain Victory: Social Democracy and Progressivism in European and American Thought, 1870-1920* (New York, 1986) and "Pragmatism: An Old Name for Some New Ways of Thinking?" *Journal of American History,* June 1996, 100-138; David W. Noble, *The Progressive Mind, 1890-1917* (Minneapolis, 1981); William L. O'Neill, *The Progressive Years: America Comes of Age* (New York, 1975); Alan Ryan, *John Dewey and the High Tide of American Liberalism* (New York, 1995); Bruce M. Stave, ed., *Urban Bosses, Machines, and Progressive Reformers* (Lexington, Mass., 1971); and Robert H. Wiebe, *The Search for Order, 1877-1920* (New York, 1967). Speaking to the disillusionment of some progressives with the American decision to enter World War I is Randolph S. Bourne, "The War and the Intellectuals," *Seven Arts,* June 1917, 133-46, and Edward Abrahams, *Randolph Bourne, Alfred Steiglitz, and the Origins of Cultural Radicalism in America* (Charlottesville, Va., 1986). Connections between progressivism and the New Deal are explored in Donald Feinman, *Twilight of Progressivism and the New Deal* (Baltimore, 1981), and Otis L. Graham Jr., *An Encore for Reform: The Old Progressives and the New Deal* (New York, 1973).

On the progressive-education movement, see Laurence Cremin, *The Transformation of the School: Progressivism in American Education, 1876-1957* (New York, 1961); Walter Feinberg, "Progressive Education and Social Planning," *Teachers College Record* (1971-72), 486-505; Patricia A. Graham, *Progressive Education: From Arcady to Academe: A History of the Progressive Education Association, 1919-1955* (New York, 1967); Martin Lazerson and W. Norton Grubb, eds., *American Education and Vocationalism: A Documentary History* (New York, 1974); Earl Russell Yaillen, "Progressive Education and Social Group Work" (Ph.D. diss., University of Pittsburgh, 1977); and Arthur Zilversmit, *Changing Schools: Progressive Education Theory and Practice, 1930-1960* (Chicago, 1993). Also worth reading are two works by John Dewey himself: *The School and Society* (Chicago, 1900) and *Democracy and Education* (New York, 1916).

Concerning the Gary system in particular are Randolph S. Bourne, *The Gary Schools* (1916; reprint, Cambridge, Mass., 1970); Ronald D. Cohen and Raymond A. Mohl, *The Paradox of Progressivism: The Gary Plan and Urban Schooling* (Port Washington, N.Y., 1979); John Dewey and Evelyn Dewey, *Schools of Tomorrow* (New York, 1915), 181-94; Richard Elwell, "The Gary Plan Revisited," *American Education,* July 1976, 16-22; Abraham Flexner and Frank P. Bachman, *The Gary Schools: A General Account* (New York, 1918); Raymond A. Mohl, "Schools, Politics, and Riots: The Gary Plan in New York City, 1914-1916," *Paedagogica Historica,* 1975, 39-72, and Raymond A. Mohl and Neil Betten, "The Failure of Industrial City Planning: Gary, Indiana, 1906-1910," *AIP Journal,* July 1972, 203-14. Further insights into the evolution of the Gary Plan may be found in a periodical called the *Platoon School,* issued between 1927 and 1936. It was published by the National Association for the Study of the Platoon or Work-Study-Play School Organization and edited by Ueland's old friend Alice Barrows. The journal carried articles by William Wirt, the founder of the Gary system, and by others associated with the Gary Plan or with progressive education in general. Ueland herself was a loyal subscriber to the *Platoon School,* a nearly complete set of the journal having been found among her personal papers.

Studies of the settlement-house movement and the emergence of social work as a profession include David M. Austin, *A History of Social Work Education* (Austin, Tex., 1986); Jill Conway, "Women Reformers and American Culture, 1870-1930," in *Our American Sisters: Women in American Life and Thought,* ed. Jean E. Friedman and

William G. Slade (Boston, 1976); Allen F. Davis, *Spearheads for Reform: The Social Settlements and the Progressive Movement, 1890-1914* (New York, 1967) and *An American Heroine: The Life and Legend of Jane Addams* (New York, 1973); Michael B. Katz, *In the Shadow of the Poor House: A Social History of Welfare in America* (New York, 1986); James L. Leiby, *A History of Social Welfare and Social Work in the United States* (New York, 1978); Roy Lubove, *The Professional Altruist: The Emergence of Social Work as a Career, 1880-1930* (New York, 1969); John P. Rousmaniere, "Cultural Hybrid in the Slums: The College Woman and the Settlement House, 1889-1894," *AQ*, spring 1970, 45-66; and Stanley Wenocur and Michael Reisch, *From Charity to Enterprise: The Development of American Social Work in a Market Economy* (Urbana, Ill., 1989).

On the subject of orphanages and child welfare, see Grace Abbott, ed., *The Child and the State*, 2 vols. (Chicago, 1938); Leroy Ashby, *Saving the Waifs: Reformers and Dependent Children, 1890-1917* (Philadelphia, 1984); Andrew Billingsley and Jeanne M. Giovanni, *Children of the Storm* (New York, 1972); Susan Whitelaw Downs, "The Orphan Asylum in the Nineteenth Century," *SSR*, June 1983, 272-90; Erving Goffman, *Asylums: Essays on the Social Situation of Mental Patients and Other Inmates* (Chicago, 1959); Hastings H. Hart, *Cottage and Congregate Institutions for Children* (New York, 1910); Marshall B. Jones, "Crisis of the American Orphanage, 1931-1940," *SSR*, December 1989, 612-23, and "Decline of the American Orphanage, 1941-1980," *SSR*, September 1993, 459-80; Ellen Key, *The Century of the Child* (New York, 1909); Jeffrey Koshel, *Deinstitutionalization—Dependent and Neglected Children* (Washington, D.C., 1973); Leroy H. Pelton, "Not for Poverty Alone: Foster Care Population Trends in the Twentieth Century," *Journal of Sociology and Social Welfare*, June 1987, 37-62; *Proceedings of the Conference on the Care of Dependent Children* (1909; reprint, New York, 1917); David J. Rothman, *The Discovery of the Asylum* (Boston, 1971) and *Conscience and Convenience: The Asylum and Its Alternatives in Progressive America* (Boston, 1980); Eugene B. Shinn, *Children in Foster Care* (New York, 1976); Susan Tiffin, *In Whose Best Interest? Child Welfare Reform in the Progressive Era* (Westport, Conn., 1982); and Martin Wollins and Irving Piliavin, *Institution or Foster Family: A Century of Debate* (New York, 1964).

Among the early writings about the Carson College for Orphan Girls and the Carson Valley School, besides those by Elsa Ueland mentioned above, are the following: Phoebe [Crosby] Allnutt, "Educational Adventures in an Institution," *Family*, June 1923, unpaginated reprint; Neva R. Deardorff, "The New Pied Pipers," *Survey*, April 1, 1924, 36-37; William A. McGarry, "A College for Wives," *Green Book*, March 1921, 17-20; *Report of the Committee on Conclusions of the Prospective Work of Carson College and Ellis College*, Philadelphia, October 13-14, 1915 (Philadelphia, 1915); Arthur Colton Willis, "The Carson College for Orphan Girls," *AR*, July 1921, 1-25.

Writings about Carson's Nursery School are C. Madeleine Dixon, *Children Are Like That* (New York, 1930) and *High Wide and Deep: Discovering the Preschool Child* (New York, 1938); and Jean MacFarland, "How Nursery Children Learn," *Parish School* (a Lutheran Church publication), September 1954, 19-20. Also helpful in understanding the evolution of nursery schools are Alice Burnett, "Pioneer Contributions to the Nursery School" (Ph.D. diss., Columbia University, 1964); Hamilton Craven, *Before Head Start* (Chapel Hill, N.C., 1993); Ilse Forest, *Preschool Education: A Historical and Critical Study* (New York, 1927); Florence L. Goodenough and John E. Anderson, *Experimental Child Study* (New York, 1931); and Caroline Pratt and Jessie Stanton, *Before Books* (New York, 1926).

A study that concentrates on the physical development of Carson is John Milner Associates, "An Architectural and Historical Survey, Carson Valley School," April 1985. Much briefer is Alice Kent Schooler, "Historical and Architectural Significance of Carson's Buildings and Grounds" (pamphlet of the Carson Valley School, c. 1990).

INDEX